GABRIEL DAVIDSON

Dr. Gabriel Davidson is executive head of The Jewish Agricultural Society which has helped develop our American Jewish farming community from scarcely 1,000 at the turn of the century to its present encouraging figure of 100,000. He is recognized throughout the country as an authority in American Jewish agricultural socio-economics, and the best of his lectures, writing and lifetime of research and study is incorporated in "Our Jewish Farmers."

Dr. Davidson was honored by the Jewish Theological Seminary of America with the degree of Doctor of Letters in 1934. Recognizing his many contributions to agriculture, Governor Franklin D. Roosevelt appointed him member of the Advisory Committee of the New York State Bureau of Farm Information in 1930. A native of New York City, Dr. Davidson was educated in the College of the City of New York and earned law degrees from the New York Law School and New York University Law School.

OUR

JEWISH FARMERS

and

The Story of the Jewish Agricultural Society

BY

Gabriel Davidson

L. B. FISCHER, NEW YORK

PRINTED AND BOUND IN THE U. S. A. BY
KINGSPORT PRESS, INC., KINGSPORT, TENN.

Contents

Dedicated

T O T H E memory of Eugene S. Benjamin, who deemed it important to perpetuate the Society's record and gave the author the inspiration to undertake this writing.

The spirit of Eugene S. Benjamin runs through the entire story of the Society. Every phase of the Society's work bears his imprint, every page of the Society's record registers his service. In his passing, in June, 1941, the Society and the Jewish farmers of the nation suffered a grievous loss. And this author lost a friend with whom it had been his privilege to serve, for more than thirty years, in a worthy cause.

Foreword

IN THESE days of facile writing and voluminous publication much has been published by men whose knowledge of their subjects is only superficial. Many a traveler has written about a continent after a few weeks in its principal cities. Many a self-styled expert does not hesitate to analyze a complex situation by compiling and editing the thoughts of more thorough men.

This book, this history of The Jewish Agricultural Society—which very nearly becomes a history of the Jewish farm movement in the United States—will not be found in the superficial category. Its author, Gabriel Davidson is the Managing Director of the Society and has been its executive for a quarter of a century. Over his desk have passed recommendations for loans totaling millions of dollars to thousands of individuals. Every phase of the farm problem as it applies to Jews has required his careful study and his ceaseless attention. This work has been his life.

The reader, however, will find more to the book than a mere marshaling and presentation of facts however thorough and profound. For Gabriel Davidson is "one who loves his fellow man." Every one of the thousands of loans was handled by him as the human problem it really was; every one of the innumerable other matters which came before him was treated not as an impersonal case, but from the viewpoint of the man or woman involved. Small wonder then that from the pages of this book shines forth the light of human understanding. I consider that The Jewish Agricultural Society, dedicated to helping Jews gain independence on the farms of the United States, is fortunate to have Gabriel Davidson as its historian.

FRANCIS F. ROSENBAUM

Preface

T H E original intent of the author was to write the story of The Jewish Agricultural Society, its beginnings, its growth and its accomplishments, during its forty years of activity. But as the writing progressed it became evident that the scope would have to be broadened. Long before the Society came into being, indeed as far back as Colonial days, there were Jewish farmers on the American scene. Agricultural colonization had also been attempted. In fact, the first concerted effort to found a Jewish farm colony took place as far back as 1837, and the five or six years beginning in 1881 witnessed dramatic and heartrending attempts to root Jews in American soil. It was the failure of these attempts which focused attention on the need of a guiding hand and led to the organization of the Baron de Hirsch Fund and of its offshoot, The Jewish Agricultural and Industrial Aid Society. Therefore, to confine this narrative wholly to the Society, would be to omit important annals and interesting phases of American Jewish agricultural history. The writer had delved into this early history and had set down his findings in articles which appeared from time to time in various magazines. These and Leonard G. Robinson's sketch of the founding of the South Jersey Colonies are therefore incorporated as a supplementary section. It became clear, likewise, that the book would miss point and purpose if it did not take the reader backstage to view the present farm scene and to make the acquaintance of some of the actors in it. Again, the author felt that it would be a serious omission not to touch upon the roles played by the Baron de Hirsch Agricultural School and the National Farm School in the agricultural training of Jewish youth. These subjects are also treated in Section II.

The history of the Society falls more or less naturally into four epochs, each of which by coincidence is practically coeval with a decade. The first epoch comprises the formative years, the period of exploration and experimentation. This was followed by a period of evolution and expansion in the fields of agricultural education and extension, a period which ended at about the time the United States entered World War I. The third epoch opened close upon the end of the war and was marked by an advance into such fields as planned settlement, rural sanitation, expanded education and support of religious and community work. That epoch came to a close with the depression of 1929, and was followed by a period which required reshaping and reorientation to conform to a restricted treasury. It also witnessed the coming of the refugee. The story told in the book falls within this general framework.

Thanks are due to the members of the Staff of The Jewish Agricultural Society for many constructive suggestions. The author also cheerfully acknowledges the debt he owes to Messrs. Francis F. Rosenbaum and Richard S. Goldman, President and Treasurer of the Society respectively, for their help in planning the book, for reading and checking the manuscript of each chapter as it came from the writer's pen, and for their valuable criticism of the work in its final form. The collaboration of Dr. Edward A. Goodwin—a devoted co-worker—ran through every stage of the writing, from planning to completion. He delved into the voluminous records of forty years, sorted and classified much material, and helped in preparing the manuscript. But for his modesty, this book would have appeared under joint authorship. If this volume possesses interest or merit, the credit must be shared with Dr. Goodwin.

GABRIEL DAVIDSON

CHAPTER I

Beginnings

THE Jews as they are pictured in biblical literature, were overwhelmingly an agricultural—and warrior—people. The story of the wanderings of the tribes reveals a nomadic pastoral civilization that determined the nature of the people and had its effect even on the character of their religion. Jehovah was a desert God; sacrificial tokens were in the form of the product of the soil and the young of domesticated flocks.

After the interval of Hebrew enslavement in Egypt where they labored as pyramid builders, as artisans, mechanics and small craftsmen, they went on to their promised land, there to become fixed for centuries in their national character as a farming people. Each man to his own vineyard was the social ideal. The national leaders, the kings, prophets or teachers (rabbis) were typical of the cultural order; men of the soil or primitive mechanics and craftsmen necessary for a farming society. Their laws were directed to maintain the independent farmer. The sabbatical and the jubilee years were devices of an agricultural people to maintain a balanced distribution of farm land and to return to their own soil those who had become temporarily dispossessed.

From Genesis through the whole of the Scriptures, the Bible is replete with allusions to agriculture. When the patriarchs wandered from Ur to Mamre, from Mamre to Beer Sheba, thence to Padan-Aram, they wandered in search of land fertile and well watered to support their flocks and herds. The land and the things pertaining to it permeate much of early Jewish thought, and the pastoral note runs through much of Jewish writing from the Pentateuch to the Chronicles, through its song, poetry, proverb and prophecy. The Lord's promise to Israel is the promise of "a land flowing with milk and honey." Blessings are invoked in agricultural metaphor. Isaac blesses Jacob with the prayer "God give thee of the dew of heaven and of the fat places of the earth and plenty of corn and wine." And, before their entrance into the promised land, Moses admonishes his people to walk in the paths of righteousness so that God "may give the rain of your land in its season, that thou mayest gather in thy corn and thy wine and thine oil, and I (God) will give grass in thy fields for thy cattle and thou shalt eat and be satisfied." And, conversely, in agricultural metaphor, Moses warns the children of Israel against turning aside lest "He shut up the Heaven so there shall be no rain and the ground shall not yield her fruit; and ye shall perish quickly from off the good land which the Lord giveth you."

Ethical and religious practices prescribed in the Bible are tied to agriculture. The corners of the fields are to be left ungarnered, the sheaves that slip from the gatherer's hands are to remain on the ground, the grapes and the olives hanging on the trees after the first harvesting are not to be picked. All these are for the "stranger, for the fatherless, and for the widow."

What a depth of compassion for man and animal is revealed in the injunctions "No man shall take the mill or the upper millstone to pledge; for he taketh a man's life to pledge," and "Thou shalt not muzzle the ox when he treadeth the corn." What a profound social philosophy underlies the principle of the year of Jubilee that "in all the land of your possession ye shall grant a redemption for thy land because the land is Mine" (God's).

The first two kings of Israel were sons of the soil, Saul and David. Only one steeped in the spirit of the land could pour forth his soul in the sublime words of David's Psalm: "The Lord is my shepherd; I shall not want. He maketh me to lie down in green pastures; He leadeth me beside the still waters. He restoreth my soul." And only one close to nature and understanding nature's manifestations could produce the magnificent 104th Psalm.

The three important Jewish festivals—Passover, Pentecost and Tabernacles—are fundamentally harvest festivals, and the minor festival in the Jewish month of Shebat is known as the "New Year for Trees" when the trees in the holy land begin to bud. So big a role does farming play in the life of the ancient Hebrew that the whole of one of the six sections of the Talmud is devoted exclusively to agriculture in its manifold phases.

The Jews were also a fighting people—out of grimmest necessity. The strip of territory on which the twelve tribes had settled as their promised and holy land was also, it so happened, the crossroads of the ancient world. For centuries the Philistines were an unruly, rebellious element within the country. And on its borders were powerful, impatient and aggressive neighbors.

Egypt, Assyria, Babylonia, the Persias, and later the Macedonian Greeks and the Romans pressed down on this small country and from time to time crossed its soil leaving testimony of the bloody destruction that is war. To have maintained the independence of this little land of Palestine for about two thousand years against numerous and more powerful neighbors was a military feat that is perhaps without parallel. The ancient Hebrews were first-rate fighting men. They had to be, to maintain themselves against the oppressive, imperialist countries that threatened them.

But if war as self-defense was a geographical necessity, agriculture, the cultivation of the soil, the husbanding of flocks were the work-a-day realities. Where some ancient peoples cultivated other forms of self-maintenance and luxury, sea-faring, trade, and even petty manufacture, the biblical and post-biblical Jews were primarily and preponderantly farmers.

It took nearly two-millennia of history to make the drastic change from rural to urban dwellers, from farmers to city folk, from a people working the land and fashioning the simple tools of an agricultural society to a dispersed people overwhelmingly petty tradesmen, professional workers and a footless proletariat. It took wars to devastate Palestine and bring about by enforced migrations a scattering of the tribes all over the known world. It took religious proscription to set these people apart for centuries; to make possession of the land impractical and later illegal for them; to deny their participation in the guilds, that is in the emerging manufacturing of commodities. It took two thousand years of denial, persecution, legal restriction and religious hostility to convert a people of farmers into a people of middlemen.

Not that there ever lacked numbers of Jews who took to and stayed on the land; or that they were without the mechanics and workers that even a self-enclosed ghetto needed. But by and large, the character of these people was transformed, slowly, with difficulty but with the inexorable grinding of the wheels of history.

By the middle of the nineteenth century the transformation had been achieved and nowhere was the change more striking than in Russia. Here in a land ruled by a Czarist despotism there were some six million Jews who had been swept together like so much dust by the incredible vicissitudes of two thousand years of history. Here they were confined in a Pale of settlement. They could not own or work the land freely; they could not move about freely. Occupations that made for a wholesome development were stunted by government hostility. The established state, the established religion and the stimulated social habits of the country in which they lived brought them to a point where externally they were in many respects worse off than serfs; and internally they were demoralized and abnormalized.

Matters came to a head in the 1880's. The oppressive governmental policy and in particular the virulent form of its Jew hatred had their effects. As one of the Czar's ministers had put it: The millions of Jews in Russia were a problem; and that problem would be dealt by bringing about, under pressure, the baptism and disappearance of one-third of the Jews; the enforced emigration of another one-third and, by sheer pauperization and starvation, the death of the remaining one-third.

This was official policy.

Such brutal condemnation of millions of people, perhaps unmatched in earlier history and not to be surpassed until the refinement of cruelty of the brutalitarian Nazi government, did not take place without protest wherever there were civilized men. All over the world and particularly in Europe and in the United States humane leaders cried out against the Czarist oppression which, after direct provocation, culminated in outbursts of pogroms, wholesale massacre, crippling, rape and terrorization of Jews and mob spoliation even of their rag-level poverty.

And along with these outcries, dreamers and practical men, visionaries and saints, idealists and fanatical saviours put forward proposals designed to rescue the terrorized Jews of Russia from prolonged submission to their oppressors.

Out of this tragedy of a group ground down by the accumulated forces of a hostile government there arose the reaction of new causes or new variations of old dreams. In some, Czarist tyranny evoked a revolutionary urge, an identification with subterranean radical parties. In others it produced a passion for Zionism, a new political version of an ancient aspiration of Jews in the middle ages and earlier, to return to the land of Palestine. On top of this broad social movement private individuals here and there pondered on this long standing calamity and came forth with proposals for rescue and resettlement.

Outstanding among these generous prophets of a happier world, possessed of greater experience than most and certainly of the largest resources, was Baron Maurice de Hirsch.

Baron de Hirsch was one of the industrial and financial phenomena of the nineteenth century. Early in his life his financial genius and industrial planning brought him an enormous fortune and while still young he retired from railroad development and other industrial projects to philanthropy. But his was an organized, planned philanthropy, and among his wide interests which covered all peoples and universal sufferings he turned more and more to the problems of the Jews in Eastern Europe. For a while he explored the possibilities of collaboration with the Russian Government. At one time he offered the Russian Government fifty million francs to establish elementary cultural and technical schools. But it did not take him long to find out that a governmental policy that was meant to exterminate could not be changed to one of generosity and sympathy. From that point on Baron de Hirsch concluded that the fate of Russian Jews was to be outside of their country; that they had to start again in more hospitable lands.

It was then that he wrote:

"The measures now being enforced against the Jews which are equivalent to their wholesale expulsion do not appear to me to be altogether a misfortune to the Russian Jew. I think that the worst thing that could happen to these unfortunate people would be to continue for an indefinite period the wretched existence which they have led up to the present time, crowded together in narrow streets, merely vegetating without hope and without a future, reduced to a condition incompatible with the dignity of human beings. The only means to raise their condition is to remove them from the soil to which they are rooted and to transport them to other countries, where they will enjoy the same rights as the people among whom they live and where they will cease to be pariahs, and become citizens. What is going on in Russia today may be the prelude to their beneficent transformation. . . .

"What I desire to accomplish, what, after many failures has come to be the object of my life, and that for which I am ready to stake my wealth and my intellectual powers, is to give to a portion of my companions in faith the possibility of finding a new existence, primarily as farmers and also as handicraftsmen, in those lands where the laws and religious tolerance permit them to carry on the struggle for existence as noble and responsible subjects of a humane government."

Baron de Hirsch did not underestimate the enormity of the problem: the heroic task involved in transplanting millions of people and on top of that to retrain and integrate these wanderers as wholesome elements in their new homes. But he was determined to show the way.

As instruments of this policy two organizations were established. One, The Jewish Colonization Association was founded in 1891 with an initial contribution of ten million dollars. The other was a committee which later became known as the Baron de Hirsch Fund.

The object of the Jewish Colonization Association was primarily to render assistance in emigration, colonization and settlement. The Baron de Hirsch Fund was to assist those Jewish refugees from Russia, Rumania and elsewhere who had of their own accord flocked to America and who needed large scale help to equip themselves for their new country. It was to provide loans to immigrants, their transportation after they had arrived in America and instruction in English and the duties of citizenship and in technical, trade and agricultural work.

Before many years had passed it became clear that the problem of resettlement of Jews on the soil was so extensive and specialized that a separate agency would be needed to deal with that subject primarily. And so negotiations were undertaken which culminated in 1900 in the establishment of a new institution under the name of the Jewish Agricultural and Industrial Aid Society.

On February 12, 1900, the Jewish Agricultural and Industrial Aid Society received its charter from the State of New York. It was formed by agreement between representatives of the Jewish Colonization Association and the Baron de Hirsch Fund. Its funds were derived from a pledge of an annual sum of eighty thousand dollars from

the Jewish Colonization Association and the income from
two funds for a like period made available by the Baron
de Hirsch Fund and estimated to yield sixty-eight thousand five hundred dollars a year. At the expiration of this
original grant, the agreement was renewed and continued
in force until the outbreak of the first World War when
the appropriation made by the Jewish Colonization Association ceased. The Fund's subsidies continued without
interruption and even increased from time to time, as
special occasions called for.

With the founding of the new organization there arose
basic problems of its machinery, its policies, its direction,
its personnel and even its field of operations. In all respects the venture was new. Records of past efforts of
smaller or related character were non-existent or meager.
The Society had to create its own work, make its own mistakes, discover, so to speak, its own soul.

Fortunately, it began with the enormous asset of the
leadership of men of vision and fortitude; experienced
leaders with sound judgment, and yet with a capacity to
consider new problems with open minds. Among these
leaders were Julius Goldman, Morris Loeb, Eugene S.
Benjamin, Marx Ottinger, William B. Hackenburg, Abraham Abraham, Sigmund Neustadt, Myer S. Isaacs,
Jacob H. Schiff, Emanuel Lehman and Henry Rice, who
had already achieved distinction in varied fields of social,
civic and philanthropic endeavor. Their grasp of the task
before them was comprehensive. It expressed itself in the
wide range of the provisions of the Society's charter: The
encouragement and the direction of agriculture, the removal of persons from crowded cities, the grant of loans
to mechanics, artisans and tradesmen, aid in the acquisition of houses in agricultural and industrial districts; the
removal of industries from tenements and shops from

crowded sections to country districts, and the encouragement of cooperatives and cooperative undertakings both
agricultural and industrial.

The very first thing to do was to appraise the situation.
And it was one to test the mettle of the most courageous.

The Jewish immigrants of that day were without agricultural background. They came from Russian, Polish,
Galician and Rumanian ghettos. For the most part they
were neither artisan nor mechanic, but had engaged
largely in petty trading. In the main they were wretchedly
impoverished. Above all they were strange to American
ways and unfamiliar with its tongue. They were dazed and
confused, harried victims of oppression and as a result suffering from all the twists of internal repression.

The task that confronted the founders of the Society to
help fashion this conglomerate mass into a normal, healthy
structure, fitted to its new environment, was enough to
stagger all but the dauntless.

As a first step the Directors decided to make an examination of the work that had been done by the Baron de
Hirsch Fund, largely in the Jewish settlements in New
Jersey which had come to be known as the South Jersey
Colonies. They realized that the Fund had been confronted with a problem overwhelming in magnitude and
novel in character; that, faced with the need of placing the
new arrivals as speedily as possible on the road to self support, the Fund had had little opportunity for pause and
contemplation. There was little if any evidence of a desire on the part of Jews to become farmers. Where efforts
to settle Jews on farms had been made, progress was slow,
farms had been badly located with respect to soil, markets
and other important factors. Farms had been acquired
with inadequate capital. Realistic idealists that the Directors were, they did not allow themselves to be stampeded

into hasty action. They perceived that only through "the gradual creation of a real class of farmers" could a solid and lasting movement be developed.

In delving into the Society's early records, one cannot help but be struck by the willingness of the founding group to explore and experiment, and by the refreshing candor with which they admitted traveling on the wrong road. At the end of the first year they did "not feel justified in congratulating" themselves upon results and recognized that "time and means must be devoted to painstaking investigation and experiments." They followed no inflexible procedure. Patiently and tirelessly they approached their task with the sole determination to build sanely and firmly.

During the early experimental period, the Society's industrial activity outweighed the agricultural. But always its activity was designed to promote the agricultural. The underlying objective in planting industry in farm regions was to strengthen and stabilize agriculture by providing farmers with a supplementary income necessary for family maintenance.

Industrial possibilities were developed by setting up small manufacturing plants, especially in the needle industry, in rural communities. In doing so, the Society realized that it was running counter to economic trends. Fully equipped factories owned and managed by the manufacturers themselves were rare. Work was done mostly by contractors, of whom there were enough in the cities ready to turn out the product at low rates. It was recognized that inducements would have to be offered to manufacturers or contractors to get them to move their shops to the country. Nearly every attempt previously made by the Baron de Hirsch Fund to remove shops had failed, and yet the new Society felt so strongly the need of relieving city congestion as well as of aiding agricultural centers that it was willing to continue these experiments whatever the risks. One plan was evolved and abandoned only to make room for another plan. New factories were erected and equipped, old factories were renovated, subsidies were granted in the form of free rent, free light and power, cost of plant removal was defrayed, bills were discounted, subventions were given in outright cash or in the form of rebates of a percentage of payrolls, the transportation of the families of the workers was paid by the Society. A home building program, initiated by the Jewish Colonization Association in 1898, was enlarged, enabling factory workers to buy or build homes on nominal down payments and on easy terms. The builder was financed on liberal conditions to enable him in turn to pass the advantages on to home buyers. A building and loan association was set up for this purpose. A plan was devised under which manufacturers arranged with contractors to move shops to the country by offering the contractors inducements for which the manufacturers were to be compensated by the Society. In that way the Society hoped to deal with responsible firms, and not with irresponsible contractors who remained in business only as long as subsidies were handed out. There was an infinite variety of experiments.

But the very next year the Directors admitted with characteristic frankness that their hopes in this direction had been entirely shattered and confessed their inability to devise workable plans. "The currents that flow into our cities," they reported, "are too powerful to be successfully diverted from their course by any body of individuals or societies."

Early in its history the Society saw the futility of pouring money into the effort of factory removal and decided against its extension. Gradually it cut down and withdrew subsidies and stipends, and curtailed allowances until, except in the South Jersey Colonies and Woodbine, it had withdrawn entirely from the field. In South Jersey the subsidies were continued until 1905 and in Woodbine they were not dropped until 1936. All told, in furtherance of this attempt, the Society assisted manufacturers and contractors in Astoria, Long Island; in Bayonne, Perth Amboy and New Orange, New Jersey; in Chesterfield and Colchester, Connecticut, besides those in Carmel, Rosenhayn, Norma, Brotmanville, Woodbine in South Jersey, and spent a total of about $200,000, most of it in the South Jersey Colonies.

When the Society appeared on the scene, the South Jersey Colonies, which had had their beginnings about twenty years earlier and had been supported by the Baron de Hirsch Fund and other agencies, were thrown into its lap. The administration of this legacy imposed serious responsibilities and caused heavy drains upon the Society's resources. According to a tabulation made at that time, the South Jersey Colonies comprised 161 farms in Alliance, Rosenhayn, Carmel and Garten Road, with a total population of 949. The farms were small, inexpensive units, averaging thirty acres (of which only 60% was arable), and worth no more than $870 of which $325 was on mortgage. They were inadequately stocked—less than a horse, one and a half cows and forty to fifty chickens per farm. The colonists' cash crops—fruits and vegetables—sold for less than $300 per farm per year. The few small factories could furnish only intermittent ill paying employment. Ninety per cent of the mortgages that had previously been advanced for home building were in default. Many farms had been abandoned. Social and communal life was at a low ebb. "The listlessness and indifference to things noble and intellectual was exceedingly depressing." Indeed there was doubt as to whether more people should be settled there unless the industries could be improved. This was the situation into which the Society stepped.

Attention was first directed to bolstering the existing industries, and, as a preparatory step, the Society built ten homes in Norma to house factory workers, loaned $4,500 on mortgage for another ten, and erected eleven houses in the other colonies, an effort toward which Leonard Lewisohn contributed $15,000. But for the industries themselves, the Directors were forced to report that they had not been able "to devise any plans that promise success," and later, "that their enterprises were as unsatisfactory as they were last year." On the other hand, "the advent of our Society and the frequent visits of our officers and employees" gave the colonists "fresh courage and thus stimulated their interest and activity."

At this point Maurice Fels of Philadelphia appeared on the scene. His generosity and constructive idealism were translated first into the establishment of a cannery as an outlet for the farmer's products, and then into setting up a demonstration farm to serve also as a social center. To both of these projects, as to others, Mr. Fels made liberal contribution over a long period of years. And he went still further. He devoted himself to the advancement of the educational, recreational, cultural and spiritual upbuilding of the residents of the colonies. He visited the colonies repeatedly, taught classes, took an interest in each individual settler, all in the spirit, not of a patron, but of a friend. His influence was enlightening and revivifying. What stands out in the mind of the historian is the selflessness with which Fels threw himself into this work.

The families that were originally settled in South Jersey did not all go there by choice. Therefore the Society felt that, since they were set down "in an unlovely region it must be our business to provide compensation." That compensation was to take the form not only of helping them earn a livelihood but of bringing to them those things which would advance and enrich their social and communal life. Fortunately the instrument for this purpose was at hand. There lived in Vineland Louis Mounier, a man of fine education who "combined with a healthy idealism a practical mind and humane instincts." First engaged to give weekly lectures alternately at each colony, he was soon made Director of a newly constituted Bureau of Educational Activities, a post which he retained until his retirement about twenty years later.

With the institution of this bureau a new day dawned. Gradually a program began to unfold which was to embrace those things which could satisfy the cravings of the colonists, especially the younger people, for a finer life. Those were days before the radio and the movies, when telephones were scarce, when roads were poor and when the automobile was just coming into its own. Little by little the mists of drabness began to lift through the activities which Mounier set in motion. The paltry collections of books which were dignified by the term "libraries" were steadily enlarged. Provision was made for instruction in music, the violin and piano, and in art—particularly painting. A brass band was organized. Young colonists were coached in dramatics and encouraged to present their own plays. Theatrical troupes gave performances. Well-known musicians came from Philadelphia and New York to conduct concerts. Lecture courses were arranged at which Mounier spoke and to which, now and then, prominent lecturers were invited. Soon these assemblages outgrew the confines of farm homes, and halls were erected either directly by the Society or through loan grants. An interesting

insight into the difficulty of getting about is furnished by
the fact that some of these halls were provided with sleeping quarters for Mounier so that he would not have to depend upon the hospitality of the colonists or drive home in
the dead of night. Incidentally the hall at Carmel was
made to serve temporarily as a factory when the factory
building was burnt down.

The religious phase was not neglected. Loans were made
for synagogues and religious education was encouraged. In
the absence of local high schools, scholarships covering tuition and transportation were awarded to bright students.
As the number of residents began to grow, a special night
school was opened for the instruction of adults in English.

The broad humanitarian policy of the Society's Directors was perhaps best exemplified in the treatment of colonists in distress. The Society granted subsidies to maintain
physicians. When necessary it paid for medical and nursing treatment. The Society made a grant to a widow whose
children were stricken with typhoid. It lent a poor peddler money to buy a horse and wagon and a small stock of
merchandise. It gave direct relief. The Directors adopted a
resolution wiping out mortgages on houses upon the death
of the breadwinners. They voted a contribution to cover
half the cost of the installation of a fire department at
Carmel. In all of this they took special care not to instill
into the colonists the feeling that they were regarded as
"wards." Wherever possible, the Directors required participation in the form of small rentals, contributions to
teachers' salaries, admission fees to functions. The colonists, too long accustomed to turning to the "Committee"
when the least thing went wrong, learned that the Directors were determined to give aid only to the extent and in
the form that would eventually make these colonies stand
on their own feet.

As a result of these efforts, the Society was able, after a few years, to report that "a very gratifying improvement has occurred in Southern New Jersey" and that "the Vineland section to which we had been obliged to refer regretfully in our earlier reports, is now in a highly encouraging condition." Comparing what was done almost forty years ago with the social program of today—evolved as a result of an economic upheaval—one cannot help but wonder at the capacity of these far-sighted men to view the needs of 1900 through the eyes of 1940.

One of the objects of the Society, as set forth in its charter, was the removal of Jews from the crowded cities and their resettlement in less congested areas. At the time the Society was organized there existed a Rumanian Relief Committee, formed for the specific purpose of helping Rumanian Jews who had come here because of oppression in the land of their origin. The Society's first step in removal activity was a contribution of $5,000 toward the work of the Rumanian Committee. But that committee was only an emergency mechanism. Soon the Society felt that the time was ripe to undertake removal on a larger scale "in order not only to clear the way for the continual stream of immigrants arriving here, but also to relieve the prevailing conditions in our ghettos." Again, the Directors did not put expectations too high. All they hoped to attain in the beginning was "almost imperceptible results." But they built better perhaps than they realized.

A bureau known as the Industrial Removal Office was established. Agents were sent to various sections of the country to discover employment possibilities and to organize local communities. Jewish leaders in the large cities were invited to cooperate and to make provision for the reception, placement and distribution of immigrants sent from New York. In the initial period of the organization's activities, the work in the local communities was immeasurably aided by the Independent Order B'nai B'rith. The Industrial Removal Office paid transportation and defrayed the expenses of local agents. But it adopted the principle to refrain from giving out and out alms.

At the outset there was the fear, on the one hand, that not enough immigrants would care to go to unknown and distant places, and, on the other, that the local communities would not be too anxious to receive them. The onrush of willing immigrants soon dispelled the first fear. But the attitude of the interior communities created a problem which took time and effort to combat. They feared that the immigrants could not be assimilated, that they would not fit into jobs, that the communities would be saddled with their care, that their own standing would be impaired. Men like Cyrus L. Sulzberger, Nathan Bijur, Leo N. Levi and others travelled from city to city to arouse these communities to a sense of their obligation; to point out that the care of the immigrants was not a local New York problem; that New York City was only the port of entry, and that this was a national problem to be solved by all American Jews.

By the end of the first two years, 2,104 people had been resettled in 256 different places in almost every State in the Union. The country was then in a period of exceptional economic prosperity and doubt was expressed that people could be induced to abandon New York. Despite that, the number of removals sharply increased from year to year through 1907, when there was a break because of the depression.

Several principles were laid down. It was early resolved not to take any side for or against union labor and not to place people where a labor dispute existed or was threatened. The IRO refused to honor requisitions for help where the work was temporary or might be injurious to health. It discountenanced the practice of some out-of-town employers of luring men holding jobs in New York with the offer of higher wages, fearing lest the better paying work prove illusory and, as had been frequently demonstrated, temporary. So far as possible, men were sent alone, with the families to follow after the breadwinner had established himself. The IRO saw value in taking people out of, or, at any rate, in preventing them from entering, the needle trades in New York in order to counteract "industrial onesidedness" and to prevent too many Jews from "getting into the one calling least desirable hygienically and economically."

The fear that Jews would not adapt themselves to unfamiliar manual work was soon dispelled. As early as 1903, it was reported that "removals were working in breweries, tanneries, tin plate factories, packing houses, railroad shops, car shops, and even at street cleaning." Later reports show that their employers testified that "their industry and sobriety make them a most desirable class of workmen." The reports mention a locksmith sent to Ripon, Wisconsin, to be followed in less than a half year by his brothers; an iron worker removed to Columbus, Ohio; a machinist sent to Pittsburgh; a man working in the car shop at Toledo; another who had found employment with the American Can Company in that city, and still another who was working in a wheel company; an upholsterer and a plasterer who had been sent to Omaha, and other cases too numerous to mention. Evidence piled up to show a wide diversity of occupation. The 1905 report cites the instance of a man who had been sent to Memphis in 1901 and who had already become the owner of a house; of three men in Nashville who had their own stores; of a shoemaker in Minneapolis who was able to buy his own home; of six removals in Rochester who had bought houses; and numbers of people who had been able to accumulate bank accounts—eloquent testimony of facility at adjustment. And later reports show that some of the very people who had been removed themselves served on committees to find openings for new arrivals.

The activity of the Industrial Removal Office grew to such dimensions that it soon functioned independently of the Jewish Agricultural Society, although the formal separation did not take place until 1907. Thenceforth the IRO was supported largely from funds derived from the Jewish Colonization Association. The Jewish Agricultural Society was left free to use its resources exclusively for agricultural work, which was assuming steadily greater proportions, and for such industrial work as would advance the growth of farm communities.

The subsequent history of the removal office is therefore outside the compass of this volume. Yet justice to this remarkable piece of work demands a few words to complete the record of its more than twenty years of unique service to American Jewry. The slump of 1907 was quickly followed by renewed and extended activity which continued until 1914. With the outbreak of the first World War and the virtual cessation of immigration, removal work began to slacken, but a skeleton organization and some activity continued until 1922, when the IRO was completely closed. During part of this period an effort was made to divert a segment of immigrants from the Atlantic seaboard by utilizing Galveston, Texas as a port of entry. An organization known as the Jewish Immigrants Information Bureau was organized, financed solely by the late Jacob H. Schiff. While it functioned, over five thousand immigrants came to the United States via Galveston, and from there were distributed to interior points. The World War brought an end to this highly significant and successful experiment.

During the life of the Industrial Removal Office, over 100,000 Jews were distributed in over 1,000 places in every State of the Union. But that is not the whole story. To get a real conception of the important role that the removal office played, we must add to the direct removals the many times larger number drawn to these places because of the presence there, and the satisfactory progress, of their pioneer friends and co-religionists.

It is impossible to write of the work of the Industrial Removal Office without paying a full measure of tribute to one man, who, apart from its generous founders and supporters, made possible its extraordinary achievement. That man is David M. Bressler, guiding spirit of the movement through its most vigorous years, and so closely associated with all that the Industrial Removal Office accomplished that he and it are, in fact, synonymous.

Figures and statistics cannot by any means describe the total impact of the work of the IRO. Had there been no such agency it is altogether possible that immigrants to this country, far from striking out to points in the interior, would be cluttering up the eastern seaboard and complicating still further the already considerable problem of the large cities.

It is probably no exaggeration to claim that the IRO is responsible for the presence of at least one half million, perhaps even as many as a million, of those Jews who are today found in the smaller cities, in towns, villages and hamlets throughout the land.

It is significant that the IRO was the first agency in the United States to give practical expression to the idea of distributing immigrants. When the work was brought to the attention of the United States Commissioner General of Immigration in 1910 he was so impressed with its possibilities that shortly thereafter his department organized a service to disseminate information regarding industrial conditions throughout the country and to call attention to employment opportunities, thus enabling unemployed labor to follow industrial expansion in the less populous areas of the country.

The story of the Industrial Removal Office is a romance —the march of people seeking security and finding it. It is to be hoped that some historian will write this epic narrative in its entirety. It should be preserved as a permanent record in American Jewish annals.

The emphasis of the new Society was primarily agricultural. But at the outset the Society had to tackle some pressing industrial problems which it had inherited. Yet it did not take long for the agricultural work to get into its stride. From 23 loans aggregating $7,500 outstanding at the end of 1900 the figures jumped to 150 loans totalling $67,500 at the close of 1902.

If the Directors were ready to experiment along industrial lines, they were even more disposed to experiment in the agricultural phases of the Society's work, though at times these experiments were against their own better judgment. Only through the process of trial and error could a relatively permanent policy emerge.

One of these projects was the so-called Tyler, Texas, experiment. This was a program sponsored by a local committee under the leadership of the Rev. M. Farber. The idea behind the plan was the establishment of a small farming community under the benevolent guidance of a local committee in a section too distant from the center of the Society's activities to be administered by its own agents. Tyler was to serve as a pattern for other communities to follow. Five families were settled there in 1904. The very next year a malignant type of malaria broke out and that ended the experiment, which was partly financed by the Society. The families had to be removed from the settlement and two of them were later placed on farms in Woodbine, New Jersey.

Similar to this experiment, if more ambitious, was the Milwaukee Agricultural Association, organized at about the same time with A. W. Rich as its guiding spirit. It envisaged the settlement of twelve, eventually more, families on farms in Arpin in the central part of Wisconsin. The start was auspicious, but before long there was dissatisfaction, manifested recurrently. The colony was run on a purely paternal system. The Society had rendered assistance in the face of serious forebodings, which proved to be fully justified. In 1908 there were only three families left and in 1910 the affairs of the association were wound up.

In the same year that the Tyler and Arpin experiments were launched the Hebrew Colonial Society of Baltimore was formed for the purpose of establishing its members, twenty in number, near that city on a three hundred acre farm which was in time to be subdivided into individual truck farms. This project differed from the others in that it was not sponsored by benevolent patrons, but was formed by the members themselves and was to be run along cooperative lines. Like the others, the plan fizzled out after a few years, but a few of the members remained in farming.

The same purposes that impelled the Society to lend its effort to the Texas, Wisconsin and Maryland projects drew it into financial relationship with the Jewish Agriculturists' Aid Society of America, popularly known as the Chicago Society because it was sponsored by Chicago Jews and had its office in that city. The Society was organized in 1900, the outgrowth of a committee formed by A. R. Levy in 1888. When the Chicago Society appealed for financial support in 1901, the Directors of the Jewish Agricultural Society saw the opportunity of making better use of local resources, both of money and of service. There began a cooperative arrangement which lasted for more than ten years.

The Chicago Society was then working with Jewish farmers who had taken up government homesteads in North Dakota. These lands were given free under certain conditions. The prospect of obtaining farms without cost was alluring; Jews were further encouraged by the support of the Chicago Society. But while the land was practically free, everything connected with its tilling was expensive. The growing season was short. Droughts and frosts were not uncommon. The chances of crop failure were therefore great. Transportation facilities were woefully inadequate. Homesteads were at great distances from railroad stations and markets. Supplies were expensive. Credit was costly (twelve per cent was the legal rate of interest). It was soon realized that it cost as much—and more—to transform free land into a real farm as to buy an existing farmstead in a section not subject to these inordinate risks nor as remote from large centers of population. Despite misgivings, the Jewish Agricultural Society felt that it had to extend its help: it made loans to homestead farmers—both through the Chicago Society and upon direct application. Though the Directors did everything to discourage further settlement on homestead land, they wanted to lend encouragement to those already there in the faint hope that the hardships of the pioneering stage might eventually be rewarded. They were bolstered in this feeling by the favorable crops of 1905 and 1906. This improvement also led to the influx of more farmers into the state, some of whom were compelled to file on poor land because most of the good land had been preempted. In the hope that the turn had at last come the Society granted fifty-nine loans in North Dakota in 1907. Besides it agreed to make $15,000 available to the Chicago Society that year to be followed by $10,000 in 1908. Neither of these appropriations was used up. The Chicago protagonists became thoroughly disillusioned. By 1911 they asked the Society to take over the administration of their remaining accounts and in 1913 the Chicago Society ceased operation. A year earlier, the Jewish Agricultural Society had established a branch office in Chicago, and all agricultural affairs in the area theretofore served by the Chicago Society came under the jurisdiction of that branch.

Contemporaneous with its support of homestead farming in North Dakota, the Jewish Agricultural Society became interested, at the instance of a committee headed by Rabbi J. Leonard Levy, in a group of fourteen former residents of Pittsburgh who had taken up government homesteads in Laramie County, Wyoming. Although included in the government reclamation plan, these lands could not be worked without irrigation. The Society's Directors believed that the settlers "could not possibly have made a more injudicious selection," yet they did not want to foreclose the slimmest possibility of success. They granted a number of loans in 1907 and again in 1908, but the colony soon thereafter disintegrated.

During the same period a small Jewish settlement on homestead land in Ferry County, Washington came to the Society's attention. Here, too, the Society made farm loan grants. This settlement lasted longer than Wyoming and was economically more successful. Similarly, the Society came to the succor of the remnant of a colony at Devils Lake, North Dakota which had its origin as far back as 1891. A little later Jewish farmers filtered into South Dakota, Montana and Nebraska, where they settled on free homesteads. In Nebraska the homesteads were opened up under the Kincaid Act, popularly known as the Desert Land Act. The latter designation aptly fitted the character of the land. These attempts also culminated in disintegration.

All these debacles tended only too well to confirm the Society's early misgivings about the prospects of homestead farming.

The quest to serve the farm-minded but otherwise untrained Jewish immigrants of slender means led to other forms of experimentation. Early in the Society's history, it became evident that the practice of first establishing inexperienced people and then letting them acquire their training in a hit and miss fashion on their farms was tedious, expensive and hazardous. As early as 1901 the Society began to study various methods by means of which families in modest circumstances could be placed upon farms with fair chance of success and without undue strain on the Society's funds.

Professor Morris Loeb, one of the Directors, proposed a plan along the lines of one that had been tried in England and Ireland and was being considered in Germany. The plan called for the purchase by the Society of a large farm to be run on commercial lines under the direction of a skilled manager who would employ the prospective Jewish farmers as farm hands on a wage basis. The laborers were to be carefully selected from among family heads. Each family was to be given a house and a small plot of ground upon which some vegetables could be raised, mainly for home consumption. A nominal rental was to be charged. Only those were to be accepted who could later invest a small amount of money in farms of their own. This method would provide steady employment during the year that these families were to remain on the training farm, would keep the family together and accustom all its members to farm living, while at the same time the wage savings would supplement the slender original capital. Finally in 1904, the Society bought a tract of 500 acres of land at Kings Park, Long Island for a "Test Farm." The first "students" were placed there early in 1905.

The beginning was promising. At the end of the first year, it was reported that "people familiar with Long Island agriculture had expressed great surprise at the quality of labor obtained from the ten or twelve Russian farmers whom we have kept on the property since early spring." Four or five families were to be transferred to their own farms before the following spring and the Society was looking about for suitable farms. Affairs ran smoothly the next year when there were as many as eighteen men on the Test Farm, thirteen of whom were to be settled on farms in Woodbine and in Hunterdon County, New Jersey upon completion of a full year's training. The graduates who had been established the previous year were reported as doing well, and while the Directors still considered it too early in the history of the Test Farm to pronounce it a success, they had no doubt "about its accomplishing good results."

The first discordant note was injected in 1907. Sources of weakness developed which the Directors sought to eliminate. Friction arose among the students and between the students and the superintendent. There were strikes and bickerings. It was therefore decided, in 1908, to place no

more men on the farm until some more suitable method
could be devised. This aim was never attained. All told,
58 families had been placed on the Test Farm—some of
whom remained but a few days or a few weeks. Twenty-
nine were graduated and provided with independent
farms, and in 1910 it was reported that twenty were on
farms, that two others intended to buy farms and that
another had been employed for the past three years as
manager of a large farm.

The subsequent history of Test Farm graduates has not
been followed up but at this date the sons of several are
still on farms. Despite all discouragements, this experiment may have been abandoned too soon.

As students began to be graduated from the Test Farm,
thought had to be given to finding suitable farms on which
they could settle. Even before the Test Farm was inaugurated, there arose the problem of finding the right farm
for the right man. It was recognized that many of the
failures recorded against Jews as farmers were due to the
initial and sometimes irretrievable mistake in the selection
of farms; that prospective buyers could not make their
choice unguided, that placing a man on the farm first and
guiding him afterwards was putting the cart before the
horse.

Back in 1903, following the Bessarabian disturbances,
the Society was earnestly considering the purchase of tracts
of land for subdivision in preparation of the expected
influx. In 1905 the Society had actually decided favorably
upon the purchase of land in the South, and in the following year had obtained from the Jewish Colonization Association a grant of a substantial amount to carry through
the program. But a change of administration at the end
of the year resulted in the abandonment of the project.
An incident happened about this time which culminated

in the Society's decision to buy, not large tracts of land but individual farmsteads and plots easily divisible—farmsteads to be made available to Test Farm graduates and to other seekers. It was discovered that an agent of the Society had, in collusion with dishonest brokers, sold farms to the Society's clients at prices which had been inflated so as to enable the brokers and the agent to receive big commissions. The agent was dismissed, the brokers were sued, money was recovered and refunded to the buyers. But the incident served to focus thought upon the need of taking steps to avoid its recurrence.

The Society's farm purchase program was the result. In 1907 the Society bought seventeen farms in Hunterdon County, New Jersey, seven of which were sold that very spring, the other ten were to be reserved for prospective Test Farm graduates. In addition, the Society bought several tracts of land in Salem and Cumberland Counties, New Jersey, for subdivision and resale. That program was pursued through 1911, the Society's acquisitions comprising 121 farms in New Jersey, Pennsylvania, Connecticut and New York, at a total cost of close to $300,000.

In time, the Society's farm purchase activity gave way to the directed settlement work which will be discussed in an ensuing chapter. It was not until 1930 that a new experiment in large scale purchase for subdivision was undertaken. That, however, had a different purpose.

But if the results proved anything, they proved that fears that Jews would not take to farming were baseless. The movement to settle on farms maintained a steady and continuous growth in all directions. This was reflected in the number and amount of farm loans, in constantly increasing accessions of new farmers, in the widening of the territory where Jewish families were located and in the progress, material and spiritual, that Jewish farmers and farm communities were making. When the Society made a survey at the end of its first five year period it was able to take "special pride" in what had been done in New England where Jewish farmers were making good on farmsteads that had been abandoned and deserted by their native owners. It spoke with satisfaction of the opening up of a "healthful" farm section in New York State. It reported favorably on the status of the South Jersey Colonies. It pointed out that Jews had settled on farms from Alabama in the southeast to Texas in the southwest, and as far north as Canada. While the picture in the northwest was not bright, the Society was able to report lessening defections and growing collections, that in general "most of the farmers are progressing very well indeed." It reported that farmers had settled and were still settling here, there and elsewhere independently of the Society.

During all this time, the Society was learning. It learned the importance of sizing up applicants, that dissuading the unfit was no less a service than encouraging the fit. It developed techniques for farm appraisal. It had an impact with dishonest real estate agents, resulting in a concerted effort to clip their wings. It learned that terms for the repayment of loans cannot be fixed by rule of thumb, but must be made to meet individual needs, as a result of which the Society liberalized its repayment requirements. Withal, the Society laid stress on bringing to farmers the understanding that a loan was a business transaction, a sacred obligation not to be lightly ignored. From the beginning, and consistently through its entire history, everything was done to extend assistance in a form which any self-respecting man could accept without sacrifice of prestige or dignity. At the end of this period (1908), the Society had helped a total of 764 farm families (4,325 souls)

in twenty states and Canada with loans aggregating $440,-
000, and had outstanding loans aggregating $282,000 as
against the $7,500 at the end of the first year.

While these matters were taking shape, a thought was
beginning to germinate which was brought to fruition in
later years. Extension work, which was to evolve into a
major activity, began to receive attention. A Yiddish farm
magazine was mentioned. A start was made in the field of
cooperatives which laid the groundwork for activity that
was to assume sizeable dimensions. After the discontinuance of the Test Farm the Society laid foundations for
organized employment service. All these subjects will be
treated in their proper setting.

In October, 1906, an agricultural exhibit was held at the
Educational Alliance in New York, a unique affair, the
first of its kind in America. It attracted 50,000 visitors in
two weeks and made America conscious that it had Jewish
farmers in its midst.

As more and more Jews were casting their eyes toward
the farm, more and more protagonists were advancing
schemes for placing greater numbers there. It is, therefore,
interesting to quote a passage from the 1907 report which
shows the grasp these pioneer Directors had of what was
involved in agricultural settlement. "If mere enthusiasm,"
they wrote, "were the proper rule for the conduct of our
work, it would certainly proceed apace. Scarcely a week
elapses in which there is not presented to us some elaborate
plan whereby thousands of immigrant Jews can be converted in a short time into self-supporting farmers. From
Canada in the North, to Mexico in the South, propositions
are presented to us which, in the minds of persons whose
interest is aroused in behalf of the poor immigrant but
who are inexperienced in the work, offer a ready solution

for all our communal difficulties." "But when the real facts are faced," the report adds, "it becomes at once apparent that no wholesale solution of our problem is possible." This observation is as apt today when all kinds of schemes are being put forth for the solution of the refugee problem, as it was thirty-five years ago.

While the Directors were studying their problems at close range—by repeated trips to agricultural colonies, through extended tours to organize the industrial removal work, at frequent meetings at which the most minute details of management and administration were considered, policies formulated and reformulated—they were also studying the structural framework of the organization and amending the by-laws in the interest of efficiency of function, increased protection of loans as well as to render the maximum of service to its clients. So anxious were they to impress upon clients and outsiders alike that, though a service agency, the Society had no eleemosynary implication, that, in the very first year, they considered the change of name to the Jewish Agricultural and Industrial Credit Society, substituting the word "credit" for "aid." No change, however, took place until twenty years after, when the present name, the Jewish Agricultural Society, was adopted.

CHAPTER II

Growth and Expansion

BY 1908 the Jewish Agricultural Society had listed 2,409 Jewish farm families, increased to 3,040 in the very next year. These families, comprising over 15,000 souls, were, in the opinion of the Society, only about half of the actual total Jewish farm population. A traveler journeying through the country from east to west and from north to south could have encountered Jewish farmers in thirty-seven states. He could have seen "the threshing machine on our western plains fed by the product of Jewish toil and many an acre of impoverished New England soil made richer by the sweat from the Jewish plowman's brow." Jews had entered virtually every known branch of American agriculture. They had "in many places received a most cordial welcome" and there existed "between them and their neighbors a spirit of helpfulness without which these newcomers would have found progress most difficult." Jewish farmers were beginning to make their influence felt in their respective communities. "The most striking feature," reported the Society in 1908, "is the raising of the educational standards and the improvement in the local schools." In several communities Jews had been elected to local school boards. Where they had settled in larger numbers, such as in parts of New York and New Jersey, they contributed to building up the village populations, drawing to these villages Jewish physicians, dentists, druggists, lawyers, and helping to make the villages self-sufficient units.

The second epoch of the Society which began about 1908, was a particularly notable one. It witnessed the creation by the Society of an educational machinery which, starting with the publication of a modest farm magazine, was step by step developed to include a system of itinerant instruction, the award of agricultural scholarships, the grant of loans to students in agricultural colleges, and similar educational features. It witnessed the extension of religious work among farmers. It saw the birth and growth of agricultural credit unions, of cooperative fire insurance companies, the formation of local farmers' organizations, which in turn were federated into a national body; the laying of the foundation for other cooperative endeavors, and the establishment of an active farm employment service.

During the formative years, the economic aspects of the problem of settlement on the soil were so pressing that little thought could be given to the educational, religious and cultural needs of the Jews on the land. What educational work had been done, was spasmodic and unorganized. "The wonder is," said the Society in 1908, "that so many have worked out their own salvation." This it ascribed to the fact that "to the Jew, agriculture is not solely the means of a livelihood . . . but the visual and tangible sign of religious liberty and political emancipation" for which he "willingly sacrificed so much to reach the coveted goal." With growing knowledge, the impor-

tance of educational activity impressed itself increasingly
upon the consciousness of the Society.

The Society began to realize that farm loans alone do
not always make farmers; that the new Jewish farmers
were left to shift too much for themselves and that as a
result some had suffered unnecessary travail and succumbed needlessly. Something more than financial help—
important as that was—was needed both to advance their
economic progress and to satisfy their cultural and spiritual yearnings.

In those years, government aid was still in the early stage
of development and where available was designed largely
for the already established farmer not for the raw recruit.
Furthermore there was the language barrier. The problem
for the Jewish farmer was not one simply of craftmanship
but also one of adjustment. He needed something more
than what government bureaus—austere and forbidding
to him—could be expected to accord. He needed a type of
service which only one familiar with his background could
offer him.

The first product of the Society's educational activity
was an idea that had for some time been in the minds of
the directors—namely, the publication of a monthly farm
journal in Yiddish. The first issue of "The Jewish Farmer"
made its appearance in May, 1908. It was the first Yiddish
agricultural paper in the world, and for a long time the
only one. Its aim was to reach a class of farmers which for
obvious reasons the English agricultural papers could not
reach. The objectives were set forth in the Society's report
of the following year: "The aim of this little paper is to
provide for the non-English reading Jewish farmer expert
advice on agricultural subjects not otherwise available; to
supply him with a publication to which he can turn for

sympathy and encouragement; to furnish him with a medium for the expression of his feelings and aspirations; to bring him inspiration by keeping him in touch with his fellow tillers of the soil."

The paper was planned and has since been maintained along these practical and constructive lines. Its contents are sufficiently scientific for the advanced farmer and yet presented in a form understandable to the beginner. They are fitted to the season and timed to deal with difficult problems as they arise.

"The Jewish Farmer" received a hearty reception. Its influence was immediate. From an initial subscription list of 138 the circulation jumped to 1,565 within one year, and to 3,100 paid subscribers by 1912. It was not long before the magazine went to every state in the Union; and in fact to Jewish farmers in other countries. A travelling social worker described a Jewish farmers' gathering round a table with an old man, the sage of the group, his wire-rimmed spectacles perched on the tip of his nose, reading from "The Jewish Farmer" and interpreting the texts in true Talmudic-fashion amidst running comment from his interested disciples. It took him back, he said, to the old Beth Hamedrash of his youth.

Letters of commendation for the new venture flowed in. Wrote one farmer, "The journal is as if sent from Heaven," and another, "It is as welcome a guest in my home, as my best friend. Although I have been a farmer for sixteen years I see that I still learn a great deal from it." The paper also received favorable recognition from the Yiddish, English-Jewish and agricultural press. Readers petitioned that the magazine be published fortnightly and even weekly, a request which it was impossible to meet. But the paper was steadily expanded in size and in content and improved in form. A question and answer column was introduced.

In response to demand, a section was added devoted to would-be farmers. An early issue featured an article entitled "Ten Commandments for Prospective Farmers" which aroused editorial comment for its applicability not only to prospective Jewish farmers but to all prospective farmers and was reprinted in over one hundred papers and in four foreign languages. Other articles were from time to time reproduced in publications of standing. In time "The Jewish Farmer" became a household companion treating matters of interest to all members of the family. An English page was added for the farm boy and the farm girl. In it, the younger members of the family were exhorted to read English agricultural literature, to join local farm youth clubs, to enter agricultural contests, in short, to make themselves fully a part of their communities. Soon these youthful readers began to make their influence felt. In 1915, a sixteen-year-old boy from Massachusetts, who had been a reader of the paper for three years, was able to write, "My father is not a regular farmer but kept poultry during the last eight years. The first few years my father did not succeed in poultry. But lately when he started to read 'The Jewish Farmer' he found out how ignorant he was in poultry culture. In 1914 I entered the contest of the Massachusetts Agricultural College in Amherst for boys and girls poultry clubs." That boy won the first prize in the state contest.

The "Farmer" persistently stressed the importance of constant study of Department of Agriculture and Experiment Station bulletins, and, to encourage the reading of agricultural literature, entered into club arrangements whereby farm magazines and agricultural textbooks were obtainable at reduced cost. Within a short time, over one hundred agricultural books found their way to Jewish farmers' reading tables. Step by step, "The Jewish Farmer" grew in influence, not only as a medium for diffusing agricultural information but also as a vehicle through which the farmers' ideas and ideals could find expression. It came to be looked upon as the organ of the Jewish agricultural movement.

"The Jewish Farmer" led naturally and almost immediately to another phase of agricultural education—a system of field instruction. In the course of the editor's travels it became evident that, to be truly effective, book learning must be implemented by personal instruction. Some personal instruction had always been given but only incidental to investigations for loans or for other specific purposes. When no investigation was made, no instruction was given. To remedy this, the Society inaugurated a system of educational visits which to this day remains the most effective instrument in its extension service. Except for a small section in Texas where a special piece of emergency work had been undertaken in 1904, and sporadic attempts by chambers of commerce, railroads and other private interests concerned in the development of their own enterprises, the Society's itinerant instruction antedated by several years systematic agricultural county agent work. Indeed it was not until the spur given by Congressional enactment in 1914 under which the Federal government undertook to match State appropriations, that governmental county agent work can be said to have had its actual beginning.

By means of its farm to farm visits, the Society has been able to bring last minute information directly to the farmer's door. These travelling teachers, picked for their specialized scientific training, their pedagogic ability, their temperamental fitness and their Jewish background, have been able to do more than impart technical knowledge.

Going from farm to farm, seeing the farmer's problems, pointing out mistakes, suggesting improvements, speaking to boys and girls, listening to farmers' hopes and fears, they soon built up a relationship much closer than that of teacher to pupil. The farmer came to seek the counsel of these sympathetic advisors in matters outside the realm of pure agriculture—matters more intimate and personal which vexed his soul and the solution of which was vital to his welfare.

This work was possible only in limited areas. Later expanded, this activity can even now be carried on only in districts where there are sizable Jewish farm communities not too distant from the Society's offices.

From individual instruction, the natural step was group instruction. Farmers were assembled to discuss problems common to their group. These meetings became the medium through which thought could be pooled on matters requiring joint action. Out of these gatherings soon emerged Jewish farmers' organizations. Prior to 1908 there were only four such organizations in existence, but with the impetus given by "The Jewish Farmer" and field instructors, they steadily multiplied until in 1914 there were sixty-three organizations in eleven states. From the outset, they took on much broader functions. It was only natural that organizations "composed of men of the same blood, having suffered the same hardships, possessing the same ideas, with interests in common and the same problem to solve" should give thought to their social, cultural and religious needs as well as to those purely economic problems—purchasing, marketing, etc.—that can best be met through united effort. These organizations opened up possibilities of entertainment, festival and religious observance and welded the farmers into stronger entities.

Not least, they made it possible to bring religious instruction to their children. The Society's activities in the religious field assumed a larger scope during the following decade.

With the inauguration of the educational epoch in 1908, events moved rapidly. In quick succession, there was "The Jewish Farmer," a system of itinerant instruction from which there emerged local farmers organizations; these, in turn, soon federated into a national body. In January, 1909, delegates from thirteen farmers' organizations met in New York City and founded the Federation of Jewish Farmers of America. The Federation was intended to provide the cohesive force necessary to bind together the Jewish farmers in the United States. Centralization of effort would, it was thought, lead to accomplishment otherwise impossible. The high level of the discussions at this very first meeting is well exemplified in the adoption of resolutions, some of whose recommendations paralleled those contained in the report of President Theodore Roosevelt's Commission on Country Life which did not appear until a month or so later.

At the organization meeting, plans were laid for the holding of a convention and agricultural fair. These took place during Succoth Week, October, 1909. Held in the Educational Alliance in New York City, in the very center of a dense Jewish population, the fair brought the spirit of the country to the teeming masses of the city. There were 952 entries from 225 exhibitors. Even distant North Dakota was represented. The exhibits included not only the usual agricultural displays but also flowers and such products of the housewife's skill as butter, cheese, preserves, pastry and bread. The National Farm School and the Baron de Hirsch Agricultural School participated and the agricultural colleges of New York, New Jersey, Connecti-

cut and Massachusetts sent educational material. Director
E. H. Jenkins of the Connecticut Agricultural Experiment
Station and Assistant Secretary of Agriculture, W. M. Hays,
came to view the exhibits and to address a public gathering. The judges included Professor K. C. Davis of the New
Jersey State Agricultural College, Professor H. L. Garrigus
of the Connecticut Agricultural College and H. W. Collingwood of the Rural New Yorker. Wrote Professor Davis:
"I was greatly impressed with the number of exhibits.
. . . Their products were, on the whole, far better than I
expected." And Professor Garrigus, who was one of the
judges of the field crops, "There were so many entries . . .
and the exhibit was of so high a grade, that it was rather
hard to pass judgment upon them." Mr. Collingwood observed, "I thought the exhibits made by your farmers excellent. As a business proposition I should consider that
the exhibit of grain, vegetables and fruit was as good as
any I have seen this year." The fair was visited by at least
50,000 persons and received favorable press comment.
Leslie's Weekly commented, "The fair demonstrated that
the Jews' entrance into the agricultural field has been
marked by signal success. . . . They are combining with
an increased knowledge of scientific farming a desire to
succeed at this their first productive venture." The Survey
declared, "The fair was extraordinary in showing the
working of the leaven preached assiduously by the leaders
of American Jews who advocate a return to the soil. The
Jew is returning."

The Federation grew to sixty-three constituent societies
in eleven states. Growth in size was accompanied by expansion in function. To reduce the cost of the commodities that farmers must buy, the Federation established a
purchasing bureau in 1910. On a capital of $300, the
bureau did over $10,000 worth of business the first year,

and it was estimated that it had saved its customers over
15%. The volume quickly mounted. By 1912, business had
been increased fivefold. In time the bureau extended
credit. This helped many a new farmer for whom credit
was tight. But unfortunately, the Federation was too liberal. Soon it had to return to a cash basis. With the discontinuance of credit, it declined and, in 1920, the purchasing bureau became inactive. But the ten years of the
Federation's purchasing bureau were not devoid of usefulness. Savings on purchases were not the sole benefit.
Farmers were made conscious of the importance of quality. Local merchants began to assume a more liberal attitude. The farmers themselves learned a wholesome lesson
in the use and misuse of credit. They also learned the value
of joint action which was to stand them in good stead in
their later cooperative ventures. With the discontinuance
of the bureau, the Jewish Agricultural Society stepped
into the breach by arranging pooled purchases for farm
groups and later in setting up a purchasing service under
its own auspices.

With the waning of its purchasing service, the Federation began to languish. While the Federation was in existence, the Jewish Agricultural Society contributed generously to its support in providing office quarters and secretarial help, in paying the salaries of two field men, and in
supplying funds for current expenses and for the conduct
of the purchasing service. In an effort to revive interest, it
helped the Federation effect a reorganization under which
commercial phases were to be eliminated and activities
confined to educational and cultural fields. But the attempt
failed. The economic problems of Jewish farm groups
were identical with those of the communities of which they
formed a part and would have to be handled in common
with other farmers. It also became apparent that the non-

economic problems were local in character, different in different communities, and had to be worked out on a local and not on a national scale.

The constituent societies of the Federation furnished the nuclei for the establishment of a system of cooperative agricultural credit. The subject began to receive the Society's attention in 1908 and the report of that year contained a discussion which is of historical interest in that it was one of the earliest public utterances on the unsatisfactory credit situation then confronting the American farmer. Said the report in part, "One of the difficulties confronting the American farmer is the want of agricultural credit. By this is meant short term credit, similar in a degree to the credit of commerce, as distinguished from long term credit, or mortgage loans. . . . Agricultural credit as such is virtually non-existent and the American farmer has been forced to depend for his annual working capital upon the generosity of neighbors, the forbearance of the local storekeeper or the cupidity of the usurer. . . . It is therefore planned to initiate a system of Cooperative Local Credit Associations somewhat on the lines of the 'Raiffeisen' system which has done so much good work among the farmers in Germany."

Owing to legal technicalities nothing was accomplished in 1910 beyond the approval of an appropriation for the installation, by way of experiment, of three or four credit unions in selected localities. Rensselaer County, New York, Fairfield County, Connecticut, and Ellington, Connecticut were the places chosen, and credit unions began business there on May 1, 1911. They were the first agricultural cooperative credit associations on American soil. The form of organization was simple. Control was vested entirely in the membership. The par value of a share was $5. The holder of one share was to have the same voice and the same rights as the holder of many shares. Loans were to be granted only for productive purposes or for urgent needs for a period not exceeding six months and for an amount not exceeding $100, and were to be secured by the promissory note of the borrowing farmer with one or more responsible endorsements. The Society lent each credit union $1,000 at 2%, which together with the credit union's own capital was to constitute a revolving fund for loan purposes.

The reception accorded by competent authorities was very gratifying. Writing in the American Economic Review (December, 1912), Professor E. W. Kemmerer of Princeton said, "To the American the surprising thing about it all is that such cooperative credit banks are practically unknown in the United States. . . . A real beginning in the direction of cooperative agricultural credit was made last year through the influence of the Jewish Agricultural and Industrial Aid Society." Under the caption, "The Jews Ahead," the Indianapolis News in an editorial on December 14, 1912, wrote, "While there are two bills now in Congress calling for a commission to go abroad and study the question of cooperative credit for farmers, the Jews in New York have organized just such a Society and are aiding Jewish farmers. . . . We do not need commissions to hunt knowledge. We need simply to follow the lead of these Jews and set to work to provide credit. And we need to do it just as they did—which is simply to do it. . . . So these practical people without waiting for anything, simply patterning after one of the German systems and on their own account, have started a credit system that all American farmers could start for themselves."

Between 1911 and 1915, nineteen credit unions were

formed in New York, New Jersey, Connecticut and Massachusetts. The Massachusetts union, formed in 1913, was the first agricultural credit union in that state, although the State's credit union law had been enacted four years earlier.

The value of credit unionism was well illustrated by reports of delegates to a convention of the Federation of Jewish Farmers. "Our credit union is keeping us on our feet" reported the delegate from Rensselaer County, New York. And the delegate from Leonards Bridge, Connecticut: "Previous to the formation of the Credit Union, when a farmer had an accident—a horse died, or a cow died—there was no help for him. . . . But now when we have a Credit Union, when a farmer applies for help it does not take more than an hour for him to get the money."

Because of the absence of enabling legislation in states other than Massachusetts, the credit unions were formed as voluntary associations. In 1913, New York State enacted a credit union law and soon thereafter four of the New York credit unions were incorporated under it. This brought them under the supervision of the New York State Banking Department and made them amenable to departmental regulations.

Unfortunately, the farmers did not fully grasp the requirements of credit union practice. It was hard for these simple people, coming from humble walks of life, to appreciate that a credit union is a miniature bank to be run on banking lines. In 1916, the Society took stock and, while it found that credit unions on the whole were serving a good purpose, it also found some pronounced defects. Because credit union loans are based largely on character, where intimate knowledge of the members is essential, and because the area of operation was limited, the membership was small. This limitation in turn meant small loaning capital. With the members resorting to the credit union solely for borrowing purposes and overlooking the fact that a credit union is as much a savings bank as a loan channel, the funds were soon exhausted in loans to the initial members with no new monies coming in. Because the officers, though well-meaning, were inexperienced, extended credit too liberally and, in cases of default, were loath to enforce payment from endorsers, it was found that these credit unions were not conforming to strict banking regulations. In 1918, it became necessary to wind up the affairs of three New York credit unions and, at the request of the New York State Banking Department, their liquidation was placed in charge of the Society. The dissolution of the other sixteen credit unions followed soon thereafter but, with one exception, these credit unions came through without loss and some were even able to declare dividends.

To offset the loss of this source of credit the Society stepped into the breach by making small seasonal and emergency loans on unsecured notes direct to farmers—a policy inaugurated in the war period and then incorporated as a permanent item into the Society's program.

The Society's experience with the early agricultural credit unions was not wasted. The lessons learned led to recommendations which have become recognized credit union practice. It is not too much to claim that the Society helped to evolve a national credit union philosophy which was embodied in later credit union legislation. Thus it was that, in 1930, the Society helped bring about the modification of the New Jersey law to make it serviceable to farmers; and was instrumental in establishing the first farmers credit union under the amended law. And when the Federal Credit Union Law was enacted in 1934, the Society immediately assisted in the formation of new agricultural credit unions in farming communities. There are now several such credit unions under federal charter in New York and New Jersey.

The outstanding rural, though not purely agricultural, credit union in the United States is that in Ellenville, New York, the fruits of the efforts of Jewish residents, and the spiritual offspring of the earlier credit unions sponsored by the Society. The Ellenville Credit Union was chartered in 1924 with a membership of 205 and a capital stock of $19,-140. Now it has a membership of almost 500, a capital stock of nearly $100,000, a guarantee fund of $15,000 and undivided profits and reserves of $6,000. Its loaning policy is liberal, its interest rate has been reduced from 6% to 4%. During its existence, it has made 5,000 loans aggregating $2,000,000 to hotel keepers, merchants, farmers, laborers and professional men. It truly represents a cross-section of rural life. During its entire career not a single loss has been sustained.

At about the time the credit union idea was taking shape the farmers turned to cooperation as a means of solving another problem that had long vexed them. Fire normally takes a heavy toll on American farms. Because of the absence of a fire code, of regulations prescribing the kind of materials used in the construction of farm buildings, the hazard from lightning and from forest fires, the insufficiency of fire fighting apparatus, because farmsteads are often scattered, and the tax involved in inspecting the risks before their acceptance and supervising them afterwards is burdensome, many stock companies are chary of writing farm insurance; some companies refuse it entirely.

About 1910, the situation was particularly acute in the sections of New York State commonly known as the "mountains"—Sullivan and Ulster Counties and adjoining territory. Farms and boarding houses were springing up rapidly and good-sized country hotels were being erected. Because of the inherent hazard and the skepticism on the part of insurance companies in the stability of the business, fire insurance was either unobtainable or obtainable only at heavy cost. This situation affected not only the owner's indemnification for loss by fire but also complicated his mortgage problem. Mortgage lenders naturally refused to place money on uninsured or underinsured property or on property the insurance on which was liable to be cancelled at any time. The residents of the district were concerned about their future and turned to the Society to help find a solution to this perplexing problem. It was apparent that the solution lay in the formation of a mutual or cooperative company managed by the members themselves and paying losses by membership assessment. Mutual companies had long existed in farm regions and had demonstrated their usefulness. Because a mutual company is composed of property owners living fairly close to one another, the members know their neighbors intimately and can size up the risks more adequately than can paid agents of a stock insurance company. Supervision is facilitated, and losses can be evaluated and adjusted with minimum bias or prejudice. A mutual company does not operate for profit, it has small overhead and no need for large reserves; therefore, the cost of insurance is governed solely by the loss rate.

With the assistance of the Society, the Cooperative Fire Insurance Company of Sullivan and Adjoining Counties was organized and received its charter from the State of New York in April, 1913. Its beginning was modest and it had many hurdles to overcome. Property owners who had managed to obtain insurance were afraid to antagonize the stock companies. Many mortgage holders refused to recognize the new company's policies. But the founders had courage and tenacity. They were fortunate in finding in Boris Fogelson a sagacious and able secretary who was untiring in his efforts to steer the cooperative wisely and safely. The Society stood squarely behind them. It assigned a field man to help write the insurance, a bookkeeper from the Society's staff did the initial auditing and the assistant manager attended the monthly directors meetings. Though it had much at stake financially, the Society readily accepted the cooperative policies, thus putting its stamp of approval upon the new company. Gradually other lenders followed suit. After nine months of operation, the company carried 296 risks aggregating $655,000 and after three years there were 504 risks aggregating $1,211,000. As was anticipated, stock companies reduced their rates, in some instances from $4 to $1.50 a hundred. It was estimated that Jewish farmers had within that short period saved $80,000 on their insurance coverage.

The growth was steady and continuous. In 1920, an affiliated company was formed and in rapid succession three others. The five companies now form a group known as the Associated Cooperative Fire Insurance Companies of Sullivan and Adjoining Counties which operates in Sullivan, Delaware, Greene, Ulster and Orange Counties. In 1941, these combined companies carried policies aggregating $19,000,000, distributed among 2,263 policy holders.

On the occasion of the twenty-fifth anniversary of the first company, a modern office building in Woodridge, Sullivan County, costing over $60,000 was dedicated. It is a building that would grace, not a country village, but any good sized municipality. At the end of 1940, the companies had an accumulated surplus of $293,000 in liquid

assets consisting of United States savings bonds and local
school and fire district bonds, including its office building.
The assessment rate in 1939 and 1940 was 15% lower than
in 1937 and 1938 and 48% lower than in 1934. The declaration of principles contained in the companies' annual
statements sums up their philosophy: "Our cooperative
companies are democratic—one member one vote—proxies
prohibited; are owned and controlled by our members;
have no stockholders—pay no dividends—no profits; employ no agents . . . ; pay no commissions . . . ; charge
no stipulated premium but assess members for losses sustained and cost of administration . . . ; educate constantly
to prevent fires . . . ; are neutral in race, religion and
politics."

The agricultural program which emerged in 1908, recognizing the importance of farm youth in the farm economy, provided for scholarship awards. The thought behind these awards was well expressed in the Society's report of the following year, "to make the child of the Jewish
farmer an important factor in the economy of the parental
farm; to instil in him a pride in his calling; and to im-
plant in him a love of the soil by demonstrating that farming is not a menial occupation but an honorable profession." The Society alloted a sum of money each year to
send farm boys and farm girls chosen by competitive test
to the agricultural colleges of their respective states for the
short courses given during the winter months, when farm
work lags and youth can best be spared from the farm.
Designed originally solely for farm youth, the scope of
these scholarships was later broadened to include others
who showed a special aptitude for farm work. By means of
these scholarships, the young folks were given the opportunity of getting a short concentrated practical course in

some specific branch of farming—such as poultry, dairying, gardening, etc. The girls could combine with it a course in home economics. Students who attained special merit in their studies were allowed to compete for a second scholarship.

The influence that scholarship students wielded on parental farms was immediately perceptible. To quote from the 1910 report, "Barns were whitewashed, cows placed on proper rations, more milk produced at less cost. . . . Those who took up general agriculture got to work on crop rotation, fertilizers and the general improvement of the farm. Poultry was a favorite course. One of the boys took hold of an old apple orchard, considered worthless and realized forty dollars from it. Another found upon his return that the chickens were dying at the rate of about forty a day. He put a stop to it." The girls who had taken courses in household economics, "started in to improve the appearance of their homes."

In 1925 a new form of scholarship was instituted—scholarships for junior short courses offered at some agricultural colleges during the summer. The courses were open only to boys and girls affiliated with agricultural clubs under government supervision and enabled these boys and girls to spend a profitable week at college.

Scholarships consisting of a complete course at the New York State Institute of Applied Farming at Farmingdale, Long Island, and at the State School of Agriculture and Domestic Science at Delhi, New York, were for a number of years given by the Baron de Hirsch Fund. The Fund also awarded a number of scholarships for the regular four year course at State agricultural colleges.

During the early years of the Society it had made a few loans to students at agricultural colleges. In 1916, the Society incorporated the student loan definitely into its

educational program. Loans were made on the promissory
notes of the students payable in instalments after graduation. Preference was given to upperclassmen because it
was felt that a man who had worked his way through two
or three years had demonstrated a genuine interest in
agriculture. Budgetary retrenchment necessitated by the
depression forced the Society to discontinue student loans
and the regular scholarships in 1930. Junior scholarships
were continued until 1932. All told, 340 scholarships were
awarded in the agricultural colleges of California, Connecticut, Georgia, Massachusetts, Michigan, North Dakota, New Jersey, New York, Ohio, Wisconsin and Wyoming, and sixty-nine student loans were granted at the
New York, Missouri, Michigan, Ohio, Massachusetts, Minnesota and New Jersey colleges.

Many scholarship students and loan recipients were
placed in remunerative farm jobs and responsible professional positions. And still others branched out into farming on their own account. Scholarship students won distinction either at college or after they had left college.
An Ohio boy won the championship of Cuyahoga County
for raising 115 bushels of corn on an acre of land and was
awarded a trip to Columbus and Washington. A girl
student became cow tester in the State of Wisconsin. Of
her, Professor Otis, in charge of short courses at the State
University wrote, "Miss B. L. to whom you awarded a
scholarship two years ago is making good. She is the first
and only woman cow tester in the state, and I note by the
program of the state Dairymen's Association that she has
been placed on the program for a paper. This looks as if
your work was bearing fruit." A scholarship student found
employment with the Indiana State Experiment Station.
Another was made assistant to the superintendent of a
government experiment station. A young woman became

rural field worker for the National Council of Jewish Women. An agricultural graduate who made his way through college partly on a student loan went to Poland to organize agricultural schools. Another went to Palestine. Still another was sent to Russia on an agricultural reconstruction mission. The Jewish Colonization Association appointed one of these men director of an Argentine colony. The recipient of both a Baron de Hirsch scholarship and a student loan won many spurs while at college and is now in charge of the Agricultural Adjustment Administration's Information Activities in twelve states.

The year 1908 also marked the inauguration of another activity in the Society's service—the institution of the Farm Employment Department. While the Society had before then found work for a few men each season, no systematic effort at job placement had been attempted. The management observed that many farm minded people, even those who had the necessary financial means, were deterred from buying farms because they feared that lack of agricultural training would spell failure. It occurred to the Directors that a period of employment on farms would give such men an opportunity to obtain their experience before starting out for themselves. In setting up a farm employment department, the aim was stated— to give "an apprenticeship which serves as a rational, practical and inexpensive means of schooling. The insight into farm life and into its problems will accelerate the progress of those who stand the test. The others can return to the city no worse off for their experience and no poorer in the world's goods, with their little treasure chest intact to enter pursuits for which they are better qualified."

The design of the department was unique. Emphasis was laid on preparation for independent farm operation and for the more skilled farm positions, not simply on supplying a farmer with a farm hand or a farm hand with a job. That has remained the underlying objective to the present day. But it is not in aim alone that this department differs from the ordinary employment agency. Its service is free. It investigates both employer and employee before bringing the two together. When wage disputes arise it helps to effect adjustments. As far as possible, it follows up workers to keep track of their progress.

The educational aim had at times to be subordinated. Such times were the war years when it was important to supply farmers with workers, and the depression years when it was imperative to supply as many workers as possible with jobs—times when too strict adherence to objectives would have worked hardship on the farmers or on the workers.

In its first year the department placed 172 men. In the following year, the number was doubled, and in the third year it was trebled. Not content with waiting for requisitions to come in, the head of the department travelled around to drum up jobs. This, likewise, gave him the opportunity to foster employer-employee understanding and to place the department on a higher than commercial plane.

The Society's entrance into the employment field was welcomed by farmer and worker alike. At the end of each year, the Society checked the season's placements. Not all the comments were favorable but some were decidedly laudatory. Farmers found the men "quite satisfactory as help," "sober, faithful and skillful," "good and honest." One farmer wrote, "My experience with this man—the first foreigner I have ever employed, and the first of his race and country with whom I have become intimately acquainted—has been a wonderful eye-opener to me. If he is typical of the people for whom Russia is making life intolerable and driving from her borders, I pity Russia." The same broad minded attitude was evinced by some Christian farm employers who had never before associated the Jew with farming. Wrote a Nebraska farmer, "I presume we might find a little difficulty for a while in understanding each other, but I will try to be fair. I should like to be informed by you as to whether the man you sent has conscientious objections to working on Saturday, feeding hogs, or eating beef, etc., that was not killed by a Jew, or any other special subject, for I should not like to antagonize his religious principles any more than I would permit another man to make me go contrary to mine." And a Vermont farmer, "Am a retired Protestant clergyman. Help can have the advantages of my home and the association of a large Hebrew population in the City, where there are two Synagogues." From Connecticut, "He is a good honest boy, and if sickness comes over him he shall have everything that can be done for him free of charge. We have taken care of him for some eight weeks and will do so again if needed." This boy remained on the job upward of three and a half years. From Maine, "S. is still with me, (after two years) has proved his worth, and has become a valued member of the family."

The employees were equally satisfied. A young man sent to a nursery in Minnesota, in writing about his job, reported, "I was going to tell you what my work is. I am now a foreman in the nursery and have from twenty to twenty-five men working under me. I am getting a lot of experience." And from a boy sent to a Connecticut farm, "Last August I came to you seeking employment on a farm. You sent me up here with the understanding that this was a three weeks job. At the end of three weeks the owner asked me to stay over winter. I did so. Now there

is an understanding between the owner and myself that
I am to remain in his employ for another year." Again
from Connecticut, "I have been here over three months
and I find Mr. S. is an experienced farmer and that I am
able to learn from him poultry raising which is the branch
of farming which I intend to pursue later on." A later
case, that of a New York City boy placed on a New Jersey
farm, "The people I am staying with accept me as part
of the family and the work is very interesting. The life
here is entirely different from that in the city and soul
satisfying."

Gradually a clientele was built up. The number of
placements rose steadily until 1917, interrupted only during the early period of the first World War. Our entrance
into the war caused a sharp increase in the demand for
farm labor, not only to offset enlistments and conscrip-
tions into the army and navy, the diversion of farm laborers to the more alluring jobs in munitions factories,
industrial plants, shipyards, etc., but also to enable farmers to meet the imperative demand for greater production. "Food will win the war" was the slogan, and farm
work was a patriotic service. The peak of placements was
reached in 1917 when 1,529 men were sent to jobs on
farms. In 1918, placements dropped to 1,009. In 1919
there was a further decline—to 830. With the exception of
the following year in which the number of placements
again rose to over 1,000, the course was steadily and at
times precipitately downward.

There were several contributing factors. The stress of
war had taught farmers the value of mechanization and,
in step with the trend in all fields, farmers came to rely
more and more on mechanical devices and labor saving
appliances. The machine began to displace the man. Another factor was the agricultural depression when farm-

ers were forced to hold paid help to the minimum, followed by the industrial depression which resulted in a veritable home-coming of farm youth, when boys who had sought their fortunes in other fields were glad to go back to farm jobs. The low point in the Society's placement record was reached in 1932 when the number fell to 143. From that time on, the curve has been upward, but the maximum attained was only 267 in 1941.

Those placed included graduates of the Baron de Hirsch Agricultural School, the National Farm School, the agricultural schools at Farmingdale, L. I., Cobleskill, Delhi, Alfred and Morrisville, New York, and of other farm schools in this country, in Europe, and in Palestine, graduates of agricultural colleges, and young men who needed a period of practical work to qualify for admittance to agricultural schools and colleges. They also included sons of farmers who sought to branch out on their own. The department's placements included wards of child-caring institutions and (employers having been fully informed) discharged prisoners and men on parole. In a limited number of cases the department was able to procure jobs for the physically handicapped—deaf mutes, men with deficient sight, mild epileptics, etc.—and those suffering from nervous ailments.

Whether many of the men placed by the Society remained in farming is a moot point. Farm employment in itself is not sufficiently attractive to provide a permanent occupation for ambitious urban youth. But a season or two of farm work amidst healthful surroundings is a wholesome and beneficial experience, and in hard times a farm position is a life-saving prescription. Besides, the step from farm laborer to farm owner is a big one. For one thing, capital is essential and it is hard to accumulate it out of the small wage farm laborers receive. But in virtually every case where a farm laborer evolved into a farm owner, the resultant farm enterprise has been successful. On this score the Society's reports record several interesting instances. In 1914 a freshly arrived immigrant was given his first job near Waterport, New York. Then he was given other jobs, each one an improvement upon the one he left, until he reached $100 per month plus maintenance. Then, in the spring of 1921, with $2,800 saved almost entirely from farm wages, he bought a farm in Rensselaer County, New York. There he did so well that he was able to build up a lucrative farm and cattle business and to clear his farm of all debt.

The largest distributor of milk produced on an individually owned farm in New Jersey is a product of the Society's Farm Employment Department. He was first placed in 1913, soon after his arrival in this country, in a small farm job. Step by step he rose until he became manager of a large farm estate on which he employed other men sent by the Society. Finally he was able to save enough money to start his own enterprise. Now he has one of the finest dairy farms in the State, a large herd of accredited cows, and a modern and expensive pasteurizing and milk bottling outfit. Both he and his wife are socially-minded and are held in high regard alike by Jew and Gentile in an elite community.

"He had the idea of knowing everything" wrote a Pennsylvania farmer of a man sent him by the department "and on the third day he was here he knew how to milk, knew how to harness and hook horses, and gradually I broke him into using the plow, harrow, two horse cultivator, mowing machine, etc. Strive to get there was his motto." On a combined capital of $2,000 this young man and his brother bought a farm near that of his employer. Some years later the brothers became employers of workers furnished by the Society, about one of whom they reported, "Victor is still with us. . . . He seems to be desirous to stay and make good."

Speaking of employee clients who later become employer clients, it should be noted that, taking the last three years as an example, about ten per cent of the job placements are with "graduates" of the department.

All told the Farm Employment Department had effected 19,212 placements in 32 states up to the end of 1941, an army of young men trained in practical fashion at minimum cost.

The end of the period under discussion saw the United States engulfed in the World War. Immediately following the declaration of war, the Society entered upon a special program designed to stimulate greater food production. It granted emergency loans without investigation and without security to encourage farmers to increase their normal crop production. With farmers crying for workers, it strained its every resource to place the largest number of farm hands in its history and, as has been stated, it reached that goal. "The Jewish Farmer" carried special articles on food conservation and disseminated information contained in official bulletins. As early as May, 1917, it issued an "Agricultural Preparedness Number." The Society placed at the disposal of several municipalities farms that had fallen into its hands. Meetings were held at which the farmers were spurred on not only to increase their production but to buy war savings and thrift stamps and to subscribe to Liberty Loans, Red Cross and United War Campaigns. The response was gratifying. The area in crop was materially increased. Large over-subscriptions to Liberty Loans resulted, Jewish farm districts having substantially exceeded their quotas.

At the close of the period (1919), the Society had granted directly and administered 5231 farm loans approximating $3,000,000. Almost 300 loans amounting to over $250,000 were to credit unions, to the Federation of Jewish Farmers, to students, to synagogues and for other miscellaneous purposes. Its farm loan operations had reached thirty-six states. The expansion of loan activities made it necessary to open a branch office in Chicago in 1912, already referred to, and an office in Philadelphia in 1916, the better to serve the people in the territory of which these cities are the hub. The Philadelphia office functioned for twenty years and had under its charge the work in the South Jersey colonies and Woodbine, and in Pennsylvania, Delaware, Maryland and contiguous territory. It was discontinued in the interest of economy forced by the depression and its work taken over by the main office.

As this chapter in the Society's history was drawing to a close, a new chapter in American farm history began to unfold. The enactment in 1916 of the Federal Farm Loan Act, the culmination of two years study by a joint committee of Congress, opened up a reservoir of credit theretofore unavailable to farmers, of which they were desperately in need. Before the passage of the law, farmers depended for mortgage money upon the banks, insurance companies and private lenders. The usual farm mortgage, even on ample margin, bore heavy interest and was payable on demand or had a short maturity. Periodic renewals entailed the payment of bonus or commission, and there were times and areas where farm mortgages were difficult of obtainment on any conditions or at any price. A federal farm loan bears a low rate of interest, is amortized within a period of from twenty to thirty-three years, the amortization payments are uniform, the farmer is relieved of anxiety and is spared expense. The farm loan law set up twelve regional Federal Land Banks which operate through local "national farm loan associations" composed of, and managed by, the borrowing farmers. The Society's then General Manager, Leonard G. Robinson, had for years been exposing the deplorable lack of agricultural credit and advocating the adoption of a system to make up this lack. He was consulted by the congressional committee and he aided in drafting the law. Upon its passage he was appointed President of the Federal Land Bank of Springfield, with jurisdiction over the New England States, New York and New Jersey. He organized the bank, framed its policies and formulated its practices. The Federal Land Bank began to do business in 1917. Immediately Jewish farmers set about to organize national farm loan associations and in the following year nineteen such associations were formed in New York, New Jersey, Massachusetts and Connecticut.

CHAPTER III

Continued Expansion

BY THE end of the war it was again possible to take stock. The period of pioneering was over. Early difficulties and problems had been met and, on the whole, dealt with successfully. The crisis of the war, with its unexpected complications and new factors not foreseen at a time when the Society was founded, was now passed. Jews settled on the farms remained there. The Society stood up, experienced and well-organized. The years ahead held out promise of major progress.

Further work was plainly necessary. The Society was not the creator of the back-to-the-land movement among Jews. Some men long for a life on the soil as deeply and as passionately as others pursue the arts or give themselves fully to the world of politics. Normally, Jews would have in some measure found their way to the farm lands and made their independent efforts to establish themselves as agriculturalists. The Society's task was to encourage this normal yearning and to help in realizing this desire by measures that removed the handicaps that blocked the way of the would-be Jewish farmer.

Looking back at its place in the American scheme of things, the Society could see that it had made a substantial contribution to a basic American concept: a fair chance for those, who, without the aid of the Society would have remained eternally victims of a vicious chain of history.

The intervening years since the founding of the Society had proven one thing above all: that given these correctives to their traditional disability, Jews could succeed as farmers, could find contentment and satisfaction in work on the soil, and could integrate themselves to a greater extent year after year in the occupational diversity of a free and democratic country.

The activities of the Society, the addition of new and the extension of old functions, had been somewhat interrupted during the war era; after the conclusion of the conflict, they were pushed forward with vigor. The next decade witnessed further growth and expansion. Systematic farm settlement activity was resumed, departmentalized and enlarged. Rural sanitation, a new field, was added to the Society's program. The educational machinery was overhauled, strengthened and extended. New educational practices were devised and adopted. A branch office was opened in the Ulster-Sullivan district of New York State, the better to serve an area that contains a rather large Jewish rural population. In cooperation with other agencies, work with the Jewish farm woman and the Jewish farm child was broadened. Religious education was given a new impetus. In general, the post-war decade was one of sustained and consistent growth, not alone for the Society but for the Jewish agrarian movement as well.

It had always been the Society's belief that an artificially stimulated farming class meant a weak farming class. The Society studiously refrained from any form of propaganda directed to the conversion to farming of large masses of urban Jews. In its very first report, it made clear that "our aim should be rather the gradual creation of real farmers than the settlement of large numbers." Report after report warned against the attempt to make farmers en masse. The responsibility was too heavy; the risk of failure too great. The Society has always preferred to follow the "slower but safer method of directing the natural flow toward the farm and guiding it along proper channels." It held to the philosophy that the prime requisite is "a genuine desire on the part of the individual to farm, that an artificially stimulated desire is apt to wane as soon as the hard realities of farm life are confronted. . . . A real innate love for the farm provides the real solid foundation upon which to build."

In the beginning, no systematic effort was made to guide the prospective farmer in the selection of his farm other than to acquaint him with the broad general principles which should govern his choice, and then to send him out on a hunt for a farm that might conform to those principles. Of course, he was cautioned not to buy until he had given the Society an opportunity to examine the farm which he had provisionally picked out for himself. Beyond that, there was little direction.

But a program of farm purchases had been begun in 1906 and abandoned after several years as not altogether satisfactory. In 1913, this general purpose was again sought when a Farm Finding Bureau was established "for the special purpose of connecting farm and farmer and finding for each applicant that farm which in our judgment is most suited to his individual needs." After a year and a half's operation, the retrenchment forced upon the Society by the outbreak of the war in Europe, necessitated the bureau's suspension and the reversion to the former unsatisfactory practice; the farm seeker was to pick his own farm subject to the Society's confirmation. Unfortunately, that confirmation was not in fact always sought. Too many buyers succumbed to high pressure agents. In 1918, when the Society's financial position had improved, the bureau was reopened and, with the growth in the number of farm seekers, it became a vital part in the Society's machine. As it developed, it was renamed The Farm Settlement Department, the better to express its real mission.

Farm settlement is a delicate, complicated and responsible task. It deals not only with physical matters, but with the human element—a most subtle factor. The process comprises four, sometimes five, distinct stages—sizing up the farm seeker, examining farms, fitting farm to farmer, conducting purchase negotiations, and in some instances granting the loan without which settlement would be impossible.

Prospective farmers come from all stations of life and from every conceivable occupation. There is the factory worker tired of his daily grind and fearful of the tenure of his job. There is the small storekeeper chafing under the enslavement of long hours and constant confinement and in daily dread of being driven out of business by big combinations. There is the white collar man obsessed by fear of the slowing down of mental faculties. There is the professional man crowded out by younger competitors. There is the man whose health or that of a member of his family demands outdoor life. There is the man of relative affluence—perhaps a manufacturer or merchant—who fears a turn in the wheel of fortune and sees in farming the means of an assured, if modest, livelihood. There is the man oppressed by the complexities of city life, who has long nourished the urge for country living. Added to these, there came later the victim of tyrannical and totalitarian oppression who saw in farming a physical and spiritual refuge.

Most farm aspirants, however, have but the haziest notion of what farming means. They must be enlightened. The lights and the shadows must be put before them in bold perspective. They must be made aware that farming is not only an occupation out of which to earn a living, but a mode of life demanding a capacity of adaptation to change which not all city folks possess but which is of prime importance because it touches every member of the family. They must learn that farming is no easy road to riches, that the average farmer must be content with a modest living, that he must look to certain spiritual satisfactions as compensation for any narrowed material gain. Not least, they must realize that as a business farming requires a capital, a knowledge of business practices, physical vigor and preferably some experience.

The second and third stages in farm settlement procedure, finding the farm and fitting farm to farmer, are closely related. Many a farm failure is directly traceable to the injudicious selection or improper purchase of the farm. There are many factors which must be considered—the size of the applicant's capital, his farm experience, if any, his age, his physical make-up, family requirements, personal predilections. The question of location is important. Most Jews desire to live within ready access not only of elementary and high schools, but also, where possible, of Jewish religious schools. Some wish to settle, if not within commuting area of a city, at least within a radius which makes occasional visits from relatives and friends possible or enables them to market their products directly to city consumers. Others want to combine boarding with farming and must choose locations from this two-fold point of view. It is no small responsibility to select for each applicant that farm which in the judgment of the Society's experts best meets his specific needs.

Important as it is for the right man to buy the right farm at the right price, it is equally important for him to buy it on the right terms. This is the fourth stage in farm settlement. Few men are able to buy farms free of mortgage. The size of the mortgage and its terms of payment are important. If the enterprise is not to be doomed at once, care must be taken to see that mortgage payments come within the farmer's paying capacity.

For the man who possesses sufficient means to finance the undertaking himself, settlement is concluded with the fourth stage. But many Jewish farm buyers do not have enough capital to buy and equip a farm entirely on their own. Good farms come high. Equipment is costly. A farm buyer may need help to complete down-payment, or if he can cover down-payment, he may require assistance for stock, equipment, operating capital. This is supplied by the Society's farm settlement loan. The completely moneyless man, save in a few exceptional cases, is outside the Society's reach. The Society is not endowed sufficiently to bear the full burden of financing; even if it were, the wisdom of settling a man who has no stake may be doubted. Unless a man has something of his own to protect, there is the danger that he will simply walk out at the first untoward occurrence or when fancy moves him.

The very first report of the re-established department brought the importance of proper selection pointedly to the fore. Upon their retirement from business, two partners, each possessing the same amount of capital, had some years earlier bought farms, one a combination farm and boarding house in an unfavorable section of New York State, the other a tobacco farm in the Connecticut River Valley. In 1918 the widow of the former was obliged to apply to the Society for a loan to pay debts, while the latter made a handsome profit from his crops.

An all-important part of farm settlement is the protection of the farm buyer against the dishonest farm agent and the corrupt real estate speculator. The wreck of many a farm enterprise can be traced to the avarice of conscienceless manipulators. Preying upon the innocent and ignorant, resorting to outrageous misrepresentation, they sold farms at prices far beyond their value, exacted terms impossible to meet and extorted bonuses which were not only usurious but which were tantamount to confiscation. Often advised by unscrupulous lawyers, they were clever enough to stop just short of the boundary line of downright criminality. The Society's reports cite numerous cases where farm buyers were mulcted through these vicious practices. These practices not only meant doing working people out of their hard earned savings, but also robbing them of their hopes, throwing them back upon the city, shorn of their means, to the very life from which they struggled to escape.

An early case of this kind was that of a poor tailor from New York City who had managed to save $800. Attracted by an advertisement in a Yiddish paper, he learned that the advertised farm had already been sold. (It is more likely that the advertisement was simply a bait.) The agent—"a landsman"—inveigled him into buying another farm represented to be a great bargain at $3,600 with $800 to be paid in cash. The buyer was prevailed upon not to seek the Society's counsel. After purchase it was discovered that there was a material shortage in acreage, that the seller had retained the best tract with a good building, that some of the cows were "dry," that the horse was worthless, that there were not as many chickens as represented. The farm produced no income and the man was forced to go back to the city to look for a job at the very time when manufacturers were reducing their forces. His wife and four small

children were left on this desolate farm and were soon on
the verge of starvation. To raise money to sustain life the
farmer sold, first a cow and then some chickens—thus eating up the very means of earning a small income. Soon the
farm had to be abandoned and the family sought refuge
back in the city in a basement on the east side where the
woman worked as janitress while the man went out to seek
employment. The Society's investigation disclosed that the
farm had a realty value of not over $2,000, and from a pro-
ducing standpoint was utterly worthless.

The problem of combatting fraud is bound up with
many intricacies. Conflicts of jurisdiction arise from the
fact that the scenes of these practices are laid in different
counties—often in different states. Criminal prosecution
is even harder than civil. The law wisely surrounds the
accused with every safeguard and it is hard to forge a
chain of legal evidence which will preclude all reasonable
doubt. In one case a prosecutor, while admitting that the
transaction bore every earmark of fraud, refused to enter-
tain a complaint because he felt certain that a conviction
could not be obtained.

The Society is always on the watch to prevent these
crooked deals and to bring malefactors to book. Through
newspaper advertisements and by means of lectures and
other educational propaganda, the Society has brought its
services to the attention of Jewish farm buyers and, while
not able to eliminate fraud completely, it has saved many
a farm buyer from the clutches of the land shark. Thus
it forced the cancellation of a contract and the return of
$250 out of a $500 deposit in a case where the victim was
a poor sexton who was induced to buy a farm for $8,000
which had shortly before been offered at $6,000 and was
not worth even that. As a result of criminal indictment it
drove a dishonest agent out of Massachusetts. Through a

civil suit it forced a band of swindlers to make restitution of their illicit gains. Real estate license laws—non existent in the early years—and even now not too general, have helped reduce the evil. In one particularly flagrant case where the Society lodged a complaint with the Real Estate License Commission of New York State, the commission's inquiry confirmed the Society's suspicion of wrongdoing but indicated that the New York City agent had himself been imposed upon by his co-agent in the country. To right the wrong he had unwittingly committed the advertiser sent the following letter for publication: "When an investigator from the office of the Secretary of State came to my office I learned that a complaint had been made on the part of the Jewish Agricultural Society because of an advertisement that was inserted by me in the . . . some time ago. At the time the advertisement was put into the newspaper I was not aware that it contained inaccurate information. Later investigation made by you and the State Department leads me to believe that the suspicions of your Society were justified, and that the 'ad' contained statements which were misleading. I plead innocence of any wrongful intention, but I owe an apology for the fact that the 'ad' appeared . . . I promise to be scrupulously careful in my advertisements."

Right after the outbreak of the depression the Society scotched a widely advertised scheme purporting to offer farms at ridiculously low figures and upon absurdly easy terms. Announcements in the press presumed to cite from government bulletins which were misquoted and misinterpreted. Exaggeration of statement, omissions and implications stamped these announcements as deceptive. People came to consult the Society, some before and some after they had made deposits, happy in the belief that they had found a way by which, with the investment of a small sum, they could make a living. Many had been out of work for a long time and were eating into their dwindling resources. Though the advertisements were patently fraudulent, the Society instituted a thorough investigation to make sure of its ground. This investigation revealed that the land was of little value, overpriced and unsuitable, that its location with relation to city, markets, synagogues, and schools had been grossly misstated. People were warned against buying and those who had paid deposits were advised to drop them. The matter was placed fairly before the Yiddish newspapers and, to their credit, it must be said that they promptly discontinued the advertisements.

Within the last few years there has been a noticeable decrease in the number of cases of this kind brought to the Society's attention and presumably a decline in the perpetration of fraud. This may be ascribed not only to the tightening of licensing laws and other legal safeguards, but also to the Society's educational campaign, and to the knowledge that the Society stands as a watch dog to protect the farm buyer from the machinations of ruthless profiteers.

In the period immediately after the war and ending with the depression, approximately 13,000 people came to the Society to seek advice as to whether they should cast their lot on the farm. This number of course, contains duplications, some men having come in more than one year. During the same period 1189 families were settled on farms in Maryland, Connecticut, Delaware, Illinois, Massachusetts, Michigan, New Jersey, New York, Ohio, Pennsylvania, Wisconsin and Wyoming. On the basis of five to the family, the settlements represent close to 6,000 souls. The number is actually larger. Most farm families include dependent parents and other relatives. Nor do these figures represent the total accretions to the Jewish farm movement

during that period. Many families settle on their own initiative, having at some time or other received the Society's
advice or the guidance of friends or relatives whom the
Society had previously settled. Taking this into account
and making allowance for those who left the farm, the
new accessions may be conservatively estimated at between
ten and fifteen thousand.

One aspect of settlement activity is particularly worthy
of note. The Jew on the farm draws others, both to farms
and to neighboring towns and villages. Many Jews, once
they leave the city, never return to it even if they cease
to be farmers. Children remain in rural districts, in business or in the professions. More than a few Jewish rural
communities have been built up in this manner. The
Society stresses the value of any tendency that lifts the
pressure from the city, even in small measure.

More than half of the 1,189 families settled during the
period under discussion needed no loans to become established but they did need the guidance available to them
only from the Society. Five hundred and forty-four "settlement" loans aggregating $809,920 were made. In accord
with the Society's policy, families were placed on farms
which were going concerns or readily made so, farms well
located, on good highways, with reasonably modern appurtenances, in or near districts in which other Jews lived.
The Society believes it unwise to place newcomers on undeveloped land in undeveloped sections.

With the growth in the number of Jewish families established on farms, fair sized Jewish farm communities
gradually developed. The Society had always been opposed
to the development of exclusively Jewish farm settlements
believing that Americanization would thus be retarded.
Yet it could not close its eyes to the fact, gained by experience, that the tenure of the isolated Jewish farmer is often

unstable. It is only natural that, like his brother in the city, the Jew on the farm should seek communion with kindred spirits and seek out the opportunity for religious observance. By settling Jewish farmers, not in compact groups but fairly close together, the Society aimed to promote adjustment to the American milieu while preserving cultural and religious Jewish identity. In this way synagogues and religious schools can be maintained, the farmers and their families can get together for various communal purposes, and yet become part and parcel of the general farm body. Thus Jewish farming communities were built up in the so-called "Mountain" districts and in other parts of New York State, in the Connecticut River Valley and other sections of Connecticut, in the middle west, in California and elsewhere. Fine examples are the Jewish settlements scattered throughout New Jersey—a favorite state because of its rounded agricultural possibilities, its proximity to large metropolitan centers and its exceptional marketing opportunities. Striking instances of Jewish farm settlements built by the steady infiltration of individual families directed by the Society are those in Toms River, New Jersey and in adjacent Lakewood and Farmingdale.

The first Jewish farmer in Toms River came in 1908. For a decade thereafter just five more straggled in. It was only with the resumption of the Society's farm settlement activity in 1918 that real life began to stir. In a little over five years the community had grown to seventy-six families. In Farmingdale, the first Jewish farmer settled in 1920 and remained the only one for almost five years until the Society picked it as a desirable extension of the Toms River-Lakewood Community. Now there are in the neighborhood of five hundred Jewish farm families in the Toms River-Lakewood-Farmingdale area, in the very center of a region noted for the magnitude and quality of its poultry industry. Jewish farmers stand among poultry leaders. They have taken the initiative in building up strong co-operatives and a commanding part in their management. There are synagogues and Jewish schools, and ample facilities for an active Jewish life. The refugee farmers who have come in lately are worthy additions.

The Society never stopped at the mere settlement of families on farms or the making of farm loans. It felt that these functions, important as they are, standing alone, would not accomplish their purpose.

Before the inauguration of the Society's educational activities, its contact with farmers was spasmodic and, as a rule, incident to loan investigations. Too often it began with an application for a loan and ended with loan approval. With the establishment of the educational department in 1908, and more so with its enlargement in 1919, the Society began to extend beyond its own walls, to bring the benefit of its teaching directly to the farm. Recognizing at the outset that the intermingling of business with education would not make for that confidential relationship which should exist between pupil and teacher and that many farmers who had not been recipients of loans would feel some hesitancy in availing themselves of educational services if these were interrelated with loan making, the department was set up as a separate entity entirely divorced from loan functions.

The federal government has always stressed the importance of agricultural education. It has built up the largest, best equipped and most comprehensive and scientific department of agriculture of any government. Each of the forty-eight states has an agricultural college and one or more experimental stations. The American farmer has long been fortunate in having access to a vast mass of agricultural information upon every conceivable branch of farming in all of its manifold phases. Yet, valuable as this always has been to Jewish farmers, it did not entirely fill the needs of the newcomers. The readjustments following their transplantation from Europe to America, and the exchange of city for country life, with the mutations in occupation and in mode of living that the twofold process of orientation entails, were not easy to make. Clearly, if native farmers, men born and bred on the farm with generations of farming behind them, need elaborate aids, people to whom farming is new and strange cannot be left to fumble and flounder. Government agencies obviously cannot stand in that intimate relationship to a special group of farmers as an organization specifically designed to promote its interests. Moreover, government county agents have under their jurisdiction a large number of farmers scattered over many square miles of territory. Close personal contact is obviously impossible and individual instruction to new farmers practically out of the question. The aim set for the Society's educational service was to open up the storehouse of agricultural knowledge and to translate it into terms of easy understanding. The service was never intended to supplant governmental extension work, but to supplement and implement it. Jewish farmers have always been urged to join county farm bureaus, to avail themselves of all sorts of government service, to read government bulletins, to subscribe to agricultural publications, to attend agricultural fairs and to exhibit at them; in short, in common with all farmers, to take advantage of all opportunities offered by governmental bureaus and farm organizations.

The Society's educational extension work is carried on with individual farmers, with small neighborhood groups, with larger groups, and with state and regional associations. The Society works with the prospective farmer, with the new farmer, with the old farmer, with the backward farmer, and even with the advanced farmer. It reaches out to the farm wife, the farm boy and the farm girl. It handles normal and emergency problems. It grapples with matters agricultural, economic, social, religious and communal. It draws upon federal and state departments of agriculture, agricultural colleges and experiment stations, farm bureaus and other agencies both public and private.

The backbone of the Society's extension service is the individual visit, possible only in the more populous Jewish farming districts, whereby instruction is carried direct to the man on the farm. This establishes personal contact between farmer and advisor, and affords the latter an intimate knowledge of each farmer's particular problems. This is of special importance to the new farmer, but even the advanced farmer is not so proficient that he cannot benefit by an occasional suggestion from an expert agriculturist. A timely visit may save the farmer from committing costly blunders. As one farmer put it, an extension visit is "a refreshing drink of cold water to a thirsty man on a hot day."

There are problems which can be more effectively tackled through group instruction. Very early the Society began to evolve a program which came to include farm meetings, lectures, demonstrations, "field days," farmers' institutes, agricultural tours, local, state and regional conferences. Pruning and spraying of fruit trees, the selection and treatment of seeds, the effect of lime on soil, the judging of cattle, the culling of poultry, fowl vaccination, caponizing are discussed and demonstrated. Collective buying, standardized production, grading and packaging, control of plant and animal diseases and insect pests, these and related subjects are thrashed out. Models, charts, stereopticon slides and movies are pressed into service. In the light of the importance attached to soil conservation in late years, it is significant that the Society preached and taught conservation methods twenty years ago. Though its preachments were not always followed, the Society was from the very beginning a strong advocate of diversification. When tobacco in the Connecticut River Valley ruled high, or when the price of grapes in Ohio soared, it was hard to draw producers away from reliance on their one big money crop. Yet, the Society was successful in introducing certain species of crops in districts where scant attention had been paid to them before.

The early Jewish farmstead was for the most part far from attractive in appearance. Few of the early Jewish farmers had enough money to buy well appointed farms or to improve the appearance of those they purchased. Their means and their energies had to be directed toward making a living. In the course of time, however, the farmer, spurred by the Society, developed some desire for home beautification. As an incentive, the children were offered prizes consisting of shrubs, trees, and books on landscape gardening. The parents were appealed to by means of lectures and leaflets. As a result a small community in New Jersey bought 150 shrubs and trees and a large quantity of flower seed during the first year of the Society's beautification campaign. Farm grounds began to be landscaped and flowers planted. A marked change was brought about.

The Society was not content to stop with the personal pedagogical approach. It recognized the need of placing before the Jewish farmer, in the language he understood best, educational material in printed form. It also wanted to reach out to the distant and isolated farmer who rarely if ever saw its extension agents. The magazine—"The Jew-

ish Farmer"—already discussed, was the first response to
that need. This was followed by ready reference texts. A
textbook covering the entire field of poultry and fully illustrated made its appearance in 1921; its first edition was
soon exhausted and a revised edition followed. The book
found its way to many foreign countries. The Joint Distribution Committee placed an order for Russia, and the
Jewish Colonization Association placed one for Argentina.

Encouraged by the reception the book received, the
Society brought out a hand book on "Diseases of Domestic
Animals" in the following year. As in the case of the
poultry book, the first issue was quickly consumed and a
second became necessary to fill an order from the Joint
Distribution Committee. A long established western cattle
farmer wrote of it; "The book gives all the remedies to
cure the diseases as a thousand page veterinary book." A
third Yiddish publication, "A Hand Book on the Farm
Horse," was published in 1923. Despite all the mechanization which has revolutionized farm practice, the horse still
remains an important factor in farm operations. The book
presents in simple language the essentials of selective
breeding, the care, prevention and treatment of common
ailments. Commending it, a farmer of many years' standing
wrote; "I studied the booklet by heart so that I may know
everything to the last word—a real well of information. To
me it is a treasure."

Texts of another kind made their appearance soon after
the enlargement of the educational department in 1919,
in the form of leaflets issued when information had to be
speedily dispatched or in contingencies of a purely local
character. Within the next five years over 25,000 copies
of 51 leaflets were distributed. Of a similar nature, were
bulletins issued as supplements to "The Jewish Farmer,"
each of which dealt with a single subject exhaustively

treated. This innovation was introduced in 1932 and within the four years that followed 41 bulletins were put out. Then budgetary curtailment forced their discontinuance. The scope and extent of the subject matter of these bulletins is indicated by some of the titles: Statistical Data on Production Costs; The Artificial Incubation of Eggs; Preserving and Canning of Vegetables and Fruits; A Simple Bookkeeping System for Farmers; The Making of Dairy Products on the Farm; The Care of Sheep on the Farm; Landscaping of Farm Premises; A Roadside Market; The Management of the Farm Wood Lot; Fire Prevention and Fighting Fire on the Farm; Electric Illumination of Poultry Houses.

Another link in the Society's educational chain was a correspondence course carried on in Yiddish for several years beginning in 1920. The course was similar to those given by leading agricultural colleges. The material was prepared by the Society's specialists and was for a time edited by Dr. Jacob G. Lipman of Rutgers University.

The correspondence course revealed an avidity for agricultural knowledge of a wider extent than can be imparted through the medium of texts and leaflets. In response to this desire a night school was started in 1924. At first the sessions were held at the Society's headquarters in New York City but these accommodations were soon inadequate and outside quarters had to be rented. In the institution of the night school, the Society harbored no illusion of turning out finished farmers. It did aim to dispel some erroneous ideas about farming, to give prospective farmers a glimpse into the realities of farm life, and to prevent the new farmer from committing those early mistakes which are so difficult to overcome later on. While a farmer cannot be made in a city classroom, there are certain principles of farm management which can be taught there and a scientific attitude can be developed which will prove of value to the "graduate" on his own farm.

Classes were held during the winter and early spring, twice weekly. During the first three years, the course consisted of sixteen sessions. Then in response to urgent pleas from students the course was expanded in 1927 to twenty-five sessions and in 1930 to thirty. At first, only the fundamentals were treated. As some students kept coming back in successive years and as farmers occasionally drifted in, advanced studies were tackled. Under the aegis of the Society's extension head, the curriculum was carried out by members of the Society's staff, the talks being supplemented by models, charts, exhibits of feed, seeds, fertilizers and chemicals, by slides and moving pictures. Successful Jewish farmers were invited to relate their experiences. As graduates evolved into farmers they appeared on the platform. Outside experts came. When, stimulated by high pressure advertising, the students evinced an interest in fur farming, Professor C. H. Thompson of the New Jersey State Agricultural College and Dr. F. G. Ashbrook, the Chief of the Division of Fur Resources of the United States Department of Agriculture—both recognized authorities—were invited to present the subject from the expert's unvarnished viewpoint.

Classroom teaching is supplemented by tours to the New York State Institute of Applied Agriculture at Farmingdale, Long Island, and to the New Jersey State Experimental Station, at each of which the students are given complete freedom; by trips to progressive Jewish farms and by visits to exhibits, especially the poultry show held annually in New York City.

Since 1938 night classes have been conducted in Chicago under the auspices of the Society's branch manager in that city. Since that time also, the Society has prefaced its regular course with an introductory series of lectures for refugees. In addition to class work, refugee students have been given the opportunity to hear talks in German by refugee farmers. Text sheets in German have been distributed.

The Society has always kept sight of the fact that students of the night school are for the most part wage earners who have put in a hard day's work before coming to school, ofttimes travelling long distances to get there. It exacts no regularity in attendance. It gives no rating. Its theory is to permit a student to attend when the spirit moves him and to let him stay away when, because of physical fatigue or mental strain or for any other reason, he can derive no benefit from attendance. The Society has made no sustained effort to follow up its graduates, and while it can make no definite statement as to how many have gone into farming, it does know that its students have taken their places among the better farmers.

In 1922 the Society set up a purchasing service to take over the functions previously performed by the Federation of Jewish Farmers of America. The aim was twofold —economy and quality. Economy is effected because purchases are made in volume and paid for in cash. But economy is not the sole consideration. Quality is stressed. To quote from the very first report of the bureau, "We bought seed that germinates, fertilizer that enriches, brooder stoves that mother the little chicks, and incubators that do not merely incubate complaints." There is also an educational value. The farmer is not always able to judge the merit or demerit of a needed commodity, and even if he is, he does not always know the source whence it can be obtained. This is particularly true of the new farmer who often does not know what he should or should

not buy. Every order is carefully scrutinized and all useless items eliminated. When a new farmer, at the suggestion of a neighbor, placed an order for a garden tractor
with a full complement of accessories, he was advised that
a $500 tractor was impracticable for his needs and that he
could pick up necessary machinery at auction sales. When
a group of farmers asked for quotations on nursery stock
and the Society's investigation, confirmed by the State's
fruit expert, proved that the suggested venture would be
unprofitable, the group was prevailed upon to withdraw
the order. Similarly, where circumstances did not warrant
the heavy investment, poultrymen were prevented from
buying useful yet not indispensable hen batteries, electrically driven egg graders, air conditioning equipment
for laying houses, alluring but inadequately tested new
devices, and high priced equipment. Since volume of business is not a consideration, the bureau can afford to discourage indiscriminate and injudicious buying. In 1929,
for instance, the demand for broiler chicks was very heavy
because 1928 had been a good year. Sensing that production would outrun demand, the Society did what it could
to check expansion. The sharp drop in broiler prices
proved the wisdom of that stand. Again, in the several
years following, when we were in the depth of the depression, the Society did all it could to keep farmers from
making any but the most essential purchases.

The purchases range from small articles to large incubators, electrically operated milking machinery, and
trucks, and the savings range from pennies to hundreds of
dollars. The purchasing service does not handle equipment which requires frequent servicing, nor does it handle
commodities that can be bought just as advantageously
through local dealers some of whom have reduced prices
to retain the trade. The service proved particularly val-

uable in 1940 and 1941 when, as a result of shortages, new sources had to be sought and substitutes found.

Reference has been made to a phase of the Society's activity which came into being during this period, rural sanitation, a service which was to win commendation from private and public health bodies including the United States Health Service.

This work was originally planned for Sullivan and Ulster counties in New York State—a territory of entrancing beauty blessed with an air that is invigorating and a climate that is healthgiving. These natural bounties had long made these regions favorite summering places for city dwellers seeking rest and recreation. For generations back there were few farm houses which did not at times accommodate summer guests. Jews began to settle there at the beginning of this century. Following in the footsteps of the older stock, they gradually drifted into summer boarding as an adjunct to their farming operations. As far back as twenty years or more, it was estimated that a quarter million people spent their vacation periods in this summer playground. As the demand for accommodations mounted, larger and more pretentious houses were built, leading up to the erection of summer hotels embodying every modern device for comfort, convenience and amusement.

Side by side with these hostelries, there grew up a type of vacation accommodation which in a way is peculiar to the district—the rooming house. The farm-rooming house is distinguished from the boarding house in that the guests rent rooms only. They furnish their own bedding, buy their own food (much of which is raised right on the farm) and do their own cooking and housekeeping. In the early days it was a common practice for rooming families to cook in a common kitchen and eat in a common dining room. This rooming institution has been spoken of in derogatory terms and at first blush there is little to commend it. In an overcrowded house with a heavy strain upon primitive sanitary appurtenances, where the housekeeping is everybody's business, therefore nobody's, maintenance of decent standards is by no means easy. Yet the properly conducted rooming house serves a benign purpose because it brings the opportunity of a summer vacation within the range of families of modest means.

In 1916, a severe poliomyelitis epidemic broke out over large areas. Panic-stricken parents rushed their children into the country. Because Sullivan and Ulster Counties were of easy access to New York City, large numbers flocked there taxing the already inadequate facilities.

That year a survey was made by the New York State Department of Health. The survey portrayed vividly the sadly deficient sanitary conditions obtaining in farming regions. It dealt primarily with the Ulster-Sullivan districts where the sanitary picture, though different only in degree from that of other country regions, was worsened because the tremendous swelling of the normal population during the summer multiplied opportunities for unsanitary conditions.

When the New York State survey came to the notice of the Society, the Society decided as an experiment to explore the situation with the view to correcting the most flagrant sanitary abuses prevailing in the territory. The work was started in 1918. The first summer was devoted largely to the making of a sanitary survey. Only the most urgent corrective work was undertaken. As a result of the survey it was decided to incorporate sanitation into the Society's permanent program.

The problem was taken up with Dr. Matthias Nicoll,

Jr., then Deputy and later Health Commissioner of New York State, and a program of operation was mapped out with Dr. Frank W. Laidlaw, the State Health Officer for the district. Dr. Lee K. Krankel and Dr. George M. Price, both noted public health workers, were invited to serve as an advisory committee. A thoroughly trained sanitary expert, released from the United States Army, was employed as sanitary supervisor.

Recognizing that results were best obtainable by confining its effort to essentials instead of dissipating it on decorative and less important details, the Society concentrated on the four major outstanding sanitary problems —sewage disposal, garbage disposal, water supply and the fly menace. With the endorsement of the State Health Department and the support of local boards of health, pressure could have been applied, but it was felt that education would be a better instrument than coercion. Duress would bring about a perfunctory compliance, but it would also call forth a resentment which, in the long run, might negate the gains. Education, though a slower process, would result in worthwhile and lasting improvement.

An intensive campaign was therefore mapped out which embraced education of the individual and education of the mass. This was gradually expanded until every recognized method of public health education had been pressed into service—demonstrations, sanitation talks to owners and guests, stereopticon lectures, moving pictures, English and Yiddish pamphlets, booklets and bulletins, posters depicting the menace of unsanitary evils, printed instructions for display in hotels and rooming houses; above all, the individual visit carrying personal instruction on basic sanitary essentials from farm to farm, from boarding house to boarding house, from rooming house to rooming house. At the close of the first year of active labor it was esti-

mated that the Society had spread the gospel of sanitation
among more than 10,000 people.

In the following year, the Society built a sanitation exhibit which still remains a unique demonstration of sanitary appurtenances. Aside from the exhibit at West Point,
it is the only one of its kind in New York State and probably in most other states. It is located on the grounds of
the Society's branch office at Ellenville, New York, the
very heart of the Jewish farm population of the "Mountains." The exhibit consists of a protected well, spring
enclosure, garbage incinerator, septic tank, double leech-
ing cesspools, subsoil absorption system, scientific dry
privy, a Lumsden toilet. All of these were planned with
the help of the State Sanitary Engineer; all are simple,
easily installed, inexpensive appliances, and yet the latest
devices of sanitary ingenuity—so built that both the details of construction and the methods of operation can be
easily studied. Later, when drought gave rise to an acute
water problem, a "home made" chlorinator for use in
emergencies was added.

The sanitation campaign prepared the soil for much
needed sanitation legislation. Local town boards were
then supreme in the domain of sanitary legislation, but
their enactments were far from adequate. In cooperation
with the District State Health Officer, the Society drew up
a model code of simple, easily observable regulations embodying the salient items in its sanitation campaign, and
went from town board to town board, from village board
to village board, to explain its provisions and to urge its
adoption. In a paper read before the New England Health
Institute in 1930, the Society's executive head took the
position that country hotels, summer camps, tourist inns
and overnight cabins are a public interest and should
therefore be subject to public regulation—preferably state

or regional—prescribing construction, equipment, management, hygienic conduct and fire protection. Ten years were to elapse before the essential features of sanitary control which the Society advocated before the Health Institute were incorporated in the New York State Sanitary Code.

Aroused by the Society to the importance of maintaining safe sanitation standards, the farmers and hotel keepers formed a sanitation league and invited the Society's supervisor to become its advisor. A code was adopted embodying the recommended township ordinances which the members pledged themselves to observe. Diplomas of merit were awarded for compliance.

Soon the effects in the Ulster-Sullivan district became manifest. Farm houses presented cleaner and neater appearances. Screening became the rule rather than the exception, garbage was properly handled. In the first years dealers reported inability to fill orders for screening material and garbage cans. The once ubiquitous open privy almost disappeared. The unprotected well of the old oaken bucket type began to be frowned upon as taboo. Water supplies were tightened and covered, sewage outfits repaired or rebuilt and "home made" septic tank systems installed. In brief, a sanitation consciousness was aroused and a sanitation morale created.

As these effects became visible, the Society made surveys either at its own instance or upon the request of authorities in other parts of New York State, in Connecticut, Massachusetts, New Jersey, and Pennsylvania. To make possible a measure of corrective work there, the Society's extension specialists were given an intensive short course by the supervisor in the practical manifestations of elementary sanitation. Very early a number of township boards in New York State appointed, at the Society's request, sanitary officers to make inspections during the summer months and the Society's sanitary supervisor was asked to train and direct them.

Soon the Society was called upon to advise on problems affecting not simply the individual farmstead and boarding house, but whole communities. In the course of the years it collaborated in the protection of village water supplies, the sanitation of labor camps, the elimination of mosquito areas, the installation of public sewage disposal plants, the safeguarding of community pumping stations, and in bringing emergency relief to flood sufferers. The Society conducted "cleanup" drives in hamlets and villages, inaugurated campaigns to prevent stream pollution by sewage which culminated in the installation of public sewage systems in some important mountain areas.

The Jewish farm woman and the Jewish farm child always found place on the Society's program. Coincidental with the inauguration of its sanitation activities, the Society enlisted the interest of the National Council of Jewish Women in those phases of the farm problem that have to do with the household, such as home economics, domestic science, and personal hygiene, where the delicate and sympathetic touch of a woman means so much. The discontent of farm women and the dissatisfaction of farm children had wrecked many a promising farming career. Farm life has its lights as well as its shadows. The aim of the work was to brighten the lights and to lift the shadows, to bring to farm families some of those things that the farm lacked and to teach them to derive those satisfactions which come only from life in the open.

Starting with a single worker in a small area with a program confined to a few simple items, the Council quickly built up a staff of field workers operating in six states in the northeast and middlewest and engaged in activity falling into five major divisions—education, health, recreation, religion and social service. The program was broad and comprehensive, comprising clubs for women, parent teachers associations, health clubs in rural schools, religious classes, hiking clubs, canning demonstrations, lectures, travelling libraries, sewing clubs, history clubs, fairs and seasonal entertainments. Above all, sympathetic messengers were sent to seek out the lone Jewish woman on the farm left out of the elaborate scheme of Jewish social service, to bring more sunshine and happiness to agrarian folk, to make their lives fuller, brighter and more livable. It did not take long before a Council worker came to be regarded as "an angel from heaven."

The Society worked closely with the Council and granted it annual subsidies, but with the onset of the depression when the Council could no longer finance the activity and the Society had to draw in its lines, the Council withdrew from the rural field. With the general improvement in the status of rural life and the more Americanized type of Jewish farm woman, this work is not as pressing as when the Council entered it. Yet the Council may derive satisfaction out of the knowledge that it did a constructive piece of work during the decade that it served in this field.

From the very beginning, the Society gave heed to the religious phase of farm living. The Council's entrance into the rural field gave fresh impetus to religious activity. But because of the many items on its agenda, the Council could touch the problem only lightly. Later the Society made a broader approach. Its attitude is expressed in a report issued at about that time.

"Religion looms large in the life of all farmers—non-Jewish as well as Jewish. Christian farmers have their churches and their religious organizations handed down to them as legacies from former generations. Present day Jewish farmers have no such heritage. They must build for themselves—no easy task for a pioneer generation. Jews cannot reconcile themselves to the idea of permitting their children to grow up devoid of religion. For two thousand years they have been ready to sacrifice for their faith and, now in the land of religious freedom, they are not prepared to surrender their ancient ideals. The lack of opportunity to give the children an adequate religious education is responsible for not a few defections from the farm."

Through outright contributions and by means of loans—payable over long periods and without interest—the Society aided in the construction of synagogues and religious centers. But it could not hope to subsidize religious education. In the early years, the Society enlisted the interest of the Jewish Chautauqua Society which conducted religious classes in South Jersey and in North Dakota for a number of years, first with a subsidy from the Society and later independently. In 1921 the matter was laid before the United Synagogue of America, an association interested in communal religious work. That organization was itself laboring under financial pressure and could do no more than make a modest contribution toward a religious school in New Jersey for the single year 1922. Toward the close of 1923, taking advantage of the fund-raising campaign then being conducted for The Jewish Theological Seminary and its affiliated societies, the United Synagogue was again approached. This time the Synagogue was in better financial condition and responded more liberally to the appeal.

The big difficulty of providing religious education for farm children twenty years ago lay in the fact that even in comparatively compact communities, distances between farm homes were large. It was hard to get together a sufficiently sizable group to pay for the services of a teacher even where the parents were relatively well to do. The plan worked out by the Society and the Synagogue called for the pooling of the resources of two or three communities close enough for an instructor to travel from one to another, and yet too far apart to assemble the children in the same school. In this way, each group could receive instruction two or three times weekly.

Early in 1924, schools were established in several sections of New York and Connecticut, and the United Synagogue granted a subsidy to a school in Benton Harbor, Michigan. Each group of schools was governed by a Board of Education composed of members selected by the farmers and of representatives of the United Synagogue and of the Society. The school boards appointed the teachers and had charge of general school matters, the Synagogue advised on questions pertaining to curriculum, and the Society on subjects of fiscal policy. Teachers were selected not only from the point of view of their pedagogical qualification but for their ability to develop into communal leaders. The Synagogue contributed half the teacher's salary, the farmers bore the rest of the expense. It was hoped that, if the Synagogue's commitments permitted, and as the schools then established became increasingly self-supporting, more schools would be opened. Unfortunately the Synagogue's funds ran short. No additional schools were opened, and after five or six years support was gradually withdrawn even from the established schools. For a while religious education languished, but with improved transportation facilities bringing the farm closer to town or village, the Jewish farm child was soon able to avail himself of the educational opportunities offered there.

Reference has already been made to the scenic beauty and invigorating atmosphere of the so-called "Mountain" sections in Sullivan and Ulster Counties, New York State. It was pointed out that these natural advantages had long made these regions favorite refuges for summer vacationists. Unfortunately the same features also made them favorite fields for the machinations of the corrupt farm agent and the dishonest farm realtor. Many a hard earned fortune lies buried in the soil of these two counties and their environs. The Society's sanitation labors early brought to light a state of affairs which led the Directors to open an office in Ellenville in the center of the territory. The office was established in 1919. In the beginning stress was laid upon protecting farm buyers against the manipulations of the unsavory brood of conscienceless real estate sharks. Signs were put up at important railroad stations announcing the establishment of the branch, and publicity was given to it through the medium of the local papers and through the New York City Yiddish press. Fraud prevention was, however, not the sole aim. The Society was convinced that, though these areas are not prime agricultural regions, they could be made more productive. Some good farms had already existed. And with the large number of Jewish residents, most of them engaged in farming and inclined to do more, the Society determined to direct its energies to the promotion of the agricultural potentialities of these boarding and rooming farms. An agricultural extension worker was appointed, whose salary for a number of years was partly paid by the New York College of Agriculture. At the end of 1920, after the extension worker had put in ten months, he reported that he had answered 1,075 inquiries either at his headquarters, through the mails or by telephone, and had held meetings attended by more than 1,400 farmers. And it was not long before the branch manager was able to report that "the swing is decidedly toward increased farming" and that "upon our advice and partly with our assistance, barns, poultry houses, milk houses were constructed and repaired. More acres were turned and more fertilizer and more and better seed purchased for sowing and planting."

The variegated composition of an area whose occupational texture was farming, boarding and rooming, interwoven with the professional and business life of the nearby towns and villages, led the Society to broaden its sphere so that the welfare of the community as a whole could be fostered. As the Ellenville branch office became better known, there were laid on its doorstep problems which were only remotely agricultural and yet could not well be brushed aside. To catalogue them is to list the innumerable social, cultural and communal problems that arise in small communities; religious schools, bible classes for adults, night schools in English, Americanization and naturalization work, arbitration, obtainment of visas, etc. Then there were the more intimate human problems such as the adjustment of matrimonial quarrels, the ironing out of misunderstandings between parents and children, the composition of partnership difficulties, and juvenile delinquency. The branch manager had a hand in settling factional disputes within communities, obtaining the improvement of town roads, procuring transportation for school children. He was active in matters involving assessments and taxation and public utility service and rates. He collaborated with the Resettlement Administration and with the Soil Conservation Commission of the United

States Department of Agriculture and other farm agencies, federal, state, local and private. Throughout the years, and in line with the Society's general policy, this branch has stimulated membership in county farm bureaus, Jewish farmers' participation in county fairs and in all affairs of the general agricultural community.

The annual Succoth festival, introduced some twenty years ago, became a tradition. At first a Succah was erected on the Society's grounds in Ellenville, to which the Jewish farmers of the entire vicinity were invited. To these Succoth festivals came people of prominence—Isaac Landman, Rabbi and Editor, Herman Bernstein, United States Minister to Albania, Judge William D. Cunningham, Jacob G. Lipman and others of distinction. The largest gathering ever assembled in any Jewish farm community in this country was the Succoth festival of October 14th, 1928. An audience of over 5,000 people, composed of farmers, boarding house keepers, business men, village residents, Jewish and non-Jewish, came together at the fair grounds in Ellenville to hear an address delivered by Louis Marshall. The memory of that event still lingers. Less than a year after that notable meeting, the great leader had passed away and a fitting tribute was paid to his revered memory at a service held in the very place where he had dined the year before.

The annual meetings served as forums for the practical discussion of matters of interest to the various components of the interdependent mountain population. Out of them grew the Federation of Hotelmen and Farmers and the Ulster-Sullivan Rooming House Association. The Society's branch manager became the English editor of the Federation's organ, the "Mountain Hotelman."

The Ulster-Sullivan territory had always been a fertile field for cooperative endeavor. It has its credit unions, buying cooperatives, selling cooperatives and the chain of cooperative fire insurance companies.

Refugees have found their way to various parts of the region. In the Catskill district, where there is a small nucleus of refugee farmers, a meeting held in a refugee farmhouse in the summer of 1939 was attended by the County Agent and the Director of Soil Conservation. Writing of his impressions, a refugee guest, after giving credit to the Society for building up "broken existences," added, "I do not want to refrain from saying that I gained a high regard for American conditions through the fact that important officials of American agriculture were present. . . . High officials in the house of a Jewish farmer to give information to a few Jewish farmers is astonishing to a European."

After twenty years, the Society was able to present a picture which was in marked contrast to its beginnings. Said the report of 1939, "Farming has grown not only in volume but in kind and in quality. In country described as hilly and stony Jews are creditably represented in every branch of farming. . . . The farm economy is better rounded and more diversified. . . . Boys of twenty years ago, now grown into manhood have joined their fathers behind the plow, in the barn or in the hen house. Some of these boys have studied at agricultural colleges"; also, "there is a lively Jewish youth movement and a wholesome community spirit."

CHAPTER IV

Depression

THE fourth decade in the Society's life dawned against a dark vista. Clouds laden with grave portent blackened the American horizon. Following the stock market crash in the fall of 1929, a storm broke with a fury unprecedented in American financial history. Not even the most confirmed optimist could derive comfort from surveying the American farm scene at that fateful juncture. In three years the cash income from farm marketings fell sixty per cent and gross farm income dropped to the lowest level in twenty years. Farm values suffered cruel deflation. Farm mortgage debt steadily mounted. Farm tenancy increased. Foreclosures were more numerous than in any previous period in the country's history. And no section was immune, no branch of farming exempt.

For the Society, these were years of stress which put its financial machinery to the severest trial, threatening at times to doom it to complete extinction. Its survival was proof that the Society had succeeded in evolving a system of farm credit which, with all its liberality, could nevertheless stand up under strain and that it had helped to develop a Jewish farm class which, though shaken, could hold firm.

The agreement under which the Society was founded provided for annual grants from the Jewish Colonization Association and from the Baron de Hirsch Fund. These subventions were designed to build up a reservoir for loan purposes and to provide means to carry on service activities. In the course of time there was created a revolving loan fund, the interest on which was used to defray the cost of administration and the maintenance of educational activity. Until the Society got into its stride, yearly balances were left for accretion to capital. At the outbreak of the war in 1914, the Jewish Colonization Association was forced to discontinue its subsidy, and the Society's sole support has since come from the Baron de Hirsch Fund and from the interest income on its farm loans. With a growing clientele, reserves were gradually absorbed and the Baron de Hirsch Fund had at times to come to the rescue with special allotments, and in later years to meet refugee requirements.

In set-up and financial function the Society is unique. It differs from the endowed foundation whose principal is invested to earn the money with which to carry on its work and without any relation to that work. It differs from organizations composed of dues-paying members or dependent on periodic campaigns. The Society is distinctive in putting both capital and interest to work for its direct objectives.

When the Society was founded and for years afterward, farm credit was woefully insufficient. The lack was acutely felt by Jewish farmers, not necessarily because they were Jews, but because they were strangers in a strange land and in a strange calling. Banks, implement dealers and local storekeepers were reluctant to repose trust in such unknown quantities. That is why the Society's initial activity was financial though in no sense eleemosynary. A farm loan department was established to extend aid through the grant of loans against security repayable with interest—a form of help that any self-respecting man can accept without the loss of prestige or the sacrifice of human dignity.

At the very beginning the cardinal principle was laid down that the new farmers helped by the Society should finance themselves as far as possible in the same way as other farmers, falling back upon the Society only where credit is not otherwise obtainable or, if obtainable, only on prohibitive terms. There were cogent reasons for this restriction. It was foreseen that the number of Jewish farmers would grow and that loan resources would not be adequate to carry the entire credit load. Furthermore, the founders were determined not to build a subsidized movement. They visioned a class of farmers who, given a lift, could stand on their own feet, free from sustained support from philanthropic or quasi-philanthropic agencies. Hence, first mortgages were ruled out where they could be obtained elsewhere.

The Jews settling on the land were to be helped only to the extent made necessary by the condition of mass migration, the abnormality of their low economic status, the complex emotional circumstances deriving from bitter European memories and, not least, their new problems of adjustment to a new world as well as to a new occupation. Once these supplementary handicaps were removed, the Jew turning to farm life had to make good. With the Society's support, he could obtain a reasonable chance to turn his back on slum and ghetto life, in a country where his religion was no barrier to his advancement. The Society did not guarantee success or permanence or a sinecure. Success not only called for help and guidance from the Society, but for resources of inner strength, a willingness to work hard and to make adjustments and sacrifices. The fact that a large percentage of those who availed themselves of the Society's services came through as settled and well adjusted farmers was a tribute not only to the procedures, principles and direction of the Society, but to the strong latent feeling for the soil among many of the Jewish immigrants.

Only broad principles of loan procedure were formulated so that every loan application could be decided on its individual merit, regardless of labor and expense of investigation and administration, with distance no bar and the man in California or Florida on the same footing in this respect as the man within striking distance of the Society's headquarters. It was stressed that a farm loan is a purely business transaction creating the relationship of lender and borrower with the obligation upon the latter to pay back upon stipulated terms.

The early human material consisted of immigrants with little or no agricultural background, who came from Russian, Polish, Galician and Rumanian ghettos, engaged largely in petty trading, strange to American ways and tongue and not overburdened with worldly goods. For the most part they were neither artisan nor mechanic. Gradually the occupational texture became more and more diversified. For instance, the 467 loan applicants in 1915 came from 72 distinct occupations running all the way from carpenter, blacksmith, metal worker and longshoreman to actor, author, dentist and rabbi. The white collar trades were represented: bookkeeper, cashier, clerk and manager. There were the civil engineer, the druggist and the teacher. There were skilled artisans: cabinet maker, jeweler, electrician, weaver and woodcarver. There were some who might be described as capitalists—merchant, manufacturer and storekeeper. Almost twenty per cent were workers in the needle and allied trades; 106 were farmers, most of them recent recruits. Today, the Society's clients are not the timid immigrants, strangers within the gates. They are not newcomers to our shores. They are either native or long resident. They may be sons or even grandsons of Jewish farmers. Unlike their early prototypes most have had the benefit of American schooling and Americanizing influences. Whereas Yiddish was once almost the sole medium of communication, the Yiddish interview is now infrequent and the Yiddish letter is rare. Finally, the refugee accessions introduced a new element.

The nature of his occupation makes the farmer a chronic borrower. This is not to his disparagement. The successful farmer plows back into the farm the money he has taken out of it. There is always some replacement, improvement or enlargement which can be made and there is amortization to be met. Progress is discernible less by the growth in bank deposits than by the increase in the value of, and equity in, the farm and in the expansion of farm inventory.

Applications made to the Society fall under five general heads—funds to buy a farm, funds to buy stock and equipment, to construct or repair buildings, to pay mortgages or other debts, and to provide working capital. Some loans, of course, are for more than one purpose, and some loans for one purpose may have an indispensable bearing on another. Loans for stock, construction or operating capital to a farmer just starting out may in essence be regarded as farm purchase loans because without them the farm enterprise could not have been undertaken.

The Society's loan policy differs from that of the usual farm loan institution. The latter looks principally to the security and appraises mainly the farm. The Society evaluates the farmer just as carefully and weighs likewise the purposes for which a loan is to be used. Loans have been denied where the purpose appeared unwise, even though the security was of the best. On the other hand, loans were granted against poor security where they could be put to constructive use or where they bridged emergencies. The emergency loan is usually not the safest loan. The man in straits is as a rule not the best risk. Yet the Society must face the possibility of loss where there is even a long chance of rehabilitating a stricken farmer. Its reliance is not tangible security as much as faith in the honesty and ability of the borrower and the prospects of the ultimate success of his venture.

The loan investigation has a distinctly educational coloring. From the lodgement of the application to the disbursement of the loan a decidedly educational strain is interwoven with what is essentially a business transaction. Farm management plans are mapped out or recast, equipment recommended, ofttimes bought, through the Society's purchasing service, live stock selected, farm buildings planned and their erection supervised. The extension of credit is in this way accompanied by instruction in the use of that credit to insure its gainful employment.

The grant of settlement loans has been governed by the state of the Society's exchequer. During periods of stress the needs of already established farmers were regarded as paramount. The Directors felt that the prospective farmer would simply have to postpone his plans until he could finance himself or until the Society's financial position had improved. At such periods, the burden of passing upon applications bore heavily upon a lending agency charged with social responsibilities. The sifting process had to be applied with meticulous care to make certain that the money would go where it could do the most good.

A farm loan, in the light of the Society's responsibilities, is not the impersonal lending of money based upon the appraisal of farm property to determine its acceptability as security. To the uninformed a loan may be a prosaic thing lacking all dramatic element. But one who is in constant touch with borrowers, who knows their problems intimately, who has watched their progress, witnessed their struggles, who sees behind each application the living flesh and blood and heart and soul—a live, breathing, pulsating human being—can see the real drama in the dry statement of the factual loan application.

The farmer's credit needs generally fall into two categories. First, there is the long term credit for the purchase of the farm, for construction, and for other capital needs, the type of credit which can be liquidated only over a period of years. Then there is the short term credit for seasonal requirements, a loan, for instance, for spring planting to be repaid out of the autumn harvest. The Federal Land Bank was created to meet the long term need, but it did not entirely fill the bill. Federal Land Banks lend on first mortgage only and then not over twenty per cent of the value of the buildings plus fifty per cent of the value of the land and make each borrower a stock holder to the extent of five per cent of his loan. The result was that a federal loan took no account of personal property and represented much less than fifty per cent of the value of the farm real estate, a wider margin than many farmers, especially newcomers, can afford. In report after report, our Secretaries of Agriculture have pointed out the need of subsidiary credit, but it was not until the Farm Credit Administration was established in 1933, under stress of the depression, that provision for such credit was made. The FCA set up what is known as the Land Bank Commissioner loan, mostly on second mortgage. At first, limi-

tations were fixed on both the aggregate to be lent out
and the period during which these loans were to be made.
These limitations were later relaxed. It is a satisfaction to
note that the Society had been making this very type of
loan for almost thirty years before its need was recognized
by the federal government.

Prior to 1933, the second type of credit, short term, was
practically non-existent. The farmer made use of so-called
store or merchant credit, purchases made on time, an expensive type of credit. Secretaries of Agriculture pointed
out that such credit was from two to four times as expensive as bank credit (not always obtainable) and that, com-
puted on an annual interest basis, the cost at times ran to
35% per annum. Yet, short time borrowing comprised
about one third of the credit used by American farmers.
The enactments in 1933 made provision for the farmer's
seasonal demands—a field in which the Society also was
pioneer.

But there still remained an area untouched by federal
aids. The new farmer, the part time farmer, the poultry
farmer, the specialty farmer were left orphaned. The dis-
tressed home owner in the twilight zone between farmer
and suburbanite was ruled out by both the Farm Credit
Administration and the Home Owners Loan Corporation.
Here is where the Society had to step in.

There are two classes of loans on which the Society has
always looked askance—loans to single persons and loans
to partnerships. It did not take long to learn that the twofold burden which the unattached man has to carry—farm
and household—plus the lack of companionship, is a
handicap which only the most rugged can overcome.
There is something to be said in favor of partnerships. It
makes possible the pooling of resources by people who
have not enough money to set themselves up separately.

It removes the fear of loneliness, especially on the part of
the city woman, but experience taught that the disadvan-
tages outweigh the apparent advantages. Farming is not
only a living, it is a life. Unlike city business, a partnership in a farm puts not only the head but the entire family
into the partnership. The families live together. They
cook in the same kitchen and eat in the same dining
room. A clash of temperament is almost inevitable. Many
promising farm undertakings have been wrecked because
of the imponderable human elements. Yet, some partnership ventures have blossomed into separate farm enterprises. The Society discourages partnership but does not
make it a hard and fast rule to bar partnerships from
borrowing privileges.

In the first years loans were small in number, small in
size and small in aggregate. At the end of the first decade,
they totalled 1,526 loans amounting to $790,416. Farms,
stock and equipment were then relatively cheap. But, in
the course of time, land values increased, construction became more costly, stock and equipment became more expensive. The standard of living rose. In short, it required
more money to become a farmer. The new farmer had to
have more initial capital, and the Society had to be more
generous in its loans. After the first decade, the demand
for loans at times outran the supply of loanable funds.
For several years it was necessary to resort to a quota system, to set a fixed amount to be lent out in any one
month. Although this was not a desirable situation, it
worked toward a more equitable distribution and assured
preference on the basis of urgency instead of priority. On
one or two occasions it became necessary to declare loaning moratoria for brief periods. Toward the middle of the
nineteen twenties the shortage became so acute that the
Society was prepared to appeal to public spirited Jews for

an enlarged loan fund. Yielding, however, to what was considered the more imperative need of stricken European Jewry, the appeal was deferred and never revived. The Baron de Hirsch Fund stepped into the breach by making additional moneys available.

The peak in loans was reached in 1920—$416,853 for the year, representing 444 loans. In 1927, 570 loans were approved, the largest number in the Society's history. But the aggregate went down to $399,103. Just as the total annual grants depended on the funds available at the particular time, so did in a measure the size of the individual loan. At those rare stages when money was plentiful, the Society could afford to be more liberal. When money was scarce it had to skimp, to cut applications to the bone, making provision only for absolute indispensables. Loans have ranged from $100, in some cases less, to $3,000 and more in special instances. The loan grants thus far have averaged about 33⅓% of the amount applied for.

During the Society's existence up to 1941, it granted 13,842 loans aggregating $8,442,318. But the eight and a half million dollars in loan approvals does not represent the sum total of the Society's financial aid. There are two procedures by which the Society has been able to be helpful in a financial way without making cash advances. The Society has sanctioned new borrowing to enable farmers to fill needs which would otherwise have gone unfilled, even where the new borrowing meant weakening its initial securities. Much of these added funds has come from federal agencies. During the depression, transactions of this kind resulted in obtaining debt concessions (in which the Society occasionally had to join), in placing farm indebtedness on a more rational basis, and in raising federal loans predicated upon subordination.

The other class of non-cash grant is the waiving of the

provision calling for payment of mortgages upon changes in ownership in those cases in which the mortgages are continued with the new owners. The figures in this class have gone down steadily, an indication that there are fewer turn-overs, and that Jewish farmers are remaining on their farms. In each of two years during the past twenty, these so-called indirect loans ran over $100,000, and for the twenty years since these figures have been kept, they reached well over $1,000,000 bringing loan grants, direct and indirect, to over $10,000,000.

Pursuing its policy not to rule out any application because of geographical location, the Society has in its loaning activity reached every State in the Union except Arizona, Iowa, Louisiana, Maine, Mississippi, Nevada and West Virginia. New York, Connecticut and New Jersey are far in the lead. On the basis of five to a family, the loans have benefited over 65,000 individuals. This takes no account of the fact that in many cases a number of loans were made on the same farm, nor, on the other hand, of the many instances where loans were made on farms on which more than one family resides.

Intertwined with financial operations, there is a large range of related matters in which the Society has been consulted by loan recipients as well as by others. These include problems pertaining to fire insurance, from the procurement of policies to the adjustment of losses, questions affecting mortgages, payments, receipts and releases, Federal Land Bank applications, dissolution of partnerships, examination of farm purchase contracts and of contracts for the construction of buildings and for the purchase of stock and machinery, matters relating to farm taxation, adjustment for land taken for easements or for rights of way, questions affecting farm titles, in not a few of which defects were discovered only through title searches made in connection with loans.

In fixing terms of repayment, many factors had to be taken into account. The aim had to be to relate terms to the borrower's paying ability. Carrying charges, margin for repairs, replacement and expansion, and family requirements had to be weighed against probable income. Experience proved that it is impossible to estimate these items with any degree of certitude. Costs vary, unpredictable emergencies arise, illness strikes, returns do not come up to expectations. At times terms were too easy, not a very serious matter; at others, they proved too hard. Where the latter was the case, the Society did not necessarily insist upon rigid compliance. It recognized that farmers had to give precedence to debts contracted on a purely commercial basis, that banks and storekeepers had to be given priority so that local credit could be maintained. It stepped aside in emergencies. The Society learned that a delinquent account does not necessarily denote a poor farmer, that arrearage may be the result of an essential installation, or of reduction in other obligations and that, despite default, the security may be stronger.

The task of collection is particularly difficult in troublous times. In every emergency there are inconsiderate people who exploit distress to get unmerited favors for themselves. When agitation for debt reduction was rife, when mortgage moratorium laws were enacted, and a new farm mortgage bankruptcy act, benevolent in design, was passed, a laissez faire attitude toward debt payment was produced which was reflected in defaults often when there was no valid reason for default. Many farmers became imbued with the feeling that all principal payments should be deferred whether or not there was just ground for postponement. There was no inclination to press the man honestly unable to pay so long as he had a chance to come back. But the Society set itself resolutely against the borrower who sought to turn to his own advantage a misfortune from which he suffered little or nothing.

A lawyer associated with the Federal Land Bank, fully conversant with the Society's work, made the observation that in its financial operations, the Society flies in the face of every accepted business practice. It makes loans on farms, not usually considered prime security. Save in exceptional instances, it rules out first mortgages and makes loans on subsidiary liens. It lends to novices who, in the light of the accepted belief that a farm is only as good as the man on the farm, are not deemed the best farm risks. Finally, it spreads its operations over wide areas, making follow-up and servicing difficult and therefore increasing the hazard. From the business viewpoint, the argument is all too true. Yet, the Society has always felt that it would not be fulfilling its mission if it failed to do these very things.

With only about five per cent of loans on first mortgage and with the other uncommon practices, losses are bound to occur, in good times and in bad. Yet up to the depression the loss rate was surprisingly low. The Society prided itself that, during its first thirty years, the rate was only slightly more than 5% of the loan turnover of the three decades. The depression drove the loss rate up sharply. Since there are no fund drives, no public appeals, no means of recoupment, losses are irretrievable. Every loss reduces the Society's capacity to serve. There are no reserves, the Society having liberally interpreted the wish of its founders to keep its funds active at all times. Losses more than slow up the rotation of the loan wheel. The lessened principal means reduced interest in-

come for educational and service functions. Slight operating deficits were thus incurred during the first three years
of the depression, but the Society was able to readjust its
program without the sacrifice of essential services.

Because the Society depends upon its interest income to
help defray administration and service costs, it has not
been able to reduce its rate below 6%. Interest normally
covers only 35% of these costs. The balance is made up
by the contributions of the Baron de Hirsch Fund. But
interest is the only charge the Society makes. Unlike most
lending agencies, even governmental, the Society exacts
no application fee, makes no charge for investigation or
renewal, imposes no penalty for delinquency—and this on
loans not elsewhere obtainable. The sole expense to the
borrower is title search and recording fees, and attorneys
are asked to be moderate in their charge. In a small loan,
the entire transaction is handled without lawyers' services. The Society, of course, asks no remuneration for a
whole range of service, whether in connection with loans
or otherwise.

To appreciate the effect of the depression on the Society's structure, it is necessary to consider the depression's
impact upon American agriculture in general. This is
strikingly brought out in the Society's reports of those
years:

"The year 1930 was a most critical one for American agriculture. The report of the Secretary of Agriculture makes gloomy reading. The year witnessed
the most disastrous drought in the history of the
country. It saw farm commodity prices slump to the
lowest point in fifteen years. The national farm income was the smallest since 1921—16% below that of

1929. Whereas in former years there were some favored spots, this year the world-wide industrial depression brought suffering to all sections. The demand for agricultural products fell off sharply due to reduced buying power. No branch of farming was exempt from price decline. Farm values suffered a further recession and the number of forced sales rose until it almost equalled the rate of voluntary sales. Farm bankruptcies stood at several times the prewar figure. The credit situation was unfavorable. Lending agencies seemed to be fearful of making loans to a depressed industry."

In 1931 conditions were still more deplorable. The Society reported:

"The economic position of the American farmer took a step backward in 1931. Passing over natural causes, such as drought, frost, pest, from which some regions in so large a territory as the United States are always bound to suffer, the fundamental cause was the world depression in trade and industry. Whether due to overproduction or underconsumption, agriculture was burdened with surpluses which demoralized markets and sent farm prices to very low levels, in some instances to the lowest point in twenty years and more. The tightening of credit, in spots its total stoppage, and country bank failures in unprecedented number, contributed still further to the farmers' woes. Conditions in the cities did not add to their comfort. Wide-spread unemployment deprived them of the seasonal jobs to which some of them or their children were wont to turn in dull times or during slack periods on the farm."

To make matters worse, farm credit was virtually in a state of coma.

"Agricultural credit in 1931 was tighter than in several years. Federal Land Banks were short of money and some discontinued taking applications. About eighty-five per cent of the Joint Stock Land Banks stopped making loans. Country banks were in no position to place farm mortgages because, confronted with heavy withdrawals, they could not afford to tie up their funds in securities not readily convertible into cash. Some, in fact, were compelled to call in mortgages. An abnormally large number failed and the trustees had to demand payment to expedite liquidation. Building and Loan Associations were called upon for redemption of shares in such volume as to leave nothing over for new loans. Besides, not a few were already loaded up with farm property taken in under foreclosure. Life insurance companies and other corporations which usually lend money on farm mortgages drew in their lines. Private lenders were wary. Second mortgage money—of which there is always a dearth—was virtually unobtainable. Short term credit was scarcer than in years. Merchant credit ruled at a low point. On the whole, the agricultural credit structure was under a severe strain."

In 1932 the picture continued to be gloomy. "The year," said the report, "brought no relief to the tight mortgage situation discussed in our 1931 report. The same condition ruled in the other forms of credit utilized by farmers—for production, harvesting and marketing purposes."

Jewish farmers suffered severely. Fortunately only a

minority concentrated on those agricultural staples which
had been in the slough for some years prior to 1929, ever
since the export markets on which these staples depended
began to decline. Most Jewish farmers were engaged in
those branches of farming—dairying, poultry, vegetable
and small fruit farming—which do not depend upon export and which suffered not so much from over-produc-
tion as from under-consumption because of lack of domestic buying power. Again, the effects of the agricultural
slump were more severe in the hinterland than in districts near large centers of population, especially in the
northeast. Most Jewish farmers are located in regions
fairly close to cities. This is a distinct advantage. Markets
are more favorable. Nearby farmers who have friends and
relatives in the city are able to engage in direct selling,
thereby eliminating the middleman's commission. Such
farmers can also supplement their incomes by using surplus housing accommodations for summer roomers or
boarders. Coming in the first place from trades, many
Jewish farmers were even in hard times able to find some
city work to add a little to farm income. While these
features by no means gave immunity, they mitigated the
severe effects of the depression.

But the Society felt the full force of the nationwide dis-
turbance. The need for economy on the one hand and the
necessity to stand by on the other meant a severe tax upon
its whole machinery. Lamented its 1930 report:

"Probably in no previous year has our work been
bound up with so much difficulty and anxiety as in
the year just closed. Probably in no former year had
we to exercise such extreme degree of discrimination.
Never before were we so torn between conflicting
emotions in weighing borderline cases. Formerly we

could work on the supposition that the man who had
lost out on the farm could go back to the city and re-
enter his former occupation. This year we could indulge in no such assumption."

The same doleful strain ran through the reports of
1931 and 1932.

"No other year in our three decades was as trying,
as taxing and as nerve-straining as the year 1932. At
no other time were problems in such number and of
such gravity laid before us for possible solution.
Never before did we have to grapple with so large a
volume of work. We had to help our farmers, in so
far as we were able, to unravel their financial tangles,
to find ways of their carrying on at a reduced operating cost, to revise farm management programs, to
improve production practices, to reform marketing
methods, to seek new outlets for farm products, to
tighten farmers' cooperatives, to save the farmer every
possible dollar—in short, we had to speed up the
tempo of our work along all fronts."

The problem was intensified because of the strong
trend farmward. The Society offered the explanation
"that in their search for a way out, many Jews displaced
by technological advance, uprooted by economic processes
or declassed by social forces are casting their eyes toward
the farm. Many city folks are trekking to the farm to avoid
starvation and destitution. Children are returning to the
parental homesteads. Parents are finding refuge with their
children. Brother is going to brother. Friend is going to
friend. Here on the farm they can find, if nothing more,
at least food and shelter." The number of farm seekers

that year was, with the single exception of the boom year
1920, the largest on record. The Society was in a dilemma.
People were crying for farms. Farmers were clamoring
for loans. The Society's loan capacity was at a low ebb,
the repayments that year having dropped to the lowest
point in almost twenty years.

Losses rose alarmingly. Within the short space of five
years beginning with 1930 they aggregated more than in
the entire period between 1900 and 1930. Yet the wonder
was, not that there were losses, but that the Society was
not wiped out altogether. Officials of federal farm lending
agencies and others expressed surprise that the Society
was able to keep afloat at a time when loan institutions,
farm and city, with their incomparably stronger structures
were experiencing rough sailing or foundering completely.
The Society ascribed its survival to its basic loan philosophy and, chiefly, to the grim determination with which
loan recipients held on to their farms. Perhaps many Jewish farmers stuck only because there was nothing for them
in the city, but the fact remains that there was among
them no general flight from farms. Though the fact cannot be established statistically the Society is convinced
that fewer Jews were driven off farms during these lean
years than out of city jobs, city businesses and city homes.

Beginning with 1933 the gloom began to lift. That year
stands out as epoch-making in the history of American
agriculture. Agricultural developments of far reaching
scope and significance were compressed into a few event-
ful months. A new farm philosophy was evolved; far flung
legislation was enacted to stabilize farm prices and to re-
plenish the dried-up reservoirs of farm credit. The Farm
Credit Administration brought into being the largest and
most comprehensive farm credit system that had ever been

devised. Henry Morgenthau, Jr., a member of the Society's Directorate and at one time its Vice-President, was named by President Roosevelt to organize and head the system. These remedial measures had a salutary effect. Soon the Society's affairs began to take on a healthier complexion. Losses could not be checked immediately, but gradually dead timber was removed and toward the end of the decade, the Society could hope that the loss rate would thenceforth decline. At that time, however, the Society began to be called upon to make loans to refugees, a new and strange element in farming. Since these loans, taken as a whole, are granted on slim margins, refugee performance will have a bearing on future loss trend. So far performance has been very encouraging.

During this troubled period the Society's collection policy, generous, yet sound, enabled those to remain on their farms who, but for its forbearance, would have been compelled to give up the battle, to return to the city, there to join the already swollen ranks of the unemployed or to drift on to heavily laden relief rolls. The men at the Society's helm have always felt that loss is simply an item in the price that must be paid in building up a Jewish farm movement in this country.

Depression had its effect also on the non-financial phases of the Society's activity. Indeed every phase felt the impact. To the Employment Department came men from the more comfortable stations of life—lawyer, rabbi, pharmacist, clothing manufacturer who had been wiped out, doctor of philosophy, students unable to continue their studies—looking for nothing more than shelter and bare physical subsistence. These are just the types that farmers are loath to employ, and they came at just the time when there was a surfeit of farm help. Eager as the Society was to relieve their distress it lamented that "only rarely can we place such men."

Working with a reduced staff, the Extension Department had to refine its techniques. The depression had taught the lesson, as never before, that many farm problems cut across regional and state lines. Farm meetings of varied types were old institutions. But, at this stage, the educational department inaugurated the larger regional and interstate conference bringing the leaders of various farm communities together to take counsel with the Society and with one another, to formulate programs to meet the exigencies of the times, and then to relay the findings to their constituents. The conference of 1930, held on October 12th and 13th, was most impressive. The main session was attended by 300 farm leaders. Products of every description were exhibited, some of which came from as far south as Florida and as far west as California. The management of the Educational Alliance in New York City, where the conferences took place, estimated that the exhibits were viewed by about 14,000 people. The public meetings were addressed by Dr. Jacob G. Lipman, Dean A. R. Mann of Cornell, Percy S. Straus and B. Charney Vladeck. That conference and the conference of 1931 were general in nature. The subsequent conferences dealt with specific branches—dairying, poultry raising, and fruit and vegetable growing. They were so well received that they have become yearly affairs.

Another manifestation had its roots in the depression. With opportunities in the city restricted, fewer farm youth cast their eyes cityward while more city youth began to think in terms of the farm. This twofold trend resulted in the holding of a Jewish farm youth conference at the

Society's headquarters in 1936, and the founding of The Jewish Rural Youth Association. The objectives, as stated, are to explore "ways and means to achieve a greater measure of happiness out of country life through (1) an adequate income (2) the right kind of work (3) a satisfying social environment (4) the development of a proper sense of values and a sane outlook on life." Said the Society's report, "Rural Youth Association seeks to inculcate in the young people a wider appreciation of the advantages inherent in country life, to develop their latent talents for recreational and cultural activities, and to carry on a program to make farm life more attractive and meaningful." During the past six years, meetings have been held periodically and miscellaneous functions carried on.

The sanitation activities felt the pressure of the economic dislocation. Property owners were unable or unwilling to make repairs or improvements not immediately or imperatively necessary. A lowered morale is never conducive to the maintenance of high sanitary standards. The Society had to fight to avoid retrogression. It brushed aside non-essentials and concentrated effort on devising means of making improvements at the lowest possible cost. Farmers were shown how old outfits could be made to function and that many sanitary installations could be provided by the labor of their own hands and with materials obtainable on their own farms.

At about this juncture, a new vacation practice began to come into vogue, influenced by the vacationist's shrunken pocketbooks. Fewer people could afford to go to summer hotels and the larger boarding houses, yet they wanted conveniences and comforts not obtainable in the average rooming house. This gave rise to a type of rooming bungalow which was to become so popular as to have an almost revolutionary effect on the summer boarding business in the mountains. The summer bungalow is a two or three room abode of simple construction, housing a single family. The family has its own cooking, dining and toilet facilities and enjoys a measure of privacy impossible in the multiple rooming house. The mushroom growth of bungalows brought added problems. Additional strains were placed on water supplies already overtaxed and on sewage disposal systems already over-burdened. Government officials—some overzealous—began to make demands for apparatus and equipment beyond the ability of most farmers to meet. Through the Society's labors, such demands were moderated and without sacrifice of safe and decent standards.

In no field of the Society's work was depression felt more acutely than in farm settlement. To the run-of-the-mill farm seekers, whose number declined, were added the victims of depression who regarded farming as an escape from city burdens. Reports describe them as "the small businessman who sees the props removed from under him; the worker who, never sure of his job at any time, feels himself all the more insecure at this time; the many who see their meager savings steadily fading and live in constant dread of being thrown upon public relief," again, "people formerly in affluent circumstances accustomed to high standards of living who had suffered in business or taken losses in real estate or in stocks, people brought to the verge of nervous breakdown by the stress of the times." "What can be done for them?" the Society asked.

In the face of the much publicized plight of the farmer, the piling up of farm surpluses, the pronouncements that there were already too many farmers, would the Society not be rendering a disservice in encouraging the move farmward? The Society felt that "to lay down a general policy of dissuasion might shatter the last remaining hope of people in despair and shut the door of opportunity to some who would win out even in the face of adverse conditions." What made the task even more intense was that already established farmers needed more than normal help. To keep an equable balance between these two sets of demands—both meritorious—called for painful decisions. Faced with doubt as to the immediate prospects in farming, working on resources already shrunken and continuing to go down, and confronted with the increased and growing needs of existing farmers, the Society's settlement program was drastically curtailed. In the five years beginning with 1930, the numbers of "settlements" was just about half of that of the five years prior to 1930.

The depression changed the viewpoint of many as to the connotation of the term farmer. The Society had always maintained that a supplementary activity did not take a farmer out of that category, whether it was industrial work, boarding summer guests, running a filling station or conducting a country store. "This may not be undiluted farming" held the Society, "but it is needless to cavil about a definition so long as a man derives a substantial part of his living off the farm." Soon such farmers began to be looked upon, not with scorn but with envy, and the Federal government recognized part time farming in its loaning program.

A movement giving expression to the part time farming philosophy gained impetus during the early years of the depression. For the Society, part time farming was not new. It had been practiced to some extent as far back as the South Jersey colonization period. There were always people who drew their living partly from farming and partly from industrial work. Some of these evolved into

full fledged farmers. But, during the middle of the nineteen twenties, a trend began to manifest itself among
Jewish city workers to settle on small farms within commuting distance of their places of employment, their farms
to serve primarily as homes, secondarily as sources of income. The Society felt that, if the passage from city to
farm could be eased, the aspirations of those who were not
ripe for full time farming could be realized. This movement will be discussed more fully in a later chapter.

Cooperation is not a depression measure. But when
times are bad, when the farmer has to make every penny
count, it assumes added significance. The hard knocks of
depression brought to the farmer a keener realization of
its benefits. The Society, and the Baron de Hirsch Fund
before it, had been consistent advocates of the doctrine of
cooperation. Long before the United States Department
of Agriculture set up a bureau to "determine the possibilities and encourage the use of organized cooperative effort
in improving rural conditions" the Society had fostered
cooperatives, assisted in their formation and extended
credit to them.

As early as 1901, the Society had lent $2,200 to help buy
threshing equipment for the collective use of a group of
twelve North Dakota farmers—a form of loan which was
the forerunner of the "Community Service Loan" adopted
some thirty years later by New Deal farm agencies. The
principle implicit in that simple form of cooperation was
later translated into cooperative activities of many varieties—creameries, bull associations, canneries, buying and
marketing cooperatives, credit unions and the chain of fire
insurance companies already referred to.

The early experience was none too heartening, but the
Society had an abiding faith in the virtue of cooperation,

and that faith has been rewarded by the sound, healthy cooperatives that exist today and by the satisfaction which comes from the knowledge that many of the principles early promulgated by the Society have become established cooperative practice. A cardinal doctrine has always been that only such cooperatives should be formed as can perform a distinctive service and which have more than reasonable assurance of stability and permanence. And since the farm cooperative has primarily an economic function, touching alike all farmers in a given community, cooperative activity should be carried on along non-sectarian lines. Since non-Jewish farmers outnumber Jewish, the membership of the present cooperatives is largely non-Jewish, but the foundations were laid by Jewish farmers.

In 1933 the Farm Credit Administration established Banks for Cooperatives in its twelve regional districts. With that embracing cooperative arm, cooperation made marked strides. Taking advantage of these liberalized credit facilities, Jewish farm communities with the lead of the Society, strengthened existing cooperatives and formed new ones. Now the Society works with associations in Connecticut, New York, New Jersey, Ohio and Michigan—having a combined membership of over 2000 farmers, which in 1941 did an aggregate business of more than $2,500,000. A fine example of cooperative progress is the Central Jersey Cooperative Association founded in 1930 by seven Jewish farmers and which in 1940 had a membership of over 800, owned a plant worth $90,000 and did a business of $585,000.

The Society's role has been to do the preliminary educational work, to help organize, to give counsel, and to act as the liaison link between cooperatives and governmental agencies. The Springfield Bank for Cooperatives has from the start looked at these associations through friendly eyes and been liberal in its extension of credit—proof of the soundness of the ventures.

The ideology of cooperation has been so well expounded that it is not necessary to dwell upon its merits. Economically, wholesale purchase and joint marketing mean dollars saved. More than that, the farmer is assured of a good and safe product. But the cooperatives have more than economic utility. They bring farmers together, become forums for educational discussion and community planning, promote self-reliance, and, what is important, they tend to break down barriers based on difference in race, religion or origin.

These cooperatives have in a measure wrought revolutionary changes in the farmer's economic life. Many farmers attribute their survival in hard times and their wholesome status today to membership in cooperatives. And it is not laboring the point to say that in a very real sense these achievements were the fulfillment of the very purpose in the mind of the founder. Baron de Hirsch envisaged his people taking their place as independent farmers at the side of their fellow farmers in sympathetic and understanding community. Viewed against the background of the Russian purgatory from which the Jewish pioneers had escaped, the transition, within the space of little more than a generation, of humiliated Luftmenschen into stalwart self-reliant "cooperating" farmers is a phenomenon of noteworthy significance.

CHAPTER V

Refugees

T H E Society had just about emerged from the depths of the depression when a new and unforeseen responsibility was thrust upon it: the problem of rehabilitation through farming of many of the refugees who fled here after the coming of Hitler to power.

The Nazi conquest of Germany set in motion a new flow of immigrants, in some respects similar to and in others different from, the previous immigration waves. The flow was never large. Our immigration laws had cut down on the movements of people to the shores of the United States. Where there had been hundreds of thousands, there were now inconsequential numbers against the total American population.

Nor were the immigrants the same. They were for the most part well educated men and women who had achieved solid status in Germany, who had established reputations, specialized skills, and, long before exile forced them out, a measure of wealth. On their arrival here they had limited funds; more important, their experiences had left them with deep psychological scars. They were, so to speak, newcomers in a world suffering from severe shell shock.

In their efforts at readjustment some of them turned to farming. This was the result of a new wisdom and understanding, of a craving for life on the land as one of the few gratifying avenues open for the wounded spirit in a world full of injustices and seething with violent hatreds. It was the choice of an enduring value at a time in history when the old values seemed to have lost their meaning.

The refugee problem was first mentioned in the report of 1935. It was then slight in scope. But it was foreseen that some of the victims of Nazi intolerance would seek to find a place on farms in this country, and the Society began preparation to meet its new obligation. Fortunately, the Society had the experience, the machinery, the personnel and the organization which could be expanded to carry the heavier load.

In the beginning, the number of refugees seeking to settle on the land was small, so small that refugee statistics were not segregated from general statistics. By the end of 1937, only 173 refugee applicants had been registered, but by the close of 1941, the number had risen to 3,359. There were calls at the Society's office by refugees or by friends and relatives of prospective emigres; there was correspondence with those still in their homelands or in transit countries. Virtually all who sought help were heads of families, some spoke also for relatives or close friends, some for groups. All in all, the Society served between fifteen and twenty thousand people, earnestly interested in farming or anxious to investigate its possibilities. This was apart from the 684 who sought help in farm matters relating to immigration.

In the beginning the refugee problem centered almost wholly around exiles from Germany, but with the spread of Nazi conquest, it came to embrace emigres from practically every country of Europe and from transit countries on all continents of the globe. In the Society's reception rooms waited the lawyer from Berlin, the bank official from Leghorn, the teacher from Cologne, the university professor from Rome, the merchant from Hamburg, the manufacturer from Leipsig, the physician from Vienna, the engineer from Naples, the executive from Milan, the industrialist from Prague, the tradesman from Lodz or Budapest; later there came the unhappy fugitive from France and North Africa. Among them were some cattle dealers and a few farmers and men who had had a short period of farm training in preparation for their emigration. Some had been twice, even thrice exiled. Some had spent periods in concentration camps. Some were veterans of the first World War who had won distinction on fields of battle. There were the old, the young, the middle-aged. Some had made their way to the Society's office almost directly from the steamer. Others had been in the country for some time and had tried their luck in city ventures which proved unsuccessful. Still others were holding petty jobs and were gradually eating into the small remnants of their salvaged capital. Some appeared to have become attuned to their new milieu. Others were still living in the past. Some came simply to explore, others with the definite intention to farm. Uncertain of their future, they were eager to cast anchor. Only a few had a balanced conception of farming and of farm living. Most harbored vague and fantastic notions of what it meant. Most had slender, some no means. All, even those able to finance their own farms, needed counsel and guidance.

The successive steps in the process of farm settlement have already been described: the initial interview, the repeated and protracted consultations, the examination of farms in different localities, the ultimate choice, the purchase negotiations, the final closing, the grant of the loan

upon which most refugees depend for their start, the map-
ping of farm management programs. All this and more,
the reports say—important enough in the case of the non-
refugee farm seeker needing no orientation to American
life—becomes infinitely more important when dealing
with the man who has come from a concentration camp,
who has trekked from country to country, whose harrowing experiences are still vivid in his memory. For the
earlier farm seeker the step to the farm was a step upward,
the realization of a long cherished dream to become the
cultivator of his own little domain. For the refugee the
change was only too often the result of a painful awaken-
ing and, in the light of the substance he left behind, a
step downward. "For him to transplant himself to a poultry farm in New Jersey, to a dairy farm in New York or
to a fruit farm in Michigan meant the adjustment to a
new economic standard, the orientation to a different social order, the complete rebuilding of life on an entirely
new pattern." The Society found many of the emigres,
accustomed to high standards of living, turning down good
farms for no other reason than that the surroundings
lacked attraction, that the grounds did not have sufficient
shade trees, that the rooms in the house were too small for
their furniture. "Those to whom money does not count
can indulge in these luxuries, but such refugees are few
in number. The others must be impressed with the lesson
that farm income comes not from the farm dwelling nor
landscaped lawn; that good soil, good farm buildings, good
stock are of inestimably greater importance."

The Society also met with more than the usual tendency
toward partnerships. Refugees see in partnership a social
advantage, the comfort of sharing responsibility, financial
and otherwise. They see, too, in the pooling of resources
the opportunity of operating on a larger scale. Compelling

as this may appear, the Society opposed, as it always did, farm partnerships. Long experience has proven that these so-called advantages are more than nullified by the weaknesses inherent in a venture which is not only a business carried on by the heads, but a mode of living in which all members of the families are thrown into close contact; where, therefore, clashes of temperament are sooner or later bound to occur. Two refugee brothers had hardly become settled before they came crying to the Society for help in the dissolution of their partnership. Two brothers-in-law took the Society's advice and bought separate farms adjoining each other. Both were getting along very well and yet the wife of one was trying to persuade her husband to sell out and go elsewhere for the only reason that she was too close to her sister-in-law. "What would have happened," asks the Society, "had these two families lived under one roof?"

In resettling refugees, opportunities for income outside of the farm were not overlooked: a roadside stand, the possibility of employment of a member or members of the family in nearby factory, store or office; the use of surplus rooms for guests. A German rabbi spent some time at the Society's Refugee Training Farm. His capital was so slim that unless outside income could be provided he could not be placed on a farm. With the help of the Society and the National Refugee Service, he was able to buy a modestly equipped poultry farm in a locality where he could also conduct a roadside stand and where his eighteen-year-old son could work in a clothing factory a mile away. The farm is near a town which has a synagogue maintained by a group too small to pay the salary of a full-time minister. Before this refugee rabbi-farmer had moved to the farm he had already received and accepted a call to act as spiritual head of the congregation. The Society's exten-

sion instructor found him dressed in overalls mixing ce-
ment for flooring in his poultry house.

By the end of 1941, 324 refugee families from Germany,
Austria, Italy, Holland, Poland, Belgium, Czechoslovakia,
Hungary, Rumania, Luxembourg and Yugoslavia had
been established on farms in Connecticut, Florida, Illinois,
Indiana, Massachusetts, Michigan, Missouri, New Hampshire, New Jersey, New York, Pennsylvania, and Virginia.
But this number did not reflect the sum total of refugees
on farms. Relatives, close and distant, also find refuge
there. A refugee farmer whom the Society settled in New
Jersey in the summer of 1937 had, within about a year,
become the nucleus of a group of twenty living on four
farms. Nineteen members of five related families settled
in quick succession on three farms in Dutchess County,
New York. A refugee farm in New Jersey bought in 1938,
has accommodated as many as sixteen refugees, chiefly
members of related families. The refugee farm has facilitated the entry into the United States of other refugees
who were granted visas because they could bring to American Consuls proof that they were going directly to farms.
In addition to those whom the Society has been instrumental in settling, it has knowledge of over one hundred
who bought on their own initiative or on the advice of
refugees previously settled. It is safe to estimate that there
are well over 2,500 refugees who have found abode and
sustenance on farms in the United States.

The 1941 report points to interesting sociological implications. Of 80 families settled during the first ten
months of that year, only 15 of the heads were below forty,
while 39 were over fifty, 6 over sixty. Only 17 had been in
the country less than one year, while 44 had been here
more than two years, twenty of these over three years.
They were men of an age whom it is difficult to rehabili-

tate in other occupations and who had already been float-
ing about in the city. A man of sixty and his wife had been
on relief almost from the time they arrived in December,
1938. In October, 1939, the Society and the National
Refugee Service gave them loans to establish a small poultry farm. Two years elapsed and the elderly couple was
earning its living, paying overhead, amortizing the first
mortgage. Had they remained in the city, the probability
is that they would still be on relief. The cost of relief
during the two years would almost have equalled the sums
lent them. The money would have been used up without
hope of return and a physically sound, self-respecting
couple might have lapsed into demoralization.

Another case: a man of 63, formerly a textile manufacturer, spent a period at the Refugee Training Farm.
In May, 1941, he and his brother bought a farm in Laurel-
ton, New Jersey. At a celebration held at the training
farm in August, he was interviewed by a reporter for the
New York Herald Tribune, who found: "D. H. was one
of the most exuberant of the training center's graduates.
Yesterday was Mr. H.'s third anniversary in this country.
. . . He said he and his brother lost money for a year
trying to peddle linings to tailors in New York but now
would not take a hundred thousand dollars to quit farming for the city. He said that in America, he was a first
class citizen because he worked the soil. 'In Germany, we
were second class, third class.' "

At the close of 1941, 225 refugee farm loans totalling
$374,176 had been approved in the twelve states above
listed and in North Carolina. This excludes $6,860 in
mortgages which the Society permitted to stand against
farms bought by refugees. The Society had to liberalize its
lending policy by making loans higher in amount and
against weaker securities than had theretofore been its

practice. To offset the drain on the Society's funds, the
Baron de Hirsch Fund made sums available specifically
for refugee purposes. Not included in the above is the
participation of the Refugee Economic Corporation to the
extent of $11,416, and of the National Refugee Service in
the sum of $25,215, bringing the total of refugee grants
by December 31, 1941, to $410,807.

The majority of refugees were settled on poultry farms.
This was a matter of practical necessity, not entirely of
choice. The Society would have preferred more diversified
farming, but experience had proven that poultry was best
suited to the newcomer. While the poultryman must be
constantly on the job, the work is not as taxing physically,
as for instance, dairying. This is an important consideration for people, some no longer young, who have not done
much manual work. There are tasks which even older
folks can perform without undue hardship. The modest
poultry farm requires less money than a dairy or fruit farm
and can in most instances be run by members of the family with little or no paid help. The refugees were located
in the vicinity of metropolitan areas where some were able
to develop their own retail egg routes. Despite fluctua-
tions, poultry farming withstood the knocks of depression,
and now under war economy promises to flourish for some
years to come. The Society sees no reason, however, why
these refugees cannot, in time, as a few already have,
branch out into other forms of farming.

As refugee activity developed it became evident that
some systematic way would have to be found to give be-
wildered and floundering emigres the chance to test their
aptitude and inclination for farming and to offer the opportunity of a practical training to those who were ready
to go forth. In the beginning, the Society advised refugee
farm seekers to visit Jewish farm districts to see what Jew-

ish farmers do and how they live. After a few refugee farmers had been established, the Society sent or took the fresh refugees on visits to them. But this was not satisfactory. At best, only vague and fleeting impressions could be gained. Training via the farm job was all right for those for whom farm jobs could be obtained but there were not enough jobs of the right kind to go round. The courses in German introduced at the night classes, though helpful, did not hit the mark. Early in 1940, the Society established The Refugee Training Farm, near Bound Brook, New Jersey, 32 miles from New York City, on property which belonged to the Society. The large farm dwelling was, with slight modification, made to serve as office, schoolroom and dormitory for about 20 trainees with accommodations for several couples.

The training farm was not designed as a school to train youth and it has no fixed term nor rigid curriculum. Since those for whom the training is intended are men of mature age who have neither too much time nor too much money to spend on preparation, the aim is to give a short intensive course, enough to acquaint the trainees with the rudiments of a few branches of farming and to give them a taste of farm life. Only those are accepted who have resources with which to buy farms or at least to qualify for loans from the Society—those who can put their training to practical and constructive use. The Society was fortunate to secure as Superintendent a man who had taught in the former Baron de Hirsch Agricultural School and managed extensive farm enterprises. Didactic instruction is related to the actual work on the farm, which is performed by trainees under supervision. As part of their education, trainees help keep buildings, equipment and machinery in repair in order to gain that facility in the handling of tools and instruments which every rounded farmer must have. Through the good offices of the National Refugee Service, an assistant to the Superintendent was employed principally to teach manual operations.

The training farm has proved a wholesome meeting ground for German and Polish, for Italian and Hungarian, for banker and salesman, for lawyer and small shopkeeper, for the man of big estate and for the modestly circumstanced, for the orthodox and for the non-conformist. Refugees of Christian faiths have been accepted. Here they sleep in the same rooms, eat at the same table, perform the same chores, follow the same routine. All are on equal footing. This wiping out of artificial barriers, though incidental, is an excellent lesson in Americanization, a fine preparation for the American way of life. The fifteen men and women who composed the class at the time a gathering was held on training farm grounds in August, 1941, came from Germany, Austria, Poland, Italy and Sweden. Among them were office worker, knitter, merchant, printer, engineer, cattle dealer, dressmaker, embroiderer, and rabbi. They ranged in age from sixteen to sixty-three.

The gathering was presided over by the Extension Editor of the New Jersey State College of Agriculture who is also President of the National Association of Agricultural College Editors. It was addressed, among others, by the Professor of Poultry Husbandry of Rutgers and by the Secretary of the New Jersey State Board of Agriculture. The Dean of the State College and Director of the Experiment Station, in a letter of greeting, declared, "Your Refugee Training Farm at Bound Brook came into being as a direct result of the march of the dictators across Europe. The program you have established at the farm for refugees goes far beyond the teaching of the principles and practices underlying successful farming. Leaders of your Society with characteristic vision have emphasized in the training courses both the obligations as well as the privileges that accompany citizenship in the United States."

By the end of December, 1941, 256 trainees had been admitted. Their stay at the farm ranged from one week to eight weeks. More than half remained four weeks or longer. Tuition is free and a small charge is made toward the cost of food and lodging. The per capita cost of this training to the Society has been under fifty dollars. At the close of 1941, 107 of the "graduates" had been established upon farms of their own and 10 were holding farm jobs. Many of the others were on an active search for farms. Of course, there were some who attended the training farm only to learn that farming was not for them. It is far better to gain that awareness through an inexpensive testing period than by a costly investment in a farm.

The trainees were virtually unanimous in their opinion of the benefit derived from their course in "gaining knowledge" and "learning the ways of country life." A forty-seven year old lawyer from Vienna, now on his own farm in Connecticut, in sending his Thanksgiving greeting to the Superintendent, wrote in appreciation, "You would smile if you heard me quoting you every day, 'All depends on the man.' I guess I shall have this, your remark, printed and framed in your honour. You know, there are times when we get tired and wish to postpone some work or other. In such moments I remember you saying, 'All depends on the man,' and there is no more procrastination."

Under the caption "Newcomer Makes Good" the New Jersey Farm and Garden of November, 1941, carried an item referring to another training farm graduate. "S. H. W. has met the labor problem on his 2200 bird poultry farm at Sutton Lane, Stelton, by installing a feed and litter carrier. W. has equipped both his laying houses with a carrier and finds that it materially reduces his labor requirements and simplifies the work involved in feeding and cleaning. A refugee from Vienna in 1938, he spent eighteen months in Paris before coming to the United States in 1940. Although a newcomer to America, he has made splendid progress in the poultry business, and it is reflected in his well-kept and up-to-date poultry farm."

In another case a man of forty-five had been trying his hand at various jobs. After a period on the training farm he bought a farm with funds furnished by friends and with loans from the Society and the National Refugee Service. Though he did not show too much promise while in training, he displayed exceptional aptitude on his own farm. Doing much of the work himself, he remodelled a chicken barn at much lower cost than the Society's experts had estimated. He did many little jobs about the premises for which less frugal men would have hired labor and, by scouting about, succeeded in picking up material for $8 that would ordinarily have cost over $100.

From the very beginning of refugee settlement, the Society expressed satisfaction with results. "The refugee farm picture just now looks good," said its 1939 report. Yet the report hastened to add, "but we dare not venture to prognosticate too far ahead. Farming is a long range business and it is unwise to draw conclusions too soon. Perhaps there is such a thing as 'beginner's luck'. . . . We do not delude ourselves into believing that the road ahead will be entirely smooth. There will be rough spots over which some will stumble. In this, farming is no different from any other line of endeavor. We have faith that, by and large, refugees possess the intelligence, the industry and the perseverence to make the grade." In 1940 the Society was able to report that "The refugee farm scene continues to look good," and to "confirm" and "strengthen" the judgment of 1939.

In 1941 the Society again reported that the refugee picture continues "to look bright." Of the 324 families who had been settled through the direct instrumentality of the Society since 1937, 309 were still on their farms. Of those who had quit, some had left not because they could not make a living but because of illness, family considerations and other causes not related to the farm enterprise. A good index, the report declares, is refugee performance in loan repayments. Of the $328,668 in loans administered by the Society, $61,538 had been paid back, in part through refunding, but the very fact that refugees could find other channels of financing is in itself an indication that their enterprises are sound. Only $300 on a single loan had been charged off to loss.

"Of course," adds the report, "it is to be expected that as time goes on losses will have to be taken. And it cannot be expected that defections from the farm will not occur. It should be repeated that refugee farm activity is too new to permit long range prognostication. But the new farmers possess qualities that should stand in good stead. They are intelligent, thorough, methodical and diligent. The Society's extension men find them avid for information and eager to follow advice. Men who have been accustomed to ease, they do not stop to count their hours of work."

The refugee surge brought forth from well intentioned but overly enthusiastic well-wishers varied plans for the rapid settlement of emigres en masse. These hastily conceived but not too well considered plans were, with few exceptions, built along a collectivistic pattern where the land and instruments of production were to be jointly employed for the common weal. The Society was looked upon as overly conservative in refusing to be stampeded into efforts which, in the light of its history and experience, seemed unwise. The story of the 1881 decade, that frenzied colonization era with its train of sorrow and futility, and the subsequent colonization failures, had taught the lesson that human beings are not eager to submit to the regimen and self abnegation of collectivistic colonization. The Society preferred to plod the less spectacular but safer and saner path, tested by experience, to establish refugees on individual farms. By settling refugee farm families in districts that already contained fairly cohesive Jewish farm groups, the social advantages on which the proponents of colonization laid so much stress, were not sacrificed. Indeed, the Society perceived in the individual method of settlement the advantage to refugees of surrounding Americanizing influences and the acceleration of the Americanization process.

Fairly compact refugee farm settlements can now be found in the districts of Vineland, Farmingdale, Toms River and in other parts of New Jersey, in the vicinity of Binghamton and Middletown, New York. Beginnings have also been made in other sections of New York and Connecticut. The Vineland district contains about 140 refugee farm families. New Jersey was favored because it has distinct advantages. It is near New York and near Philadelphia. Prices of farms have in general thus far not been out of joint. Prices paid for farm commodities, especially milk and eggs, have been good. That is why New Jersey's Jewish farm population has grown more rapidly than that of other states. With Jewish communities already established, it seemed wiser to settle the newcomers where they could find kindred spirits instead of throwing them abruptly into far off hinterlands. Fortunately, transportation and communication facilities stretch the periphery of the community and provide social and communal opportunities not possible in the days when roads were few and poor, and before the automobile and telephone were in common use. The Society admits that a wider range and a more equable distribution of refugees would be desirable. "But," it adds, "there should be positive advantages before refugees are sent from New York down South or out West. That is not to say that all refugee farm work should be concentrated in a too constricted area. But as long as there are just as good farms and just as good possibilities near home, there is no valid reason to look for distant horizons, save where special circumstances exist or special inducements are offered."

The Society's reports contain thumb nail sketches of some refugee farm enterprises in action and, though they stress that it is too early for prophecy, see in refugee achievement thus far hopeful augury for the future. A few sketches gathered in 1939, 1940 and 1941, are of perennial interest.

The official of a bank in Southern Germany who was robbed of part of his possessions en route to America and who, drifting about in the city, was on the verge of despair, settled on a general farm in New Jersey which, in a little more than a year, was able to support eight people in modest comfort. Not only has this man shown marked success on his farm, but he has displayed remarkable facility in integrating himself into his community. He has been invited to address the Lions Club and the Men's Club of the Methodist Church, and to conduct a bible class on the Old Testament in the same church. He has procured affidavits from his Christian neighbors to bring over other immigrants. For several summers he had a camp for refugee children on his farm at modest rates, thus relieving working parents of their care while taking the youngsters

out of stuffy lodgings into green fields and cheerful sunshine. Dr. Albert Einstein, a neighbor, takes great delight
in visiting this farm.

The former editor of a well known trade journal in
Europe, a lawyer by profession, who with his wife under-
went training at the Refugee Training Farm, are established on a poultry farm in New Jersey. Formerly accustomed to spacious living, this man limited his household
setup to beds, tables and a few chairs. When visited shortly
after he had been on the farm, he spoke of his desire to
have his twelve year old son join the Boy Scouts, because
he wanted him to become a good American as rapidly as
possible.

From Frankfurt am Main, came a wholesale produce
merchant, a man of forty-seven. He was rigidly orthodox
in his religious practices. At first, it seemed that to encourage him to go on a farm would be courting disaster.
But he insisted that he would be lost in the city, that the
farm would give him his one chance. With no little misgivings and after much search, a farm was found in an old
Jewish farm community where the man can work and live
in conformance with his religious convictions. He has
been on the farm a little over two years and is faithfully
meeting his obligations.

At Toms River, New Jersey, an active and sizable Jewish community, a refugee was elected to the Board of Directors of the Jewish Community Center—a distinction
for a newcomer and a good token of mutual respect. In
the same place, a refugee of three years' standing runs a
combination poultry and vegetable farm and has his own
wayside stand. He has acquired enough skill and experience to do poultry breeding and the young stock he has
sold to other farmers has brought good results. His son of
sixteen is taking courses in pedigree breeding at high

school and is doing trap nesting, an advanced practice. Also in the same district an Austrian Jewess, holder of a doctor's degree, former teacher of languages, who had for some time been employed as a psychologist in a New York child caring institution, bought a poultry farm in partnership with an elderly woman whose husband, son, daughter and son-in-law are all lawyers and still in Europe. According to last reports, they have a flock of 1,500 layers doing well.

After spending six weeks in New York City upon his arrival in 1938, a young farmer from Essen, Germany, found a job as manager of a farm in New Hampshire whither he took his wife and infant daughter. By thrifty living and devoting his spare moments to dealing in cattle, he managed within a year and a half to acquire stock and machinery valued at over $2,000. When the farm on which he worked was sold, he was able with the help of the Society to buy a farm close by. He got off to a good start but in January, 1940, while hauling lumber on his place, he was seriously injured—so seriously that it was feared that he would never be able to walk or work again. Although a newcomer in a community almost exclusively non-Jewish, his neighbors rallied to his support in a manner which bespeaks the esteem which he had gained during his brief residence. The best of hospital and medical and nursing care was provided without stipulation as to the time or manner of payment. Neighbors called at house and hospital. Christian clergymen offered prayers. School children sent flowers. The Society dispatched a man to make a special investigation as a result of which an additional loan was made to pay for changes in farm management demanded by the new conditions. At the instance of the Society, the National Refugee Service made a supplemental loan. The last reports show that the man is able to carry on, with difficulty, but hopeful that as his physical condition continues to improve, his economic position will become stronger.

A young couple in their late twenties, who arrived in the United States in the fall of 1937, were farmers in Germany, had farmed in France and in Palestine and had brought their agricultural implements with them. The Society placed the couple in farm jobs. After working a year and a half, they succeeded in saving $600. In the meantime, a son had been born. Their small means narrowed the field of selection. The Society found a farm which because of unusual circumstances could be bought for $2,950 with $220 cash. As might be expected the farm had some undesirable features but the young couple brushed all objections aside. The Society lent them the money to make a start. In the fall of the year a storm severely damaged their crops. Nevertheless, overhead, including interest on the Society's loan, was kept current, and the confinement expenses of a second child were met.

In South Jersey, a young refugee and his wife bought a farm for which they paid as little as $1,000 with only $100 in cash. They came to the farm with a suitcase, a violin and a few hundred dollars, their sole possessions. The Society made loans to get them started. The following fall, in announcing the arrival of his first born, the man added "everybody including the chickens are doing well."

A language teacher in Germany, a man of forty, with wife and two children had been adrift in New York City for more than a year. He possessed no manual skills and, of course, no farm experience. The family was partly dependent upon outside assistance. Through the instrumentality of the National Refugee Service, a gift of $1,500 was obtained from a philanthropically inclined Christian woman. With that as a start and loans from the Society and the National Refugee Service, the family was located on a farm, the buildings on which needed remodelling—a job which this soft novice himself did remarkably well. He has also shown real skill in handling his poultry flock.

The greatest asset on the farm, it is often maintained, is the farm wife. The wives of refugee farmers have displayed a thrift and an industry which have commanded general respect. A woman in the late twenties came to the United States with her husband, formerly a cattle dealer in good circumstances, and settled on a farm in Chenango County, New York. Then they sent for their three-year-old girl who crossed the Atlantic in care of the steamship officers. Besides taking care of her household, this young woman tends the poultry flock and looks after the vegetable garden. She takes in occasional tourists and, being a trained dietician, bakes and sells cakes, cookies and other dainties.

The wife of a refugee farmer who had been a well-to-do grain dealer in West Prussia, herself a lawyer with degrees from two universities, built up a large and remunerative egg and poultry route through her own efforts. She is the driving force on the farm. The wife of a former textile manufacturer in Austria, a rich man's daughter who had never been unchaperoned until her marriage at the age of seventeen, at thirty went from house to house to build an egg route of well over one hundred customers. Similarly the wife of a former furniture manufacturer who had shied away from animals now takes pride in her skill in milking the family cow.

There were never many Jewish farmers in central European countries in proportion to the Jewish population, but there were some who would rate as outstanding "master farmers" even by American standards. Three related families of this type with whom the Society had corresponded while they were still in Europe are now located on a 535 acre farm in a dairy district in New York State. One had owned and operated a farm reputed to be one of the largest and best known in Austria, with a herd of over one thousand cows and a large poultry flock. Another partner came from a long line of farmers and had managed extensive estates. Here they have a modern creamery including a pasteurizing and bottling plant. Their daily retail distribution is one thousand quarts. Besides, they put up and sell milk products. In a recent test they ranked high in cleanliness and quality as a result of which they were given a contract to furnish milk to the local hospital. They have rehabilitated a declining business and are giving employment to twelve local residents.

The Society has been criticized by overzealous enthusiasts as being too slow and too cautious in diverting refugees to farms. But the Society holds that refugees cannot be flung on to farms with regard only to speed and numbers, that those who think only in numbers fail to grasp reality. It has worked in the spirit of the Talmudic precept that he who saves a soul saves a world. The Society maintains that agriculture can play only a part in the refugee problem, it cannot entirely solve it, but that meanwhile, no effort should be spared to settle those who possess the qualities which give fair promise of success. "On farms," it asserts, "refugees cannot be accused of cluttering cities, taking away jobs, intruding themselves into the professions and competing with established business. On farms, refugees can build a future in useful and productive occupation with the satisfaction that comes from the good will of fellow craftsmen with whom they are brought not into competition but into cooperation."

CHAPTER VI

Today

IN VIEWING the growth and development of forty years in the life of a movement and in the life of an organization, appraisals, reviews and estimates are in place. But the reality is more elusive, indeed, more impressive and more significant than the marshalling of fact upon fact. Summed up, there is a picture of Jewish farmers— many of them, more than ever before in American history —contented and successful farmers, who, with every advancing year, are playing a greater role in the total of our farm life.

How can the part played by the Jewish farmer be appraised. Statistics? There are statistics, not too many perhaps, enough to be revealing; but at best statistics cannot convey the reality. Who can appraise the full contribution of the pioneer; who can really weigh the changes brought about by the first family to go into virgin territory or into a new occupation? Numbers and graphs cannot tell the full story.

Personalities? There are scores of them, hundreds to challenge admiration. General progress? The story speaks for itself. Failures and disappointments? They, too, are to be found in all too full measure. There are all these—and

more—in the emergence of Jews into farming in the
United States. Before attempting evaluation or judgment,
let us take a summary view.

No census has ever been taken of the number of Jewish
farmers in this country. Before a census could be undertaken, the connotation of the term farmer would have to
be established. Is the absentee landlord of a large plantation or of an extensive ranch a farmer? Is the man who
tends a small garden on a home plot a farmer? The United
States census classification is rather vague. But even its
definition makes the task only slightly less difficult. The
taking of a census would require a staff to travel the highways and byways of forty-eight states, at a prohibitive cost
and one out of all proportion to the benefit sought. The
Society has, on occasion, tried to gather relevant information. The nearest approach to a census was made by Dr.
H. S. Linfield, who in a study of Jewish populations in the
United States made in 1927 for the Statistical Department
of the American Jewish Committee, estimated that there
are 109,600 Jews in rural territory. The writer estimates
the number of Jews wholly or partly engaged in farming
and in agricultural pursuits akin thereto, as between
eighty and a hundred thousand.

With the average size of the American farm as a base—
and this is not conclusive because size varies with region
and type of farming—the total Jewish farm holdings would
thus probably reach about one million acres. With personal property these holdings may, under normal conditions, be considered as having a total gross worth approximating one hundred and fifty million dollars. They are, of
course, subject to mortgage. Jewish farmsteads range in
size from the small intensive nursery to the vast grain
domain. They are found in all sections of the country.
The largest numbers are in the northeast and in sec-

tions of the middlewest, conforming to the bulk of the Jewish population. The natural tendency is to settle in or near places which already contain Jewish farm groups. This affords a freer outlet for gregarious inclinations and opportunity for stricter conformance with religious practises. Long urbanization has led Jews to settle not too far from the cities of their former residence where they are able to maintain ties with relatives and friends. But there are also independent spirits to whom proximity to urban centers or propinquity to Jewish neighbors is of no concern.

There is no type of agriculture practiced in the United States which is foreign to the Jew: dairying, poultry raising, truck farming, floriculture, orcharding, viticulture, cattle raising, tobacco, grain, cotton, sugar beets. Jewish farmers engage in those branches of agriculture which are generally practiced in the sections in which they have settled and raise those crops to which their land is best adapted and which are most profitably marketable.

Tenant farming is extremely rare. The Jew to whom land ownership has so long been barred, wants a spot that he can call his own. To attain this, he is ready to assume the obligation of mortgage with its attendant burdens. A good productive farm can rarely be rented and a tenant is not apt to put his best effort into a farm that will revert to the owner at the termination of the lease. The rental on a leased farm often amounts to as much as or more than the overhead on an owned farm. Stock and inventory cost the same. The difference is the initial downpayment, and when that can be raised, ownership is far preferable to tenancy. Then, again, the tenant farmer cannot get the credit which the owner of even a heavily encumbered farm can command. The Society naturally favors ownership, but is not opposed to tenancy where financial stringency

makes it imperative. There are more than a few cases
where farm tenants have evolved into successful farm
owners.

Like the general Jewish population, the Jewish farm
population is unevenly distributed. The states of New
York, New Jersey and Connecticut contain an overwhelming majority. But these states have over two and a half
million of the country's almost five million Jews, almost
three million if Boston and Philadelphia are included.
These regions contain the largest concentrated consuming
public and therefore the best markets in the land. And
there the Jewish farmer has ready access to services, principally those rendered by the Society, which, because of
monetary limitations, have to be confined to eastern territory. The Society would prefer a wider range, but the advantages offered in distant locales have thus far not been
sufficiently attractive to wean Jews far away from their
old homes. The Society believes that, had its resources
permitted it to stretch over a wider area, the Jewish farm
population might today be larger and more evenly distributed.

Connecticut contains some of the oldest Jewish farm settlements in the United States. Those in Chesterfield and
Colchester both had their beginning in 1891. The former
have declined but the latter still constitute an active agricultural community. Besides Colchester, the chief Jewish
farm centers are those around Hartford, New Haven,
Bridgeport, New London, Norwich and Middletown. In
addition, Jewish farm families are scattered throughout
the entire state. There are probably more diverse forms of
farming practiced by Jews in Connecticut than in any
other state. The Connecticut River Valley contains fertile
fields especially adapted to tobacco raising. Large tobacco

plantations were developed by Jews where both broad leaf and shade grown tobaccos are produced. During the World War period and for several years thereafter, the tobacco planters enjoyed great prosperity. Tobacco acreage was expanded. Dwellings which would grace the suburbs of a metropolitan city were constructed. Communal life was at its height. Then came the slump in the tobacco market. A hard period for the tobacco farmers ensued. Many farmers turned from tobacco to potatoes, and Jewish potato growers are now among the foremost in the state. Probably the largest individual producer of this crop is a Jew who raises close to 80,000 bushels. With the advent of the Agricultural Adjustment Administration, an upswing has set in and these farmers' prospects have shown marked improvement. Dairying, poultry raising, vegetable and fruit growing, constitute the other chief lines of farming in the state. The Jewish farm unit is large in size, an eighty or hundred acre farm being not uncommon. Except for pasture and woodland, farms are fairly well cultivated and well stocked. Connecticut Jewish farmers make their living almost wholly from the soil. While summer boarding forms part of the farm economy on farms in scenically favored sections, it is carried on largely as a subsidiary rather than a major source of income.

The state contains intensive industrial areas which provide splendid outlets for farm produce. The state's agricultural policy is directed toward the stimulation of the home market for home-grown products. Outside competition is reduced by regulations strictly defining marketing requirements. As a result, milk, poultry and other products command higher prices than in the neighboring states.

Jewish farmers have their local organizations for social, religious and recreational activity. Several of the large sized groups have their communal buildings. Some settlements are so close to towns and cities that they can participate in Jewish life there. Connecticut is the one state where local Jewish farm associations (whose membership is not exclusively Jewish) are federated into a central state organization.

New Jersey has been properly termed the cradle of the Jewish farm movement in the United States. The Jewish settlements in South Jersey are the sole survivors of all the early attempts at Jewish colonization in this country. The so-called South Jersey Colonies—Alliance, Rosenhayn, Carmel, Norma, Brotmanville, Garten Road—have provided historical themes for many writers, among them Charles S. Bernheimer, Jacob G. Lipman, Leonard G. Robinson, Philip R. Goldstein, Katherine Sabsovich, Samuel Joseph, Boris D. Bogen, Gustav Pollak, and lately "Yovel" published on the occasion of the fiftieth anniversary of the founding of the Alliance Colony. Although still popularly referred to as colonies, these settlements were never colonies in the accepted sense of that term. From the beginning to the present time, farm ownership has been vested in individuals. The farms were originally developed as truck farms, with strawberries, beans, sweet potatoes and peppers as the principal crops. Later, poultry was introduced and is now the primary source of income. Although the high hopes entertained by their founders were not fully realized, the colonies have been able to maintain their continuity as farm centers, and today, though most of the original settlers have died, the children of some are still there, and a third generation of Jewish farmers is beginning to grow up. Within the last two or three years, there has been an infiltration of refugees.

Founded as an agro-industrial settlement, Woodbine has of late years developed a fresh agricultural impetus. Aided

by the Baron de Hirsch Fund and the Jewish Agricultural
Society, new farmers have come in and modern poultry
plants have been built up. As in the South Jersey Colonies,
some Woodbine farms are in the hands of the children
of the original settlers. A recent mayor was the grandson
of a Woodbine pioneer.

With metropolitan New York near its northern extrem-
ity, Philadelphia dominating its southern end, and its
many shore resorts, New Jersey has a large consuming public within short range, affording many farmers the opportunity to market without the intervention of middlemen.
The same factors are favorable to the development of agro-
industrial settlements such as have grown up around New
Brunswick, Plainfield and Bound Brook, within the New
York City radius, as well as around the district contiguous
to Philadelphia. Hence, the state has long been a favored
locale for Jewish farm seekers. Jewish farm settlements
and individual farmers are found in every part of the state,
and New Jersey contains more Jewish farmers in proportion to the general Jewish population than any other state
of the Union. These considerations weighed cogently in
the selection of sites for refugee settlements, and New Jersey received the largest influx of refugee farmers.

Poultry and truck farming are favored. In Monmouth
and Ocean Counties, around Lakewood, Toms River and
Farmingdale, Jews are predominant in poultry farming.
Cumberland County is rapidly coming to the forefront as
well, because of recent refugee farmers. Jews have displayed unusual aptitude in mastering both the scientific
and practical phases of poultry husbandry and are engaged in all branches of the industry. Their commercial
plants range from one thousand to ten thousand bird
capacity, entailing considerable investment for building
and equipment, and requiring large operating costs. Mon-

mouth County, which ranks among the first ten agricultural counties in the United States, contains more Jewish farmers than any other county in the state. Jewish farmers around Freehold, Perrineville and Englishtown raise substantial acreages of potatoes, the county's leading crop; also many acres of tomatoes, sweet corn and a large variety of other vegetables.

Buying and marketing cooperatives exist in virtually every one of these settlements. Though organized mostly for Jews, they are not exclusively Jewish in their membership and afford a splendid example of a union of effort which, though economic in its primary aim, also makes for better understanding among groups. The Central Jersey Farmers Cooperative Association, already mentioned, is a good example. Founded by a handful of Jewish farmers, it has grown to a membership of over eight hundred, consisting of Jews and non-Jews. Jewish poultry farmers also took an active part in federating local marketing associations into a state federation. The Jewish farmers in and around Perrineville formed the first credit union organized by farmers under the New Jersey law. Other Jewish groups were likewise the first to apply for charters for credit unions under the recently enacted federal law.

The Jewish farming communities of New Jersey are well integrated, facilitating social activity and cooperative endeavor. Local Jewish organization is stronger here than among Jewish farm groups elsewhere. Practically every settlement has its own community center for religious, educational and social purposes.

Not until the turn of the century was there any marked farm activity in New York. Now, Jewish farmers may be found in various parts of the state. The densest Jewish rural population in the entire United States is centered in

Sullivan and Ulster Counties. Since Jews began to go there (about 1900), there has been a steady stream of migration, attracted, no doubt, by the scenic beauty of these pictur-esque regions, their invigorating climate and their accessi-bility to metropolitan New York. These counties had been favorite summering places for people from the city even before the advent of Jewish farmers, and following the economic pattern of the older stock, the newcomers com-bined summer boarding with farming. Side by side with the humble rooming house farm, there sprang up preten-tious boarding houses and luxurious hotels. These summer enterprises have screened the agricultural activity of the mountain regions. There is a tendency to frown upon the so-called "boarding house" farmer. Yet a volume of farm-ing, by no means inconsiderable, is carried on in this vaca-tion center, not a little by the very people who conduct the boarding and rooming places. There is probably more farming done in these two counties now than at any time in their entire history. The virtue of the combination of farming with boarding or rooming lies in providing an additional income and in bringing a ready market to the farmer's door.

Dairying still predominates in this region. Dairy herds have been improved with tested cows. Poultry farming on a commercial basis has been appreciably developed and up to the minute poultry plants have been constructed. Pota-toes are raised in large quantities and cauliflower as a commercial crop was introduced by Jewish farmers.

The Jewish farmers of the mountain districts have brought many Jews engaged in business and professions to these districts. The Society regards this trend as important, even though tangential. It tends, even if in a small way, toward a better population distribution. The population of the villages of Woodridge, Mountaindale, Hurleyville and South Fallsburgh, is preponderantly Jewish. The larger villages, Ellenville, Liberty and Monticello, have considerable Jewish populations. Ellenville contains 145 Jewish families, half of which were drawn from neighborhood farms.

Groups of Jewish farmers are located in Rensselaer County in the environs of Nassau, East Nassau, Schodack and Brainard, within easy access of Albany and Troy. The first settlers went there in 1894, but it was not until ten years later that the movement thither actually began. Here, dairying, poultry raising and a mixed form of farming are practiced. Summer boarding is on a modest scale when compared with the Ulster-Sullivan districts. Within the last decade, Rockland County has had an influx of Jewish farmers. This section is unique in that, though it is almost at the door of the metropolis and land values are high, there are Jewish farmers who carry on an intensive type of farming on sizable farms. The regions around Binghampton, Middletown and Catskill have lately received new accessions from the ranks of refugees.

Between about 1910 and 1920 Jews located on farms in the Mohawk Valley sections, principally around Utica, Syracuse and Rochester. They grew mainly grain and hay. During 1917 and 1918, they expanded their acreages to meet the crying demands of war. And they prospered. But with the cessation of hostilities grain and hay markets slumped. As in other parts of the country surplusses began to go up and prices to go down. The wider use of farm machinery which began with the war, the displacement of the horse by the tractor and of the buggy by the automobile still further reduced the need for forage and hay crops. Some Jewish grain growers, like many others, found the going too hard and dropped out. Latterly, however, these sections received new accessions and the newcomers, profiting by the experience of their predecessors, follow a diversified farm economy.

Talmud Torahs, synagogues and Jewish community center buildings are found in every sizable farm community throughout the state. Some villages have more than one. In Sullivan and Ulster Counties, farm and village are close enough together to fuse activities. There are local Jewish organizations of all kinds, branches of the large national Jewish organizations. Monticello and Liberty have hospitals built under Jewish auspices and maintained largely by Jewish contributions. Jews are members of school and village boards and hold civic office. Jewish farm girls teach in neighboring grade and high schools. Jewish young men raised on local farms have returned to these sections to practice professions.

The earliest historical record of Jewish farm effort in Michigan is the Palestine Colony, 1891—discussed elsewhere in this book.

The actual settlement of Jewish farmers in Michigan began over forty years ago, encouraged by the late Rabbi A. R. Levy of Chicago and the Jewish Agriculturist's Aid Society of America of which he was the founder. Today there are Jewish farmers in the vicinity of every fair sized city in the state. The largest number are in southwestern Michigan, whither they went from Chicago. South Haven was originally a general farming area and diversified farming is still practised there. Jewish farmers also turned to poultry and developed into one of the largest commercial poultry groups in the section. In and near South Haven there have long been summer resorts, but the boarding business of the district is confined almost wholly to the area bordering Lake Michigan, and few Jewish farmers cater to summer guests.

With the coming of the farmers, the Jewish urban population of South Haven gradually increased. Assisted by a
loan from the Jewish Agricultural Society, the urban and
rural residents erected a synagogue and community center
building which would do credit to a community of much
larger size. In the fall of 1941, the members celebrated the
burning of the mortgage.

In the neighborhood of Benton Harbor, Jews specialize
in fruit growing of various kinds. They have become expert in raising berries, fruits and vegetables. Farms range
in size from ten to two hundred acres and choice land sells
for as high as one thousand dollars per acre. Benton Harbor is the hub of the fruit belt of southwestern Michigan
and has one of the largest fruit and vegetable markets in
the country. In a total population of about eighteen thousand, there are two hundred urban Jewish families and a
Jewish farm population of about forty families. In the
eastern part of Michigan, the Jewish farmers near cities
mostly raise truck and poultry, and those in the outlying
districts run dairies and practice general farming.

Though hard pressed, as all farmers were during the depression years, the Jewish farmers of the state donated
several truck loads of foodstuffs to farmers in drought
stricken areas, and contributed quantities of farm produce
to soup kitchens in Chicago.

The Jewish farm settlements in Ohio are grouped
around Cleveland and Youngstown, and there are individual farmers scattered over the state. The largest group in
the state is in the vicinity of Geneva, about forty-five miles
from Cleveland, where Jews commenced to go on farms
about thirty years ago. Conforming to local practice, they
engaged in viticulture as a specialty. They made rapid
strides, increased their grape acreage and built up their
vineyards until, at the height of that industry's prosperity

(in the middle of the 1920s), the Jewish group, though a small fraction of the total farmers, produced over sixty per cent of the grapes raised in that section. Neighborhood banks and business men regarded the new element as a strong factor in the upbuilding and progress of Geneva. Unfortunately, specialization was pushed too far. When the cumulative effects of prohibition and competition from other grape areas made themselves felt, grapes dropped drastically in price and the grape growers had little else to fall back upon. Depression added to their woes, and the farmers of this section have for a number of years been confronted with critical conditions. Benefiting by their tough experience they have in late years begun to diversify their fruit culture and to raise other products. Hard times thinned the ranks of the oldtimers and the section has not attracted new blood. But Jewish farmers are taking active part in the struggle to lift the grape industry, and there are indications that the industry is finally on the upswing.

Not a few Jews have entered farming by way of an intermediate route; by part time farming, a good way, the Society has always held, of establishing those who for one reason or another are not ready to launch immediately into full time farming. The Society's reports point out that the central thought is settlement on farms of small acreage within commuting distance of cities where a moderate but appreciable amount of farming can be carried on by the farm wife and farm child while the wages of the head of the family continue to come in, thus making possible entrance into farming without immediate severance from city occupations. About twenty years ago, part time farming appealed increasingly to city workers of moderate means and "agro-industrial" settlements grew up near

New Brunswick, Chatham and Plainfield in New Jersey, and in the vicinity of Peekskill, New York. Lacking guidance, they made mistakes which retarded their agricultural growth. To give this type of project direction, the Society helped build up an agro-industrial settlement at Bound Brook, New Jersey. Before the depression, the settlement grew steadily and by 1930 there were forty families, and fourteen others had bought land preparatory to embarking later. The settlers lived in comfortable houses mostly newly constructed, on farms ranging in size from four to fifteen acres. The family heads commuted to their jobs and, with the help of wife and children, also did a measure of farming, mainly poultry. A few had already become sufficiently adjusted to be able to give up city work.

Encouraged by this demonstration, the Society in 1929 decided to embark on a project embodying the salient features of the Bound Brook plan. Percy S. Straus, a former President and long a Director of the Society, contributed $37,500 to get the project started. A tract of land was bought two and three quarter miles from the center of New Brunswick, New Jersey, a city of forty thousand, in which are located Rutgers College, the State College of Agriculture, the Agricultural Experiment Station, the New Jersey College for Women, high schools, synagogues, Talmud Torahs, Jewish fraternal organizations—in fact all facilities to meet full cultural and religious needs. The site was picked because it is on the main line of the Pennsylvania Railroad, with seventy trains plying between it and New York City and an average running time of one hour, which was cut still further after the electrification of the road. The land was subdivided into farms of from five to seven and a half acres, and buildings were erected. A group of interested farm minded workers, each possessing at least $3,000, was assembled, a series of meetings was held at which plans were perfected and those chosen whose qualifications with regard to steadiness of employment, temperament and general intelligence stood highest. Nine families constituted the initial group. The start was auspicious.

The agro-industrialists had hardly had a chance to become oriented when the depression broke. Some lost their city jobs, the hub of the plan. The wages of others were drastically reduced. To compensate for decrease in city income they expanded their poultry operations, using up reserves and even going into debt. Soon the depression reached the poultry industry and these people had to struggle on two fronts. When the plans were formulated, the horizon was bright. Men had jobs and money. It was natural to yield to the argument for better type houses on the plea that they were to last a lifetime. When things went bad, it was difficult for the owners to meet the overhead, which in the case of Bound Brook, included monthly amortization on building and loan mortgages. Defaults occurred. Some farmers had to give up. Others, however, managed to struggle through, the small farms a boon for them, providing a source of income, even if small, to help tide over a trying period. The Society deplored the fact that the depression set in so soon after the inauguration of this constructive sociological experiment that there had been no time for a real test. Meanwhile operations at New Brunswick were held in abeyance, to be resumed as soon as conditions returned to normal. But, with the greater demands that came in the wake of the depression and then because of the refugee, resumption has not as yet become possible.

The Society continued to express its conviction of the soundness of the agro-industrial idea. Writing in 1935, it reiterated that "our faith in this type of settlement remains unshaken," and added, "The underlying principles appeal to us as sound. It is our judgment that the combination of city employment with farming near industrial areas is a good way for farm minded city workers to gain entrance into farming. But experience has taught that it is prudent to start an enterprise of this kind on a more modest scale than was the vogue in the good years and that agro-industrialists should stick to their jobs until mortgages have been extinguished or substantially reduced."

The Society did not stand alone in advocacy of the part time farming plan. Soon after the establishment of the Division of Subsistence Homesteads in the United States Department of the Interior (1933), that division launched a project, "Jersey Homestead, Inc.," proposed by a group of Jewish needle workers and sponsored by several Jewish leaders in New York City. The government made an initial grant of $500,000 for the purchase of a 1,200 acre tract near Hightstown, New Jersey and the construction of dwellings for 200 families. Each homesteader was to invest $500 as a payment on a house and two acres of land for home consumption planting. This investment was to include an interest in the cooperative features which were part of the plan. A factory, privately financed, and a dairy, a poultry plant and a large truck farm were to be operated along cooperative lines. The Society's report of that year essayed the simple statement that "it will be interesting to watch the development of this venture." In 1935 the Resettlement Administration, which had taken the project over, made an additional grant of $350,000, which was materially augmented later. The original plans were changed and subsequently underwent still further modification. It was not until the summer of 1936 that the first fifty families moved to Hightstown and that the factory started opera-

tions. The factory, the heart of the project, worked inter-
mittently. The cooperative farms were, after a few years,
discontinued and the stock was sold. In 1940 the project
as a cooperative was liquidated and the government assumed full control. At this writing the factory is in operation under lease to a firm manufacturing millinery. The
houses are now occupied on a rental basis and the occupants work either in the factory or elsewhere.

In the same year, 1933, a group of 97 families drawn
from the radical elements in the large cities bought 9,000
acres of land with 80 buildings near Saginaw, Michigan
and founded the "Sunrise Cooperative Community." The
land had belonged to a large estate and was acquired at
what was considered an extremely low price and on ex-
ceedingly favorable terms. A large quantity of live stock,
farm machinery and crops planted on 2,000 acres were included in the purchase. The colony was conceived as a
strictly collectivistic enterprise with the land and all personal property belonging to the community and all farm
operations conducted for its collective benefit. The colony
had a brief and checkered career. Members dropped out
and new ones came in. Internal strife and economic pressure made the going tough and by 1936 the colony had
become a matter of history. Fortunately for its members,
as well as for its creditors, the Resettlement Administration bought the property for a government resettlement
venture, enabling the colony to liquidate its debts and to
make refunds to its members. A small segment of the Sunrise Community tried again in Samos, Virginia, but that
colony had even a shorter existence.

The Society played no part in Jersey Homesteads or
Sunrise Community but treated them in its reports only
because these ventures were in some circles regarded as
having significant possibilities for the rehabilitation of

large bodies of displaced Jewish workers. The Society had little faith in these expansive attempts. "The entire history of Jewish colonization," it reported, "argues against them. Colonization implies tying the weak with the strong, a regulation of labor, a regimentation of living, a submergence of personality, which people who have breathed the free air of America cannot readily accept or easily endure. Where Jews have succeeded in farming it was as individuals—not as members of organized colonies. The individualistic urge, the desire to be possessor of one's own farmstead, has apparently been stronger than any seeming benefit or alleged advantage to be derived from what is euphemistically termed cooperative but is in reality collectivistic farming.

"It is too bad," the report concluded, "that this failure will be charged by the uninformed against Jewish agricultural endeavor, instead of written down as due to the weakness inherent in collectivistic colonization."

In 1935, the Society conducted a sociological study covering three hundred Jewish farmers residing in seventeen states, the majority in the northeast and middlewest—a fairly representative cross-section. The findings give a picture of Jewish farm life through the eyes of those who live it. Almost sixty per cent of the farmers were under fifty; only ten per cent over sixty. The largest age group was that between forty and fifty—thirty-eight per cent. Eighty-one per cent had been in this country twenty years or more, while only a fraction of one per cent had been here less than ten years. Only four per cent were natives. It is evident that the bulk of present-day Jewish farmers are foreign-born who came here early in life, probably young enough to reap the benefit of some American schooling. Less than one per cent could not speak English; eighty-eight per cent claimed ability to read and write it. Eighty-three per cent were citizens and three per cent declarants.

The study disclosed that American Jewish farmers are recruited from a large diversity of occupations: labor, skilled trades, white-collar occupations, business and manufacturing, and even the professions. The needle and fur trades made up the largest group—twenty-eight per cent. Farmers and farm laborers constituted seven per cent. Seven per cent had attended farm schools or agricultural colleges here or abroad. Manifestly, the American Jewish farmer is not indigenous to the soil, but simply the immigrant Jew transplanted from American city to American farm.

The figures as to capital revealed that many Jewish farmers made their plunge into farming on slender means. Over twenty-one per cent had a capital of not more than $500. Thirty-seven per cent boasted of accumulations up to $1,000. Only fifty-seven per cent had as much as $2,000, while but fourteen per cent were in the over $5,000 class. The farmers in the smaller financial brackets are those who settled earliest, when farm lands were cheap.

The survey brought out the fact that sixty-one per cent went to the farm not to gain economic advantage or, as many believe, for health considerations, but to exchange the restraints and inhibitions of the city for the peace and freedom of the country. As they put it, they wanted "to seek a quiet life," "to live close to nature," "realization of life's ambition," "tired of city life and working in shop." Health, either of the head of the family or of some member, was a factor in only thirteen per cent of the cases. Eighteen per cent gave economic reasons. One man vouchsafed the information that he went for "speculation" and another "as an experiment."

When the survey was made, general farming predominated—thirty-three per cent—with poultry ranking next at thirty-two per cent. Then came dairying (eighteen per cent), followed by truck farming (ten per cent) as major, not necessarily exclusive, lines of production. Close to half the farmers surveyed, had supplemental sources of income, chiefly boarding or rooming or other work on the part of the head or of some other member of the family.

Thirteen per cent of the surveyed farmers had been on their farms less than five years, while sixty-nine per cent had been on their places over ten years, twenty-two per cent over twenty years—which the Society interprets as a fine indication of stability. Ninety per cent said that they would rather be on the farm than in the city, eight per cent expressed preference for the city, the rest were uncertain. In giving these figures, the Society commented: "Probably this singularly large percentage in favor of the farm is attributable not so much to smug satisfaction with prevailing farm conditions as to the realization by farmers that, with city conditions what they are, the farm is the better place for them." It should be noted that this survey was made when the nation was still suffering from the effects of the depression.

The survey disproved the notion still held by many that farm living is primitive. Seventy-six per cent of the farms had sanitary plumbing; eighty-two per cent, electricity; fifty-two per cent, furnace heat. This is much higher than the average for American farms, owing partly to the fact that Jews had become accustomed to these conveniences in the city and partly because some cater to summer boarders as an adjunct to farm operations. Sixty-nine per cent had telephones; eighty-two per cent, radios; sixty-nine per cent owned passenger automobiles—again high figures.

Data pertaining to farm children showed that thirty-seven per cent of those over eighteen remained on the farm. About fifteen per cent of those who left went into professional callings—medicine, law, engineering, dentistry, pharmacy, nursing, science, accountancy, pedagogy and social work. Forty per cent had received a high school, and twenty-two per cent a college education. Some of the high school students no doubt later entered the college group. Less than forty per cent of the children in the cases studied received formal religious instruction.

The farmers were almost unanimous in saying that they were getting along well with their non-Jewish neighbors. Over ninety per cent described the relationship as good, nine per cent as simply fair. "Just fine," "excellent," "splendid," was the tenor of replies to this question. Only one farmer out of the three hundred was not on friendly terms with his Christian neighbors.

In view of the lively interest that then existed among some Jewish groups in a back-to-the-land movement and their advocacy of farm colonies, the opportunity was seized to obtain the reaction of farmers themselves to colonization. The question was: "Do you believe in a form of farming where the land and equipment are owned by a colony and not by the individual farmer, and where the farm work is done under central management on a colony farm?" The arguments in favor were based on the premises that a colony would make possible the utilization of heavy machinery beyond the means of individual farmers, that it would meet the competition of the "big" farm, that it would provide security in case of incapacity, that it would enhance the opportunities for cultural life. On the other side, it was maintained that this form of settlement runs counter to the American spirit of freedom, that it robs the individual of initiative, that it dulls his incentive and destroys his independence, that it is "too difficult for farmers to work in harmony," that "even with competent management such a colony would not be better than its most incompetent individual." One hundred and fourteen out of three hundred recorded themselves in the affirmative, but most of these hedged their replies with reservations and qualifications, for example—"theoretically it is better to do farming cooperatively, but we have not such human material that would make it possible." "Yes, if such could be controlled by federal or state government with individual privileges." "It may succeed when the members are tied by a single religious or social ideal, when the members fit in physically and financially and have the backing of a strong organization (outside) or the government." From the replies, the Society concluded that the desire to be the possessor of one's own farmstead outweighs any benefits that may be derived from "colony" farming.

A "Who's Who" of Jewish farmers is neither within the scope of this book nor the intention of the author. But there are stories of human achievement buried in the Society's archives that deserve a wider public. They are not typical or average examples; rather do they show what can be accomplished by an urbanized folk once opportunities are opened up and energies are permitted to have full sway. These cases were selected without regard as to whether the individuals were recipients of the Society's service.

There is the story of the young man from the East side of New York City who started farming in Suffolk County, Long Island. He began on a neglected piece of land with a small shack for a home, twelve dollars in his pocket and a wife of a few weeks at his side. Steadily he worked to bring his farm up to a high level and to raise and educate four children. Now he is known as a vegetable grower of rare proficiency and his fields are selected by the New

York State Experiment Station for research studies. He is crop reporter for the United States Department of Agriculture—a post given only to leading farmers. One of the organizers of the Suffolk County Farm Bureau and a committeeman since its beginning, he was awarded a gold medal for distinguished service and elected a life member. He was chosen one of the eight members of the Suffolk County Vegetable Committee for 1941. At a county fair, noted throughout the country for the excellence of its exhibits and the stiffness of its competition, this former East Side boy has, year in and year out, won the highest prizes for his vegetable displays. With all his agricultural activities, he has served for years on the local school board and for a time was its treasurer. He was also the founder and is the president of the local synagogue.

A former shoe manufacturer bought a farm in New York State. In time he developed into one of the foremost breeders of white leghorns in the country. One of his entries was judged "The Hen of the Year" at the 1937 Poultry Industries Exposition, the highest individual award of the poultry industry. He also raised a bird called "The Hen of the Century" which made a new world's record for five years of production. Eggs from his flocks have been sent to foreign countries, and breeders from Great Britain have paid high prices for them.

A graduate of the former Baron de Hirsch Agricultural School was appointed hog expert for the Bureau of Animal Industry and was sent to South Dakota. Later he became a producer of seeds and won prizes in statewide competitions. He specializes in alfalfa seed, of which he raises 1,400 acres. He served several terms as president of the South Dakota Seed Growers Association and at one time was offered the nomination of United States Senator on the Farmer Labor ticket, an offer which he declined.

In 1937 he was invited by President Roosevelt to inspect the fields of the President's farm sown with seed which he had furnished. In the summer of 1939 he went as a member of a group which included United States Senators, Governors and several college presidents to visit the All Soviet Agricultural Fair. There he delivered a radio message to Russian farmers which he was told had reached forty million listeners.

In Greene County, New York, along the banks of the Hudson, a former laborer for the Knickerbocker Ice Company started raising mushrooms in a run down icehouse leased from the company. Later he bought the property, added to it and developed it into a $75,000 plant with private docks and an annual turnover reaching as high as $60,000. Upon his retirement he turned the business over to one of his sons. Another son and a son-in-law are operating in the same neighborhood a mushroom farm of equal, if not larger, dimensions.

Two young men, brothers-in-law, started their career on a modest farm in the Connecticut River Valley soon after their arrival in this country. They had a combined capital of $500. The Jewish Agricultural Society lent them $400. Their farm has since become a model of successful diversification. A poultry flock of 7,000 producing hens, a herd of forty high grade cows, large acreages of tobacco and potatoes are combined into an enterprise of which each component would in itself be a good sized farm operation.

In the same fertile valley, a Jewish farmer raises 250 acres of potatoes—one of the largest acreages in Connecticut. For several terms he served as president of the Connecticut Potato Growers Marketing Association. This acreage is exceeded by a Jewish farmer in the well known potato district of Aroostook County, Maine, who grew over 500 acres of certified seed potatoes in 1940 and several hundred acres of uncertified seed—the largest acreage, and largest selection of varieties in the state. His nephew, also in Maine, runs him a close second.

There are four principal onion growing districts in the United States, the largest of which is in Orange County, New York. An immigrant Jew started there on a very small scale and with the help of his sons built up an enterprise which is the most extensive in this area.

Vineland, New Jersey, is regarded as the cradle of modern commercial poultry husbandry. A Jewish family, the head of which has been farming in the United States and Canada for over fifty years, operates poultry plants of which the combined output in eggs and chicks is the biggest in the state. Numerous prizes have been won at poultry shows and official egg laying contests. The senior classes of the State Agricultural College are frequently taken to study the poultry methods practiced on these farms. As part of the farm economy, an appreciable acreage of vegetables is intensively cultivated under overhead irrigation, the pet project of the patriarchal head, a man around eighty.

Near Milwaukee, a graduate of an agricultural school in Germany operates hothouses, raising products that have won many medals and trophies for their excellence. A graduate of the National Farm School, who started his farm career on the proverbial shoestring, conducts a nursery in Connecticut the output of which goes to a wide wholesale trade. He also maintains a local landscape service of no mean proportions. For a time, he supplied evergreens to the Conservation Department of the State of Connecticut for use in forestation work. A Jewish florist produces the largest volume and the greatest variety of flowers raised by a single individual in the metropolitan

New York area. His output for retail sale is said to be the largest in the country. On Staten Island, two Jews operate a farm which ranks among the extensive orchid growing plants in the east. Incidentally, the biggest independent establishment for the construction and equipment of greenhouses is owned by two Jewish brothers of Brooklyn.

An agricultural enterprise unique in its value to pharmaceutical and medical research is the creation of a man who has come to be known as the "Jewish Pied Piper of Good Hope." After an unsuccessful try on a small farm he bought a small piece of land in the outskirts of Washington, D. C., where he raised broilers and also tried raising rabbits for experimental laboratories. Upon the advice of experts in the Bureau of Animal Industry of the United States Department of Agriculture, he started raising albino rats. From a foundation stock of sixteen bought from the famous Wistar Institute, his stock leaped within a few years to 50,000. But his reputation derives not from size but from the impeccable honesty with which he fills orders for a commodity that requires absolute compliance with exacting specifications. He numbers among his purchasers, Harvard, Yale, Johns Hopkins, the Universities of Michigan, Virginia, Ohio, Pennsylvania, Massachusetts Institute of Technology, the Mellon Institute, the National Institute of Health, the Rockefeller Institute, Squibb, Merck, Parke Davis, Fleischman, Sharpe & Dohme, and others. In the course of time he bought two farms in Maryland and added guinea pigs and white mice. Today his brother-in-law and son-in-law are associated with him not only in raising the animals but also in producing much of the food consumed by them.

The March, 1940, issue of "The Jewish Farmer" related what it captioned "Horatio Alger's Story in a Rural

Setting." It told of the son of a Jewish farmer who began his career on the parental dairy farm in Rockland County, New York. With a few dollars he had saved, he bought an adjoining tract of land on which he planted fruit trees as a side line. This gradually became his major activity. On this farm, within thirty miles of New York City, he now has a hundred acre orchard in apples and peaches of the finest assortments. The average output of apples alone is 25,000 boxes annually. A modern cold storage house is part of the plant. The mother, a woman past eighty, still tends her own flower garden. Another fruit farm—more than four times its size—in the Finger Lake region of New York State, is owned by a father and two sons, one of whom is a Cornell graduate.

An immigrant from Germany went west some fifty or sixty years ago and settled in Idaho, where he engaged in cattle raising. As his sons grew to maturity they joined him and succeeded to the business upon his death at the age of 83. On a trip east about five years ago, one of the sons called at the Society's office. He told of their home ranch which contains 3,600 acres with annual production ranging between 2,000 and 2,500 head of beef cattle. The trip east was on invitation from Swift and Company. The company had taken twenty leading cattle growers in various states on a tour of inspection. This cattle raiser was the guest selected from Idaho.

A man who started in farming as a result of a job obtained through the Society is now one of the largest producer-distributors of high grade bottled milk in the State of New Jersey. His farm is located in fashionable Morris County where he raises 180 acres of fodder crops for a 140 cow herd. His daily output is 1,900 quarts. He has a perfect record with the health department and takes special pride in the relationship he has been able to main-

tain with the twenty-five or so employees on his farm, in
his pasteurizing and bottling plant and in his distribution force. He is a director of the local Jewish community
and of the Jewish Cemetery Association and head of the
local division of the National Refugee Service. For a time
he was a member of the State Board of Agriculture. His
wife is equally active in communal affairs.

An excerpt from an article in the California Cultivator
of March, 1940, tells of a man who started on nothing and
whose courage, intelligence, industry and probity lifted
him to heights during the very period when farming was
in the doldrums. The story follows:

"S. H. was born in Russia about forty years ago to Jewish parents whose ancestors went from Germany to Russia
centuries before. While still a boy, he was sent to Palestine to be educated and to grow up with the Zionist movement. About the time he got out of school, the World
War broke out and he served in a Jewish regiment of the
British army. Although he knew little English, when the
war was over he came to California to study agriculture
at the university with the intention of returning to Palestine and teaching Jewish immigrants scientific agriculture.
However, California's opportunities looked so good that
without either money or friends, he decided to go into big
scale farming. Being endowed with abundant initiative,
energy and ambition, he was able to start lettuce farming near Couchilla in the early 1920's on nothing but
credit. The first few years saw about as much money lost
as made, but with increasing backing from men who believed he could make good. In 1925, he was able to ar-
range for some land near Los Banos still on little but
credit, and to get financing. He moved there with his
bride, a college graduate, living in a tent to begin with.

Real progress began but the collapse of prices of cotton and other crops at the beginning of the depression left him worth at least $100,000 less than nothing. However, the land had to be farmed and he could farm it as well as anybody and better than most, so his mortgage was not foreclosed and he was given credit to raise more crops. At one time, he owed $100,000 for tractors, farm equipment, wells and pumps. Now he farms 8,000 acres of as fine land as the state boasts and is out of debt. In no other country on earth could a young man without money, friends or influence get backing to go ahead like this. America is still a land of opportunity. From an agricultural standpoint, the achievement is especially significant because both yields and quality are tops on the H. farms. . . . The main crops of the West Side are flax, cotton and barley. Particularly where irrigation water is pumped from wells, big scale farming is necessary. . . . H. is the pioneer in some of the practices followed so successfully on his lands for that section at least, and his methods are watched closely by the other big farmers of the district. . . . While these methods are being applied to large scale farming many of them could be adapted to small farms in other locations with profit."

The irrigation outfits in his lands, he told the Society in January, 1941, cost $165,000 and the tractors and other equipment are worth over $200,000. His permanent labor force, working under his personal direction, ranges from 45 to 50 and seasonal laborers number between 500 and 600. In 1940, the turnover was $340,000. Success has not turned this man's head. He is modest, unassuming and warm hearted.

Formerly a dairyman, a Connecticut Jewish farmer of the second generation changed to poultry. Within a dec-

ade, and despite a difficult struggle, he became so outstanding a breeder that within the past three years alone
he won no fewer than thirty-eight medals, trophies, cups
and sweepstakes at national exhibits and at the 1939
World Poultry Congress. Recently his pen of Barred
Rocks attained the highest egg production record in government supervised contests in thirteen northeastern states
—an area in which the best poultry stock in the country
is to be found. Shipments of his chicks have gone to poultrymen in Central and South American lands. In the
summer of 1940, at the time of the annual convention of
the International Baby Chick Association, he was invited
to deliver a radio address over a national hook-up on the
"Advances Made in Poultry Breeding."

   Children of Jewish farmers have made their mark. The
son of a Connecticut poultryman, a boy of 16, won awards
for poultry judging. These included the state championship, which made him eligible to participate in interstate
contests, in which, in turn, he attained equally high distinction. The son plays an important part in the conduct
of the paternal farm. The boy's young sister is the winner
of the county championship in poultry raising and similar awards.

   The seventeen-year-old son of a Perrineville, New Jersey, farmer ranked highest in individual scores on his high
school team which won first place in a state-wide milk
judging contest at Rutgers. The team again came out first
at the Eastern States Exposition at Springfield, Massachusetts. Finally, the team won second place at the American
Royal Live Stock Show held at Kansas City, Missouri, and
the young contestant ranked fourth in the United States.
While at Kansas City, he was New Jersey's delegate to the
convention of The Future Farmers of America. Last Sep-

tember this versatile lad was a member of the team that attained first place in a tri-county potato grading contest. Several months later, he was tied for first place in a potato disease identification contest conducted at Rutgers.

The son of a Michigan farmer, an honor student at the State College, was appointed assistant research worker at the College while yet a senior in the Division of Veterinary Medicine. An early report of the Society records the appointment of the daughter of a Wisconsin Jewish farmer to the position of cow tester when the system of cow testing was a new practice. She was the first woman cow tester in the state and one of the very few in the country. The daughter of a graduate of the Baron de Hirsch Agricultural School who settled on a farm in Massachusetts, showed early signs of interest and ability in matters agricultural and was for years champion of the 4H Club in both county and state. At the State Agricultural College, where she took the home economics course, she became president of the College 4H Club, and upon graduation was appointed assistant county 4H club leader in a county where the agricultural population is overwhelmingly Christian.

But it is not only as "dirt" farmers that Jews have made their mark. Jews have also made contribution to American agriculture in the realms of science and economics and in related agricultural fields. They are found on the staffs of agricultural schools and colleges, experiment stations, in extension service, in state and federal agricultural bureaus, and in scientific work for commercial concerns. To call the full roster or to give lengthy biographies would take the author beyond the bounds of a volume of this scope. He must content himself with setting down briefly the achievements of the more eminent figures. Here, again, the individual's relationship to the Society, if any, has not been taken into account.

Selman A. Waksman, Professor of Soil Microbiology at Rutgers since 1930, and Marine Bacteriologist at the Woods Hole (Mass.) Oceanograph Institute, is a member of scientific bodies in America, Europe and Asia and author of papers and several volumes on soil microbiology, enzymes and microbiol physiology. He is a consultant microbiologist and is regarded as a foremost authority in that field. He has received the Nitrogen Research award from the American Society of Agronomy. In December, 1941, Dr. Waksman was elected president of the American Society of Bacteriologists.

Jacob S. Joffe, Associate Professor in Soil Research at Rutgers, working with Waksman, discovered a new soil organism and has otherwise contributed notably to recent advances in soil chemistry. He is the author of "Pedology" and of numerous papers which have appeared in American and foreign scientific journals.

Moses Naphtalison Levine, Pathologist in the United States Department of Agriculture, who at various times held important posts at Kansas State Agricultural College and the University of Minnesota, is a phytopathologist who has won special distinction through his researches in the diseases that attack grain. He is the editor of "Phytopathology," a prolific writer and a member of many scientific and pedagogical societies not only in this country but in Holland, France and Palestine.

Jacob Joseph Taubenhaus, whose untimely death occurred in 1939, had been Chief of the Division of Plant Pathology and Physiology at the Texas Agricultural Experiment Station from 1916 to the time of his death. Before going to Texas, he was associate plant pathologist at the University of Delaware. The titles of some of his books, all standard texts, are "Culture and Diseases of the Sweet-Pea," "Diseases of Truck Crops," "Diseases of Green House Crops," "Diseases of the Sweet Potato," and "Culture and Diseases of the Onion in America."

Walter Naphtali Ezekiel, Taubenhaus' successor at the Texas Agricultural Experiment Station, was educated at the Maryland State College and at the University of that state, from the latter of which he received his Ph. D. Before going to Texas he worked at the Maryland Experiment Station and at the University of Minnesota where he was research fellow. He is author and co-author of seventy articles on plant pathological research.

The late Myer Edward Jaffa was for many years Professor of Nutrition at the University of California. For a long time he was also Chief of the Bureau of Food and Drugs in the California State Department of Health, and Consultant Nutrition Expert in the same department. His studies in the healthgiving properties of fruit did much to advance the interests of the fruit growers of California and elsewhere.

Joseph A. Rosen, the last superintendent of the Baron de Hirsch Agricultural School at Woodbine, was the discoverer of "Rosen Rye," a variety which grows on soil of moderate fertility. It won prizes at the Chicago Grain Exhibits for more than ten consecutive years. Rosen was in charge of the monumental Jewish agricultural reconstruction work in Russia under the auspices of the Agro-Joint and is now the vice-president of the Dominican Republic Settlement Association.

Benjamin Israel Masurovsky came from Russia at the age of 21. He studied at the Baron de Hirsch School, at Rutgers and at Nebraska, and specialized in dairy chemistry. Masurovsky is the inventor of the dairymen's slide

rule known as Masurovsky's Milkmeter, an important aid
to dairymen. Articles on his specialized field have appeared in various scientific and trade publications.

Arthur D. Goldhaft was brought up on a South Jersey
farm, studied at the Woodbine School, worked on farms
in Pennsylvania, New Jersey and Illinois and received his
doctorate in veterinary medicine from the University of
Pennsylvania. For many years he has been practicing in
Vineland, New Jersey, of which he is Health Officer. He
was the first veterinarian in the United States to take up
the practice of poultry diseases as a specialty. He developed valuable poultry vaccines and has been called as
consultant to such distant places as Utah, Idaho, California, Oregon and Washington. His son, daughter, son-in-
law and a nephew are all veterinarians, associated with
him in the running of a laboratory complete in scientific
equipment and modern in its practice, from which vaccines go to all parts of the country.

Robert Marshall, the son of Louis Marshall, who died
in 1940 at the age of 39, was the Chief of the Division of
Recreation and Soil Conservation in the United States
Forest Service. Before that he had made silvicultural ex-
plorations for the Northern Rocky Mountain Forest Experiment Station and engaged in ecological studies and
anthropological research in Northern Alaska and served
for four years as Director of Forestry in the Office of Indian Affairs in the United States Department of the Interior. His map of 12,000 square miles of uncharted country
in Northern Alaska was published by the United States
Geological Survey in 1934. Marshall was the author of
"Arctic Village," "The Peoples Forest," "The Forest for
Recreation," "The Universe of the Wilderness Is Van-
ishing."

Raphael Zon had already received degrees at the Classical Gymnasium in his native Simbirsk, Russia, and the Imperial University of Kazan, and had studied at the L'Universite Libre, Brussels, before he came to the United States in 1897. In this country he studied at Cornell University. In 1905 he organized the first forest research unit of the Forest Service of the United States Department of Agriculture and for twelve years was its chief. Since 1923 he has been the Director of the University of Minnesota Forest Experiment Station and of the Lake States Forest Experiment Station. He is Professor of Forestry at Minnesota and non-resident Professor at the University of Wisconsin. Zon has for twenty-five years been the editor-in-chief of the "Journal of Forestry." He is the author of several hundred papers and pamphlets and co-author of "Forest Resources of the World."

Jacob Joshua Levison, Master of Forestry, Yale University, was forester for the New York City Department of Parks from 1905 to 1915. Since then he has been consulting landscape forester. He was lecturer for the United States Forest Service, instructor at the Forestry School, Yale University, lecturer at Florida University, at Syracuse University, at Brooklyn Institute of Arts and Science, and at other places. He is forester for the American Association for Planting and Preservation of City Trees, and was instrumental in organizing shade tree bureaus in various cities. Levison is the author of "Studies of Trees," "The Home Book of Trees and Shrubs" and he has written extensively on his specialty.

Edward K. Kotok, for thirty years in the forest service in California and since 1926 Director of the California Forest and Range Experiment Station, recently received an important post in the government's reforestation service. He is the author of articles on fire control, water problems and erosion control.

Max Kriss, who died recently at forty-seven, came to the United States at the age of twenty-one. He worked his way through Pennsylvania State College, received his Ph. D. from Yale and was a member of the Pennsylvania State College faculty for twenty-three years; author or co-author of more than fifty scientific papers on animal nutrition on which he was an authority.

The late H. L. Sabsovich, a graduate of the Zurich Polytechnicum, organized an agricultural department in the University of Colorado, which was probably the first of its kind in the west. He was the first superintendent of the Baron de Hirsch Agricultural School.

Louis Pyenson, Harry Pyenson and Maxwell Pyenson are the sons of a long-established Jewish farmer in the Berkshire district of Massachusetts. All three were born on the farm and studied at the State Agricultural College. Louis, 31, received his doctorate in entomology and plant pathology at Cornell. He worked for the Brazilian Government and helped organize the entomology department of the State Agricultural Institute at Pernambuco. Now he is a member of the faculty of the New York State Institute of Applied Agriculture at Farmingdale, Long Island. Harry, 29, received his Ph. D. in dairy bacteriology and chemistry from the Pennsylvania State College, where he was graduate assistant in dairy manufacturing. From there he went to the Federal Surplus Commodities Corporation and now he is Federal Milk Market Administrator in an area which covers Wisconsin, Illinois, Indiana and Michigan. The youngest son, Maxwell, 25, a master of science, supervised student agricultural projects at the West Springfield (Mass.) High School and was in the extension service of the Jewish Agricultural Society until called to service early in 1942. The career of the father of these three young men, though cast in a more modest role, deserves a word or two. A graduate of the ICA Agricultural School at Minsk, Russia, he came here in 1905 at the age of 20. Almost immediately he went to work on a farm in the Berkshires. In two years he saved $250 with which he was able to make a down payment on a neighboring farm costing $900. It is on this farm that he raised the three sons and a daughter. And it is on this farm, vastly different from the original humble purchase, that he is living today, a successful and respected citizen.

Jacob G. Lipman, who died in 1939, made the campus of Rutgers College of Agriculture the mecca for agricultural scholars the world over, who came to seek knowledge and gain inspiration from the man who ranked as the world's authority on soil chemistry. For twenty-eight years Director of the New Jersey Experiment Station and for twenty-four years Dean of the State Agricultural College, Lipman had at times lectured at Cornell and at the Universities of Illinois, Iowa, Tennessee and Nebraska. He served as President of the International Congress of Soil Science in Washington in 1927. He represented the United States at the International Institute of Agriculture at Rome and at other world congresses. He wrote textbooks recognized as standard, was editor-in-chief, associate editor, consulting editor and contributor to scientific journals in the United States, France, Germany and Russia. His affiliation with scientific bodies was legion and extended to England, Italy, France, Czechoslovakia and Sweden. The French Academy of Agriculture awarded him a silver medal. From Chile he received the Nitrate Award and an Honorary Doctorate from the Catholic University of Santiago. His alma mater honored him with a Doctor of Science Degree and with the Rutgers College Award. Columbia University gave him the Chandler medal—a rare distinction. Lipman served on the Board of Directors of the Jewish Agricultural Society for twenty-five years. He took an active part in all phases of the Society's work. His special talents were of inestimable value in helping to frame and mold the Society's educational program.

His brother, Charles B. Lipman, has been a member of the faculty of the University of California since 1909, Professor of Plant Pathology since 1925, and Dean of the Graduate Division since 1923. He holds doctorates from Rutgers and California. Like his brother, he has risen to be one of the foremost soil scientists in the country.

Louis H. Bean was a member of the research staff of the Bureau of Agricultural Economics of the United States Department of Agriculture from 1923 to 1933, when he became Economist in the Office of the Secretary of Agriculture and Chief of the Agricultural Industrial Relations Section in the Division of Program Planning of the Agricultural Adjustment Administration. In 1939 he was designated as Counselor in the Bureau of Agricultural Economics.

Nathan Koenig, a graduate of Connecticut Agricultural College (now University of Connecticut), joined the staff of the Agricultural Adjustment Administration in June, 1933, as special agricultural writer. Later, he became Assistant Chief of the administration's press section and in November, 1934, he was placed in general charge of the administration's information activities in the twelve northeastern states. In August, 1940, he was named Assistant Chief of the Information Division in the newly organized Surplus Marketing Administration of the Department of Agriculture.

Mordecai Joseph Ezekiel, the brother of Walter Naphtali, is the Economic Advisor to the United States Secretary of Agriculture. He played an important role in shaping the policies of the old Federal Farm Board and of the present Agricultural Adjustment Administration. He represented the United States at the World Wheat Conference held at Rome in 1934.

Joshua Bernhardt is Chief of the Sugar Division of the Agricultural Adjustment Administration. With others, he drew up reports for the United States Tariff Commission on the relation of tariff on sugar to rise in price and on difference in cost of production between the United States and Cuba. He has also made numerous studies and written many publications on the economic aspects of the sugar industry.

Bernhard Ostrolenk received his Ph. D. from the University of Pennsylvania after having studied at the National Farm School, Massachusetts Agricultural College, Boston University and University of Minnesota. From 1916 to 1927, he was Director of the National Farm School and lectured on agricultural finance at the University of Pennsylvania. Now he is Professor of Economics at the College of the City of New York. He is the author of "Social Aspects of the Food Surplus," "Harvey Baum, A Study of the Agricultural Revolution" (with E. S. Mead), "The Surplus Farmer" and other works. Ostrolenk is a contributor to a number of leading publications.

Leonard G. Robinson, a former general manager of the Jewish Agricultural Society, assisted in framing the federal farm loan law enacted in 1916, and organized and became the first president of the Federal Land Bank of Springfield, Massachusetts, one of the twelve regional banks of the federal system.

Henry Morgenthau, Jr., the Secretary of the Treasury, who served on the board of the Jewish Agricultural Society and as its Vice-President, was selected by President Roosevelt to organize and head the Farm Credit Administration. In that capacity he brought into being the largest and most comprehensive farm credit system that has ever been devised in any country.

David Lubin, in founding the International Institute of Agriculture at Rome, Italy, rendered a service to agriculture which was world embracing. At a meeting held in October, 1934, a tribute to Lubin's memory was paid by delegates from the sixty-three nations represented in the Institute.

This is the scant outline of the record. True, these men possessed endowments above the average. But, in assessing this record of achievement, it must be remembered, even if it must be repeated, that for two millenia, since the Jew lost his homeland, he has been wandering over the face of the earth with only brief and intermittent interludes of relative security of residence and occupation; that nowhere for any length of time did he have that firm anchorage which would permit him to lead an agrarian life. With land ownership proscribed, membership in occupational guilds closed (preventing acquisition of manual skills), with expulsion edicts constantly hanging over his head, the Jew had to seek such form of livelihood as would permit him upon short notice to pull up stakes, load his possessions on his back and move onward to some more friendly, yet uncertain, refuge.

Even after emancipation in some European countries, few Jews had access to the soil. Most still lived in the benighted lands where their lot was not much better than in the days of medieval darkness. It was only when he came to the country which threw up no barriers between man and man that the Jew could give vent to a long repressed agricultural urge. What the Jew has accomplished in America proves that he can break with his narrowly circumscribed past, that he can make reunion with the soil in a country which gives him the opportunity to take his place as a free man at the side of free men in a free land.

This history presents the record down to the close of 1941. Since then a great war is being waged. The pattern of farm life, as of all life, will undergo profound changes. It has already undergone changes. To give a fleeting glimpse of how these changes have affected Jewish farmers and The Jewish Agricultural Society, the introduction to the Society's 1942 report is added to the story.

The war has set in bold relief the important role agriculture plays in our national economy—in world economy. With sudden and startling clarity it has made us aware of our utter dependence upon the products of the soil. And the war placed mighty responsibilities upon the shoulders of American farmers, responsibilities which are bound to grow heavier as the war progresses.

American farmers are meeting that responsibility. They have geared their energies to war demands. They have made themselves a vital part of the gigantic war instrument by which the United Nations will win through to ultimate victory. Just as war brought its added responsibilities so it brought its added problems. Faced with the imperative necessity to step up production and to make shifts in production, the farmer found himself short of hired help, his sons in service, with priorities restricting purchase of machinery and equipment, limitations placing rigid curbs on new construction, with lack of commodities normally considered essential and with transportation and other difficulties. The records of 1942 demonstrate that the American farmer is able to face problems and to lick them. The production of 1942 topped all records. More crops, more livestock, more milk and dairy products, more eggs and more meat birds were produced than in any previous year.

As a result of increased production and, thanks to favorable weather conditions, the national cash farm income reached a total of fifteen and a half billion dollars, the highest ever—four billion dollars more than in 1941, itself a peak year, and two and a half times the low in 1932. Normally, the farmer plows back a good share of his profits into farm plant—a new piece of machinery, a new barn, a new refrigerator or electric washing machine for the farm home. But with spending circumscribed, the farmer made maximum use of such plant, equipment and material as he possessed and bent his back under longer and heavier toil. In accord with the preachments of the heads of federal farm agencies, he used a bigger part of farm income for debt reduction. As a result the total national farm mortgage debt went down to the lowest point in more than twenty years.

Like his fellow farmer the Jewish farmer toiled and sweated in the performance of his part in producing the abundance needed to stoke the war machine. Like his fellow farmer he shared in farm prosperity. Like his fellow American, he threw himself unsparingly into every phase of the war effort.

The conditions alluded to eased the Society's work in some respects and made it more difficult in other respects. Since the cycle was upward and because of restrictions on purchases and construction, there was a lessened demand for loans from old farmers. More than fifty per cent of the loans made in 1942 were to establish new farmers. Principal repayments reached the highest point in the Society's forty-two years. Interest collections yielded more than in any year since 1929. By and large farmers did not have serious financial troubles to lay before the Society, a comforting contrast with the grim depression years. That was the light side.

But there was a serious side. Besieged with cries for farm help, at times desperate, the shortage of farm labor was so acute that despite redoubled efforts the Society could not nearly meet the call. To keep the farmer's plant functioning the Society had to ferret out sources of equipment and material and to dig up substitutes when the usual commodities were not available. It had to help sharpen the farmer's ingenuity to make existing machinery serve and to resort to home made improvisations. In the effort to help attune farmers to the emergency the Society had in a sense to bring about changes not only in methods of practice but also in ways of thinking.

The settlement of new farmers weighted the normally heavy responsibility in this all important activity. The bright farm picture and the resultant increased demand for farms shot up prices of farm real estate in many districts, in some to fantastic levels. The Society could have followed the path of least resistance by discouraging all farm purchases during the period of boom. But that would have been a distinct disservice to those who might thus have been tempted into unprofitable ventures or forced to fritter away their savings to the point where postponement would mean abandonment. The difficulty was to discard old standards of farm values where rises were justified and yet not establish a measuring rod which might plague both the buyer and the Society in the future.

This difficulty manifested itself particularly in the case of refugees. The rapid strides made by refugees heretofore settled aroused a spirit of restlessness, if not of envy, among those who had toyed with the idea of farming but who had been afraid to take the jump. It was hard to restrain them from making injudicious purchases and it was equally hard to settle them on suitable farms at suitable prices under conditions that would yield a living after the era of high prices shall have passed. The settlement of seventy-seven emigre families this year under these circumstances was no mean job. The more than 400 Jewish refugee families so far settled directly by the Society and the several hundred who went on their own initiative are by their intelligence, their industry, and their frugality, contributing their meed to the much needed food supply.

The pressure upon the Society was intensified because of the curtailment upon transportation and because of the entrance of members of the staff into the armed forces. This pressure is likely to become more acute as the war progresses. More and more resort will have to be had to group rather than to individual contact, where that is feasible. At the present writing four men are in the army, two with the rank of captain—one of the latter on a battlefront overseas. A member of the secretarial staff joined the Women's Auxiliary Army Corps. Not only has the Society's staff been depleted but the complexion of its directorate has undergone a change. Five of the Directors including the President are either in the Army or Navy or serving in other capacities directly related to the prosecution of the war.

It is yet too early to call a service roll. But the few and meager reports that are beginning to trickle in from farm communities already give ample promise that, when the complete story is written, it will set forth a record of credit and distinction. Young Jews from the farm, in some instances two or three from the same family, are serving in every branch of the combat forces, as enlisted or drafted men, in all ranks from buck private to commissioned officer of advanced station, on all fronts and on all the seven seas.

On the home front the Jewish farmer has joined with his fellow American in giving of himself and of his substance. He has, of course, increased production in the face of harder conditions. He has bought war bonds. He has joined the state guard. He has become a fire warden, an air-raid warden, a watcher in the interceptor command. He has given his blood to the Red Cross. His daughters are nurses. He has pushed scrap and salvage drives. Synagogues, community houses, cooperative headquarters have become collection centers and centers for all kinds of Red Cross activities. A newly erected Jewish house of worship in a small Connecticut community has turned over a part of its building to the Red Cross for sewing and knitting. And there are others. Jewish farmers have collected money for Hanukah and Christmas presents for the soldiers and sailors. Through the columns of "The Jewish Farmer," at group meetings, at farm gatherings, at individual visits, the Society supported and encouraged every phase and aspect of war service.

Last year the Society pledged itself "without reserve to use its every energy, its last resort, to meet and to help Jewish farmers meet the demands that will be made upon it and upon them in these days of fateful destiny." This year the Society pledges itself anew to this consecrated purpose.

Conclusion

By and large, Jews have, for two thousand years, been turned away from farming. The vast majority lived in countries where land ownership had been proscribed and where they were forced into occupations which did not require a firm anchorage, where, when pressure became compelling and oppression unbearable, they could pull up stakes and move on. Urban dwellers for two millennia, they became habituated to city life, and it is not easy to change firmly ingrained habits of thought and action. It takes generations to create a background. Even where, in recent times, there was relative freedom of movement and of action, Jews saw farming for the most part in lands where it was in low estate, where the farmer was the dull serf. The early Jewish immigrants in America brought with them this lowly concept of agriculture and though American agriculture has always been on an incomparably higher plane, Jews of immigrant origin long retained the European picture.

Then there was the financial problem. Not all who felt the urge to farm possessed the needed capital. Some may speak loosely about settling masses on farms, but they are oblivious to the fact that farming is an enterprise which requires an investment for the farm plant, stock, equipment, operation and, in the case of the beginner, maintenance over an initial period. The Society's funds were derived exclusively from one source—the foundations set up by Baron Maurice de Hirsch. No attempt was made to tap American support. The Society's activities had to be geared to its financial capacity. Had there been funds available for more generous lending, more Jews could have been turned landward—and this without creating a subsidized element.

Yet, important and significant results have been accomplished. Thousands of Jews have been made farm conscious. Thousands of Jewish families have wended their way to the farm. It has been demonstrated beyond question that Jews can farm and that they do farm. And, this should be noted, the ratio of the Jewish agrarian population to the general Jewish population has increased many fold during the very forty years when the general drift was from country to city, when the ratio of the national farm population to its total population went down from almost forty per cent to less than twenty-five per cent.

Note should be taken, also, that, while the Society served a special clientele, it made definite contribution to American agriculture. It developed techniques and practices, not a few of which were adopted by other agencies, even state and federal. The Society created what was in a sense the first "farmers bank" in America. It collaborated in drafting the first federal farm loan act and its executive head became the first president of the Federal Land Bank having jurisdiction over the New England States, New York and New Jersey. The Land Bank Commissioner loan which was initiated upon the advent of the New Deal is in essence the type of loan which the Society had already been making for more than thirty years. The Society was

a pioneer in the evolution of the agricultural credit union
and its early recommendations became recognized credit
union practice embodied in later credit union legislation.
The Society set up the first specialized farm employment
agency and founded one of the first farm papers in America to be published in a foreign language. Its system of
field instruction antedated systematic government county
agent work by seven or eight years. The Society's entrance
into the rural sanitation field was characterized by the
United States Public Health Service as "of statewide and
national importance. . . ." The Society was the first to
engage in planned farm settlement activity. Its executive
head was consulted in the planning of New York State's
Bureau of Farm Information, and appointed a member of
its advisory committee. The plan of the Farm Security
Administration in resettling farm families is in a broad
sense akin to the Society's settlement work.

Fundamentally all Jewish agricultural activity must be
based on the capacity of the family to wrest a livelihood
from the farm. From the standpoint of the individual, no
such considerations as relieving congestion, redistributing
population, combatting anti-semitism, demonstrating Jewish ability to farm, dare count. The Jew who chooses farming should be impelled by precisely the same motives that
cause people to select other occupations—the reward, material or otherwise, that he expects to derive. But looking
beyond the individual settled, there is a much deeper significance, and that deeper significance is being brought
home in this day more forcefully than ever before. Too
often is the charge heard that the Jew has neither inclination nor aptitude to toil or to till. The Jewish farm class
which has been built up in America within a comparatively short span of years emphatically refutes that charge.

The Jews on American farmlands signify a major social phenomenon not to be measured by numbers alone. They represent a positive gain in normalization. Jewish farmers have tapped for themselves a precious lode of self-reliance and self-respect. In rediscovering the satisfaction of life on the soil, their ancient tradition, they have also rediscovered themselves. In no field as much as in farming, does the American Jew have the same sense of pride of achievement, the same quiet strength of inner dignity. Responding to man's innermost urge, many Jews have hewed out for themselves a life on the soil. They are growing in numbers, adding to their acreage, and prepared in times of war as in times of peace to make their fullest contribution to the basic economy of this blessed land of hope and opportunity.

Supplement

JEWISH COLONIZATION IN THE U. S. IN THE
NINETEENTH CENTURY

From the earliest period of American history, Jews engaged in agriculture. Abraham de Lyon brought the vine and silk cultures from Portugal to Georgia. In the South Jews were engaged in the production of indigo, rice, corn, tobacco and cotton. But Jewish immigration to the colonies and later to the young republic was insignificant; there were not many more than 3,000 Jews in the United States when Mordecai Manuel Noah in 1820 announced his plan to establish a Jewish agricultural colony on Grand Island in the Niagara River—a plan that proceeded no further than the purchase of the land.

The first concerted effort to found a Jewish farm colony came in 1837 in Sholem in New York State. For more than thirty years following, no organized attempt at Jewish colonization was made but Jews in small numbers settled on farms as individuals. The year 1881 witnessed the beginning of what was at once the most active and the most dramatic period in American Jewish agricultural history.

The persecutions which broke out in Russia upon the accession to the throne of Alexander III led many Russian

Jews to seek refuge in other lands. Some went to Palestine. Some came to America. Transatlantic steamers loaded with immigrants arrived in quick succession. The ingenuity of American Jewry was taxed to the limit to provide for the newcomers and to put them on the road toward self-support. Farming was conceived as an outlet—the more so because some of the immigrants had come here with that in mind. Within a few years sixteen known attempts at agricultural colonization were made in such far flung places as New Jersey, Louisiana, Arkansas, Dakota, Kansas, Colorado and Oregon. These were followed in the next decade by the Palestine Colony in Michigan.

The story of this era is a saga in American Jewish history. Its material is to be found in old records, and in correspondence the author had over a period of years with some of the colonists. There was agreement on most essential points and it is therefore possible to present accounts which are substantially authentic.

Unfortunately, these colonies were short lived. The only survivors are those in New Jersey whose proximity to New York and Philadelphia saved them from the common fate. In Louisiana it was flood, in Arkansas malaria, in Dakota hail and drought, in Colorado aridity, in early Sholem, in Kansas and in Michigan, a combination of circumstances that doomed these ventures. In Oregon the cause lay not in the physical but in the spiritual domain. But the underlying causes were the same in each instance. These colonies were conceived in haste without adequate thought to those factors upon which successful colonization depends. Geographical location, the character of land, the fitness of colonists, capital needs, farm experience, leadership—none of these vital requirements received sufficient consideration. Though ill fated, these agricultural adventures were not altogether bare of result. These very failures led to the

creation of the Baron de Hirsch Fund and of the Jewish
Agricultural Society whose guidance gave the Jewish farm
movement form and direction and helped a sizable section
of Jews to attain the goal for which these pioneers struggled so valiantly.

Following are sketches dealing with these early farming
ventures. Except for the report on the South Jersey colonies, written by L. G. Robinson and included for the sake
of completeness, they are from articles by the author of this
book, which first appeared in various magazines.

The Tragedy of Sholem *

Among the hills in the extreme western part of Ulster
County in New York State, there is a rocky stretch of
plateau land, sterile, lonely, forbidding, reached by difficult mountain paths and in places almost impossible of
access even to this day. A bare half-score families, mainly
descendants of old inter-related German residents, constitute the sole population of this lonesome mountain fast-
ness. There are a few none-too-well preserved houses, ill-
kept farm buildings, small cultivated fields and large
stretches of rough and stony land, unused and untillable.
Farm animals are few and inferior. The few residents are
for the most part elderly people. There is a complete absence of child life. Indeed, an atmosphere of brooding and
desolation permeates the entire region. Yet in this forsaken
spot a stirring human tragedy was enacted a century ago,
in which the actors were Jewish colonists.

Sometime in the year 1837 a small group of New York
Jews banded together for the purpose of founding a Jewish
colony. They selected as the site for their settlement a
tract of land in the northern part of the township of Wa-

* From articles published in "The Jewish Tribune," June 16 and 23,
1922.

warsing, about six miles west of the village of Warwarsing and four miles north of Lackawack, part of a large stretch of land belonging to one Edmund Bruyn. The land was subdivided into plots of about five acres, a site was set aside for a village and village lots laid out. This projected village with the surrounding area was given the name Sholem, a name that it retains until this day, and to reach it the colonists travelled by boat up the Hudson to Rondout and then by way of a canal to Wawarsing, a journey that took probably three days or more.

The Ulster County Clerk's Office shows that a total of 484.54 acres and eleven lots in the Village of Sholem were conveyed in December, 1837, by Edmund Bruyn to William N. Polak, Marcus Van Gelderen, Elias Rodman, Benedict Cohen, Jonas Solomon, Edward May, Zion Berenstein, Solomon Samelson, Ignatz Newman, Joseph Davies and Moses Cohen. (Polak immediately conveyed his holdings to Moses Content at the same price that he paid for them, and, apparently dropped out of the venture at its inception.) The land was owned in parcels ranging in size from 20.7 to 70.5 acres. With the exception of Ignatz Newman, the purchasers also bought village lots—one-half lot to two lots each. The aggregate price paid for the land was $3,631.18, an average of $7.50 per acre. Of this $2,724.84 was taken back by Bruyn on first mortgages. Only $903.34, therefore, was paid in cash by the purchasers. The individual payments ranged from $38.81 to $130.75 and the mortgages ranged in amount from $116.44 to $398. All mortgages were payable in five years and bore seven per cent annual interest.

About three years after these eleven purchases, Charles S. Saroni bought 187 acres in Sholem. The deed is from Edmund Bruyn and is dated September 4th, 1840. On the same day Saroni gave Bruyn a purchase money mortgage for $1,052.44, the identical amount which appears in the deed as the purchase price of the land. The mortgage was payable in quarterly installments with seven per cent interest. It is worthy of note that Saroni paid $5.62 per acre as against $7.50 paid by the earlier buyers, despite the fact that he made no cash investment whatever. It is believed that the original agreements called for the full payment of the land in cash, but that a re-arrangement was effected for partial cash payments and mortgages for the balance, as already outlined, due to the panic of 1837 which struck the country between the initiation of these negotiations and their consummation.

Contracts were awarded to build houses, probably eight —the exact number is not definitely known. The cost seems to have been around $300 or $400, ample for the erection of a very comfortable house in those early days. Indeed, the houses were out of the ordinary for that primitive time and that primitive country, and the fact that the newcomers could afford the luxury of a frame house in place of the primitive log cabin commonly in use caused them to be regarded as men of means by their neighbors. A plot was set aside for a burial ground and a synagogue was erected. How hard it must have been to accomplish this can be judged from the fact that a petition was sent to the Shearith Israel Congregation in 1838 for financial help toward the erection of the building. While action was deferred on the petition, the Synagogue, nevertheless, was built.

The newcomers cleared and fenced their lands; dug wells; built roads. Wisely they did not depend upon farming alone, for they evidently realized the futility of trying to make a living from barren soil. They engaged in the manufacture of goose quill pens and fur caps. They became cobblers, peddlers and tailors. Davies conducted an inn and general store, and it is narrated that before he waited on his customers he took them into a room behind the store and served them tea and cake. One of their number, Samelson, served as Rabbi and Schochet.

The settlers were men of education and culture, people who for the most part had lived on a good, even though modest, standard in the city. This is indicated by the comparatively luxurious houses, and also by the character of the household furniture, their oil paintings, and the art objects which they brought with them. Thomas E. Benedict, an old, distinguished resident and the historian of Ulster County, maintains that they even had a small museum and art gallery.

For a time the newcomers were able to get along—how well is doubtful—but by combining farming with their other occupations they managed somehow not only to eke out an existence but even to reduce their mortgages. But— it is surprising that sagacious men should not have foreseen it—the odds against them were too heavy. Farming, especially for new recruits, was impossible in that bare, cold, mountainous country where the soil was poor and the growing season short. Even the native farmers who had had their lands free of mortgage, and the German immigrants who followed in the wake of the Jews, experienced though they were, could make no headway. The country was sparsely settled. Removed from markets and from centers of population, the colonists soon found the road too thorny to travel. Their sufferings at times were intense, but they held on tenaciously. On one occasion their condition was so desperate that they slaughtered a day-old calf to assuage the hunger of their families, despite the fact that the Jewish law prohibits the use of an animal for food before its eighth day and although these people were conforming Jews.

The troubles of the Sholemites reached their climax with the temporary shutting down of the local tanning factories in the neighborhood, one of which was owned by Edmund Bruyn; some of the Sholemites worked there in order to stave off starvation. Deprived of even this meager source of income, the condition of the colonists became desperate. They could no longer meet the payments on their mortgages, small as these were. Foreclosure suits were instituted, and in 1842 nine of the twelve were sold out. The other three mortgages were satisfied by payment— that of Ignatz Newman on November 22, 1842, that of Joseph Davies on July 24, 1843, and that of Zion Berenstein on November 24, 1846. All of the mortgages seem to have been considerably reduced, showing that the colonists strained to clear their properties as quickly as possible. The records show that at the time of the foreclosure the amounts owing on the mortgages ranged from $24.45 to $673.56, whereas the mortgages ranged from $116.44 to $1,052.44. The nine foreclosed parcels were bought in by Edmund Bruyn. Davies conveyed his property to Rowland Davies, a brother, in September, 1851, and he in turn deeded to David H. Divine in the following month. Divine later acquired the other nine parcels. Further than this it is not necessary to trace them. What disposition was made of the Berenstein and Newman properties, we have not been able to ascertain.

There is an atmosphere of mystery surrounding this colony. Why did this handful of immigrant Jews in that early day leave their homes in New York and select as their future abode a sterile, inaccessible and forsaken country more than one hundred miles from the metropolis? Surely there was better land closer to the city to be had for little, if anything, more than the price they paid in Sholem. They were people, if not of affluence, at least of comfortable circumstances. What was it that induced in them a desire to change? Why did they select farming as the means of a livelihood? What was the composition of the colony—what the common bond that brought these colonists together?

To find the answers to these questions we took a trip to Sholem and, with old residents acting as our guides, made observation at the spot where this old colony was located. We interviewed old settlers of Sholem and its environs, made search of official records at the County seat, and traced descendants of five of the twelve Sholem founders, and a descendant of Bruyn. We heard many interesting human stories—some perhaps legendary—woven around these early settlers. In the traces of a by-gone habitation we saw mute evidence of industry and toil. Even the musty records in the County Clerk's Office in Kingston, though containing merely the formal documents of conveyance, mortgage and foreclosure, unfolded a stirring story of this heroic undertaking, idealistically conceived but doomed to failure—a failure that put the quietus upon the Jewish agricultural movement in America for the succeeding forty years.

On our trip there our car, light though it was, found it impossible to make some of the ascents. The spot where the colonists lived is now a wilderness covered with a second growth of timber. The stone foundations of houses, fences built out of the rocks gathered from these very lands, a lane, and abandoned wells, are all that is left to mark this old habitation. We saw the place where the Synagogue is supposed to have stood. It was moved from Sholem several decades later, and we took a picture of a house near Wawarsing, part of which is purported to have been the Synagogue. We saw the spot which is said to have been the burying ground, but found no evidence of graves or tombstones. It is said, however, that there were at least three graves over which had been placed ordinary rectangular field stones without inscriptions. We saw an abandoned well, blocked up with stones, and met an old resident of Ellenville, formerly of Sholem, who told us that this well was formerly referred to as "Der Yudenbrunen."

Some of the colonists' furniture is still in existence, a number of pieces being in possession of a Mrs. Leibolt of Napanoch. We saw an inlaid mahogany wall mirror, a folding table, a chair and a rocking chair—all made of mahogany—and a combination bureau and secretary. It seems that when misfortune overtook this colony it was found necessary to dispose of part of the belongings. The story is told that when the last of the colonists reached Lackawack on his way to New York with his household furnishings loaded on a wagon, he was obliged to sell a fine mahogany bedstead to realize enough money to pay for his own food and for the feed of his horse until he reached the city.

Our quest for information from Sholem descendants was more successful, but the facts, fragmentary as they are, only tend to deepen the mystery, for the settlers were of different nativity, different occupations, different ages, and different shades of belief.

Elias Rodman was born in Poland probably about 1790. His wife, Esther, was German. Before going to Sholem, and after his return, Rodman was a peddler—what later became known as customer peddler. Possibly his territory included Sholem and its environs. A son, born in Sholem shortly after the family settled there, still survives. He lives in New York and has for many years been in the city's civil service.

A son of Charles A. Saroni also lives in New York. He is 72 years old, connected with a prominent Fifth Avenue business house, and a man of considerable education. His father was born in Frankfurt am Main, Germany, and came to the United States as a young man. He was a furrier, and after his return from Sholem became a hatter, a member of the firm of Saroni & Archer. Drawn by the gold fever, he went to California in 1850, and while on a voyage back to New York in 1857 he was lost in the wreck of the sailing vessel "The Central American." It is an interesting coincidence that in our research we met an old gentleman, who told us the story of the wreck as related to him by the mate of the vessel, who was the sole survivor. As the son was only eight years old at the time of his father's death, he has but a faint recollection of him, but he remembers having heard that he farmed for a short time in Ulster County.

The ancestors of the well known New York Contents seem to have been related to the Moses Content of Sholem. We have not been able to trace Moses, except to ascertain that he was the brother of Simon Content who came here in 1803, was naturalized in Philadelphia in 1813, and later moved to New York. The minutes of the Spanish and Portuguese Synagogue list him among the seatholders in 1820. The Contents were a French Jewish family who moved to Holland whence they emigrated to the United States. One of their ancestors was an officer in the French army.

Joseph Davies was born in Holland, educated in England, and came to the United States in 1798. His early history is not known, but he seems to have been well along in years at the time he settled in Sholem. It is said that he was the last to leave the colony. The fact that the deed from him to his brother, Rowland, cites his residence as Cleveland, leads to the inference that he went there from Sholem. Later, however, he returned to New York City, where he died at an advanced age in 1857. A great-grandson is J. Clarence Davies, the well known New York real estate man, and a great-granddaughter is Mrs. Max L. Levenson, both prominently identified with Jewish affairs. From these descendants we learn that Davies was well educated, well read, rather interesting, with a fund of stories and a keen sense of humor, but that he was not a man of means nor much of a moneymaker—just the type of a man who would be expected to serve tea to his customers, as tradition tells of his Sholem experience.

Marcus Van Gelderen was born in Holland in 1798 and came to the United States at the age of twenty-four. In 1828 he acted as temporary Schochet and Bodek of the Shearith Israel Congregation during the illness of Mark Solomons. From 1860 to 1871 he was the regular Schochet and Bodek. He seems to have died in the latter year. We found a grand-nephew, Abraham Van Gelderen who is in business in New York and lives in Brooklyn. He could add nothing to this except that his grand-uncle died a bachelor.

The records of the Spanish and Portuguese Synagogue contain the name of John Solomons as a seatholder in 1820. Was this the Jonas Solomons of Sholem?

Pioneers in the Land of Cotton *

The scene of the first of the episodes of the eighteen eighties was laid in Louisiana. Late in 1881 a group of immigrants left for New Orleans under the leadership of Herman Rosenthal, who had come to the United States earlier that year. Rosenthal had been a wealthy merchant in Kiev, a man of erudition and culture, a writer and poet. Later in life he conducted a book establishment in New York City and became head of the Slavonic department in the New York Public Library. The group comprised

* From an article published in "The Jewish Tribune," September 27, 1929.

twenty families and some single men, in all about 125
persons. A more motley aggregation can hardly be imag-
ined. Its membership was composed of students, teachers,
artists, merchants, craftsmen and peddlers—educated and
illiterate. None had ever farmed and few were accustomed
to manual work.

Louisiana had been selected as the site for the colony
after correspondence between a "geographical committee"
of the prospective colonists and leading Jews in various
parts of the country. A tract of land located on Sicily Island
in Catahoula County on the Ouachita River, a tributary
of the Mississippi, about 160 miles northeast of New Orleans, was bought. There is uncertainty as to the exact area.
One of the colonists gives it as 1,000 acres, another as
2,400, and Leonard G. Robinson in his "Agricultural Activities of the Jews in America" (1912) records it as 5,000
acres. The price was $8 an acre. Easy terms were extended.
The "Alliance Israelite Universelle," through a New York
committee, granted a loan of $8,800 to help the undertak-
ing. There is a difference of opinion as to how this land
came to be selected. One of the colonists maintains that it
was the voluntary choice of the geographical committee,
another that the selection was forced upon the committee
because the sale "was to the advantage of a politician." All
agree that a more injudicious choice could not have been
made.

Upon the arrival of the group in New Orleans, it was
met by Sol Marx, a prominent Jewish resident, acting as
representative of the New Orleans Jewish community. The
new arrivals were given a cordial reception. Writing over
forty years later one of the colonists said, "I have not sufficient words to describe the kind treatment we received
while in New Orleans." After a short stay in the city, the
colonists set out for their new abode. Most of the women

and children were left behind. Some accompanied the men to the colony to take over the household duties.

The colonists were divided into three groups and worked cooperatively. All resources were pooled. The business was conducted and the profits were to be divided on a communal plan. But the intention was to establish each farmer on an individual basis as soon as the colony was on a strong foundation. The colonists found much of the land in splendid timber. The clatter of the axes soon mingled with the rhythm of Russian folk songs as these big trees yielded to the blows of the amateur woodsmen. Cotton and corn were to be the main products and a small amount of gardening was to be done for home use. A German farmer was employed as agricultural adviser, but he came only once or twice a week and his instruction was of little value.

There were three big houses on the plantation and a few old shacks where negro slaves had been quartered. Rosenthal, the president, and A. Peissokovitch, the secretary, (who, by the way, is now farming in California) occupied a room in one of the big houses. Another room was used as an office. The rest were herded ten and more to a room. From this it may be surmised that the buildings which the colonists found were not in habitable condition. New Orleans Jews planned to help build forty small houses, each of which was to serve for a family or for four single men. Ten or twelve houses were actually put up.

To the credit of the Jews in New Orleans it must be recorded that they showed a commendable interest in the colony, even if at times they allowed their zeal to run away with their better judgment. A general store was opened in the colony and the good New Orleans people supplied it with things "both necessary and unnecessary." At a banquet held in New Orleans a prominent Jew offered to pay

$2,000 for the first bale of cotton raised in the colony. Cotton was then selling at $40. He was never called upon to make good because not a single bale of cotton was produced.

The community developed an active social life. At night the colonists gathered in the "big house" and indulged in debates and discussions lasting until after midnight. One Borowick, who had been in the United States before, and Rabinowitz, a linguist, taught English. A small school was organized for the children. Rosenthal regaled the colony with his poems. Borowick, for many years a member of an operatic company, entertained with song. A weekly news bulletin written in Russian was issued. The caricatures of the various colonists showed that serious minded as they were and serious as was their undertaking, they nevertheless could see the humorous side of life. One cartoon portrayed the vice-president, a big strapping fellow and a former Russian banker, with penknife in hand trying to chop down a big tree. Another represented one of the grumblers as a barking dog—"he, too, is necessary to complete the Colony."

Isolated though they were, romance was not lacking. To quote from Peissokovitch, "Busy as I was with the affairs of the colony, I found time to court and win the most beautiful girl of the whole group." Another colonist also wooed and won "the most beautiful girl." As is to be expected, the group contained its malcontents ready to heap abuse on its leaders. In truth, this epic can best be summed up in the impressive words of one of the members: "Work—mostly useless, hope, despair, love, song, poetry, happiness and misery—life as we lived it there in Louisiana."

The Colony's life was short. Surrounded by deserted plantations, cut off from the world, with negroes of the most ignorant type as their neighbors, with rattlesnakes infesting the country, and mosquitoes "eating them alive," with malaria taking its toll among the children, is it any wonder that the thoughts of these impractical young idealists soon reverted to the city? They had been receiving letters from relatives and friends telling of city success, in contrast to which their own plight seemed all the more unbearable. And as if the cup of misery were not full enough, the Mississippi overflowed in the spring of 1882, washing away houses, cattle, implements and the small crops.

That was the last straw. The New Orleans committee was willing to continue its aid, but the colonists were utterly discouraged. Rosenthal and a companion went to New York to raise funds to enable the rest to leave. Some of the colonists, impatient at the delay, simply walked away. One sold his watch and chain to pay for the transportation of his wife and himself to New York.

Despite all the suffering and disappointments, many of the colonists did not lose faith. Their failure in Louisiana simply strengthened their determination to prepare themselves for a new start under more favorable conditions. The back-to-the-land urge persisted so strongly in these sturdy Chalutzim that many actually joined colonies launched shortly thereafter, in Arkansas, Dakota, Kansas and elsewhere. There the tragedy of Louisiana was re-enacted.

An Arkansas Colonization Episode *

Probably the most tragic of all the projects took place in Arkansas. As far as the writer is aware its history has never been recorded. Nor was the writer able to trace more than a few of the survivors. The story that is here set

* From "The Jewish Tribune," July 12, 1929.

down was pieced together from fragments furnished by them. The writer believes it substantially authentic, making allowance, of course, for the frailty of human memory of events that occurred almost a half century ago.

Late in 1882 or early in 1883 a tract of land in the eastern part of Arkansas about midway between Little Rock in that state and Memphis in Tennessee was offered for Jewish colonization. The offer seemed attractive because a lumber company had agreed to buy staves to be cut by the colonists at $20 per thousand, paying half on the completion of cutting and half upon delivery. A ready income seemed thus in sight. A group of about 150 people, families and single persons, was formed in New York to be sent to Arkansas.

Early in the spring of 1883 this motley band packed their few belongings and started for their new home. There, a virgin forest greeted them—a forest so dense, so thick with underbrush, that not even the natives had ventured to penetrate it. The sight of a tree was a novelty to these Ghetto dwellers and these immense wooded stretches in their spring garb appeared to them like a veritable Eden. In their ecstasy they wrote back home of the Paradise they had discovered. What a fool's paradise it turned out to be will appear as the story develops.

Upon receipt of these glowing reports a group of thirty Odessa immigrants belonging to one of the Am Olem societies, three families and the rest single men, decided to follow the early settlers. This group had already been formed and was waiting a favorable opportunity before venturing forth. Unlike the first group it was not dependent upon philanthropic support. Financed by their own organization, they bought a tract of land near the site of the first colony. The land was of similar character—a thick forest. For this timber land the purchasers paid $150 per acre, $25 down, the balance to be paid out of the proceeds from the sale of wood. To this group there attached themselves Solomon Menaker and one Spies as delegates representing a remnant of the Louisiana Colony which had failed the year before. Made wary by their unfortunate experience they determined to investigate before making another attempt. Menaker was selected as one of the investigators because he had had a little farm experience, having worked for four months on a farm in Connecticut.

When the second group reached Arkansas in the beginning of the summer they were shocked at the conditions which confronted them. They perceived immediately that agriculture as such was impossible. The only visible means of making a living was to cut and sell staves. When the contract was made for $20 per thousand staves, the settlers had no conception of the labor entailed. Because of their inexperience it required two men working two weeks to cut a thousand staves. They got $10 when the cutting was completed. The balance was payable on delivery—a very uncertain date. The staves had to be floated down the streams. During flood conditions—and these prevailed during the whole short life of the colony—delivery was virtually impossible. The saving element was a good market, and, had the colonists been more adept, they probably could have managed to eke out a modest living.

The colonists had hardly settled down before the hot season was upon them. Temperatures of 105° to 108° in the shade were not uncommon. Unaccustomed to this torrid weather the settlers endured much suffering. One relates that the men worked in overalls and shirts and would have discarded the shirts had they not been afraid that the sun would burn their bodies. So intense was the heat that work between twelve and four was impossible. The woodcutters went to work at four in the morning, re-

turned at eleven for a lunch of beans and corn bread, and
worked again from five until nightfall.

Living conditions were crude and primitive. The only
buildings were two log shacks in the larger settlement and
a ramshackle barn in the smaller. A larger log house was
started but never finished. The buildings sheltered the
women and children. The men slept in the open. It was
not uncommon for the sleepers to find snakes crawling
on their crude headrests. To add to these discomforts
there was a long succession of torrential rainstorms—
veritable cloudbursts. A survivor relates that during a violent thunderstorm the whole small settlement crowded
into its single little shelter. Lightning struck a giant tree
just outside of the building and it was by a mere hair's
breadth that the occupants were not crushed by the falling trunk. All the members of the colony joined in blessings to the Almighty for their deliverance.

Bad as these conditions were, they were mild in com-
parison with the horrors that followed. The excessive heat
and frequent rains produced myriads of mosquitoes. Without a vestige of protection against this pest and without
lotions to assuage the sting, the colonists suffered agony.
What was worse, malaria and yellow fever soon raised
their grizzly heads. In July, when the heat was at its
height, ninety per cent of the colonists were down with
these maladies. Fever racked, men dosed themselves with
quinine before going to work. A neighboring physician
helped minister to the stricken. He supplied quinine and
other drugs and agreed to wait for his pay till returns
came in from the staves. Within a short time eighteen or
twenty persons had succumbed to disease. Intensely tragic
was the death of both parents of three young children. A
neighboring Jewish business man helped care for the sick
and bury the dead. The sympathetic physician urged the

sufferers to write to their friends for money to quit the
colony.

With farming impossible, with money from the staves
slow in coming in, with mosquitoes making life intolerable, with the heat sapping the energies of the few who
had escaped the ravages of illness, with the constant rain
interrupting their labors, with sickness and death taking
their toll, the colonists were continually on the verge of
starvation. They had no livestock, therefore neither milk
nor eggs for the children or invalids. The mystery is that
a much larger number did not perish.

But the thickest of gloom is often penetrated by a gleam
of light. When conditions were most desperate and starvation stared the sufferers in the face, a call came from the
owner of a tobacco plantation three miles away for forty
men to clear his fields of weeds. The men were supplied.
After two hours' work it became evident to the planter
that his workers were unfitted for the strenuous, back-
breaking job. All but two—Menaker and one Vasa—were
discharged. At the end of the first day one complained to
the other that it was impossible to stand the strain. Only
the inducement of a good supper to be followed by an
equally good breakfast, and the thought of what a $1.75
daily wage for each could buy for the colony, spurred the
two toilers to remain. They stuck for ten days. Their combined earnings amounted to the munificent sum of $35, a
princely fortune in the eyes of these worn but undaunted
laborers. It never entered their minds to use this money
for themselves, urgent as their needs were. The welfare of
their starving companions was uppermost in their
thoughts. Instead of taking their wages in cash they took
them in foodstuffs. Their employer, a good natured man,
loaded a big wagon with provisions and sent it back to
the colony. This provender would have fed the smaller

colony—that to which the two were attached—several weeks. Here again the unselfish generosity of Menaker and Vasa asserted itself. They knew that the larger group was suffering from famine and so they divided their stock between the two colonies. Many years later Menaker visited Carmel, N. J., where one Goldstein, a former Arkansas pioneer, had settled. In the old days religious differences had divided the two men. Yet the lapse of years had not obliterated the memory of Menaker's noble deed, and Goldstein took pride in introducing him to his Carmel neighbors as the savior of the Arkansas colonies.

The life of the colonies was short. It could not have been otherwise. The marvel is that it lasted as long as it did. The smaller group was helped to leave Arkansas by fellow members in New York. The larger group had no one to fall back upon. Before leaving, a letter was dispatched to Am Olem leaders in New York describing the sufferings and misery of the colonists and begging for aid to get away from the plague infected country. This plea was heeded and by September, 1883, the Arkansas colonies had become a matter of history. But even these harrowing experiences were not sufficient to shatter the ideal cherished by these colonists. Some remained in the city just long enough to earn money for a start elsewhere.

An Epic of the Prairies *

After the Louisiana colony, the earliest of this period, broke up (1882) some of the colonists immediately made plans for another attempt elsewhere. Some went to Arkansas, others to Kansas. The moving spirit, Herman Rosenthal, had hardly returned to New York before he set plans on foot for the establishment of a colony in what was then the territory of Dakota. Two main reasons governed the

* From the "Detroit Jewish Chronicle," January 29, 1932.

choice of a northern locale. First, attributing the debacle in Louisiana to heat and malaria, the projectors sought a more temperate climate, a climate which more closely resembled that to which they were accustomed in Russia. Besides, the United States government had just thrown open a former Indian reservation for settlement by homesteaders, and this free land served as a magnet.

Rosenthal was a man of considerable means, who had been a successful merchant in Kiev. He was a man of wide culture and profound learning, the leader of the Am Olem groups of young Jewish idealists which sprang up in Russia about this time and whose objective was the return to the soil. Associated with Rosenthal was Benoir Greenberg, a young Russian immigrant who had lived in the United States about one year. Greenberg was the son of a noted architect and bridgebuilder in Russia, reared to wealth and brought up in an atmosphere of luxury and culture. Early in life he developed an idealistic bent. He became imbued with the longing to demonstrate that the Jew was a creator, capable of earning his living from the soil. In furtherance of this ideal he was prepared to surrender a life of ease and comfort, to tear himself loose from home and family and throw himself heart and soul into the effort to establish a farm colony. He had corresponded with Rosenthal and found in him a kindred spirit. By coincidence he met Rosenthal on the steamer on which he came to the United States.

Upon his return from Louisiana, Rosenthal got in touch with Michael Heilprin who, though not a colonist himself, was a prime mover in all of the colonization ventures of this period. A fine soul, whose heart bled for his suffering brethren, he spent himself in the efforts to ameliorate the condition of the immigrants poured upon our shores. These three men formed a loose organization among the Am Olemites who were holding themselves in readiness to go to the land anywhere as soon as arrangements could be made for their reception.

On July 1, 1882, two families, Greenberg and Samuelwitz, left New York, arriving at Mitchell, Dakota, on July 5th. Upon alighting from the train, the newcomers celebrated the event by procuring a large can of boiling water and brewing and drinking Russian tea, right in the streets of Mitchell. So strange was this sight that practically the entire population of one thousand turned out to see the immigrants. A local Jewish businessman, one, Weil, with whose brother, a merchant in Milwaukee, they had had some correspondence, took them in hand, helped them obtain temporary quarters and advised them on registration of land claims. But nothing was done until the arrival of Rosenthal a week or so later. He came with a Jacobowitz family and was followed almost immediately by the Pflicht family.

The site selected was on the division line between Davison and Aurora Counties, South Dakota, and about 20 miles from Mitchell by country road. This land had never before harbored the white man. It was beautiful prairie country, with black, fertile, virgin soil. Word was dispatched east that a location had been selected and other families immediately began to come, so that within a short time the colony numbered 50 people. It grew steadily until at its height it contained about four times that number. Rosenthal and Greenberg acquired their land by purchase, the former buying four quarter sections—a whole square mile. The others filed government claims. Government regulations permitted the adult members of the family to file separate claims. Taking advantage of this, some filed two claims, some even three, and thus obtained a half and even three-quarters of a square mile. The area that came under their control stretched over a distance of 15 miles.

The colony was called Cremieux, in honor of Adolphe Cremieux, president of the Alliance Israelite Universelle.

In the choice of land this colony was more fortunate than most of the others of the period. But like them, it suffered from inexperience and lack of trained leadership. Like them, therefore, it had a short though interesting history. Its very first step foredoomed it to failure.

The initial arrangements completed, a committee of colonists was sent to Milwaukee to buy lumber, stock, equipment, etc. There they engaged in a reckless orgy of extravagant buying. They bought beyond their means and their needs. They bought the best horses, paying as much as $800 for a single team. They bought quantities of fancy lumber for their houses. Soon a trainload of stuff rolled into Mitchell. Only after the livestock had arrived at the colony did they wake up to the fact that they had made no provision for its housing, and no preparation for its feeding. Worst of all, only then did it dawn upon them that animals needed water, of which there was a woeful shortage. At first, water had to be carted a distance of three or four miles from a small pond on one of the claims. Then some of the colonists dug wells. But in this they encountered enormous difficulties because of the topography of the prairie country. Two expert well diggers were employed who, with the assistance of the colonists, had to excavate to a depth of 50 to 60 feet before reaching the water level. The cost of individual wells ran up to $200, $300 and even $600, and even then the supply was meagre. This scarcity of water plagued the colony all through its existence.

As soon as the lumber was unloaded, the building of houses began. Here again reckless expenditures were incurred. Buildings beyond the means of the settlers were erected. The leaders, being people in more affluent circumstances, built eight, ten and twelve room dwellings. The others put up less pretentious structures, but even these were far above the shacks used by the average homesteader, many of whom contented themselves with sod houses. This was also the case with a number of the colonists who were ready to put up with inconveniences until financially strong enough to build more elaborate homes.

It was during the course of the construction of one of the first of these houses that an incident occurred which, but for the prompt action on the part of a German carpenter, would have had tragic consequences. While at work on the roof of this house, the carpenter saw a haze of smoke in the distance. Realizing its significance, he immediately raised the cry "prairie fire." In Paul Revere fashion, he aroused and gathered the neighboring colonists and set them busily at work starting back-fires, to create a barrier against the raging conflagration. Men, women and children were pressed into service at firing a stretch of land several hundred feet in diameter, to denude it of all inflammable material. It is hard to imagine the terror in the hearts of these poor people, with the roaring of this fiery furnace in their ears, and the sight of the onrushing clouds of flame before their eyes, fighting grimly to save their possessions and their very lives. Fortunate it was for them that this carpenter understood the portent and knew how to ward off the danger. Otherwise the colony would have met immediate extinction and many of the colonists an appalling death. The drama of this event is heightened by the fact that it was enacted on the eve of Yom Kippur in 1882.

As a result of this prairie fire, every bit of the standing hay was destroyed, and not a speck of fodder was left for the cattle. Yet, buoyed by their enthusiasm, the colonists went to work. They made the rounds of the older farmers—few and far between—to buy the small quantities of feed that were purchasable. Somehow their spirit pulled them through the first winter.

And a severe winter it was. The cold was so intense that the kerosene would freeze in the lamps, and one's very breath congeal on his pillows at night. The water, which had to be lugged in barrels over a distance of three or four miles, ofttimes became solid ice en route. Added to the extreme cold, were the severe blizzards which raged that winter, blizzards of such intensity as to make even the short trip from house to barn a hazardous journey. One of the survivors relates how some of the colonists used ropes, one end fastened to the door post and the other end tied around the body, to prevent losing themselves in the blinding sheets of ice and snow. For days at a time the cattle had to go without water. It was fortunate that, despite the rigors of the climate, the colonists remained healthy. In fact it is worthy of note that no serious illness developed during the entire existence of the colony and no deaths occurred.

In the spring crops were planted, mostly corn and flax, but also vegetables. Everybody worked, even the women, some of whom had been brought up in the lap of luxury. When harvest time came the men worked on the threshing outfit while the women went from house to house cooking and baking for the hungry workers. A good crop was harvested but, unfortunately, prices were generally low and the settlers fell behind financially.

Yet they were not discouraged. Flax brought fair returns and they simply decided to plant more the following year. But nature seemed to conspire against them. The crop of flax showed wonderful promise, and the fields in their delightful coloring were a glory to behold. Came a hailstorm and laid it low. With the flax went their hopes for the second year. The exodus from the colony began. Some of the younger men started to work for the railroad. All but a few of the families were heavily in debt. They had by this time obtained title to their lands and the process of mortgaging began. Money seemed plentiful, but borrowing was expensive. The exactions of the lenders were extortionate. Bonuses of 20 per cent plus other charges brought the cost almost to 50 per cent.

Still the people persevered and looked hopefully forward. But again nature was unkind. Protracted drought the following summer and intense heat ruined their crops and broke their spirits. With the scarcity of both feed and water, many head of cattle were dropping and the farmers began to sell off their stock. As one man put it "the cattle began to diminish and our capital diminished with the cattle." The colony continued to dwindle, though more persevering spirits hung on.

Strange as it may seem, hardship did not prevent these amateur farmers from getting joy out of life. They regarded this as an adventure and were willing to accept the consequences, whether good or bad. An active social life prevailed. Meetings were held at various houses. Parties, dances, lectures were frequent. The spacious homes of Rosenthal and Greenberg were used for entertainment of various kinds. The former had a piano, a rare thing on the prairie at that time. The colony had its own glee club and choral organization. Native farmers who came to the concerts marvelled at the artistic ability displayed in these affairs. Rosenthal employed the daughter of a prominent neighboring farmer as tutor for his children. With the same generosity that he showed in helping some of his fellow colonists over desperate periods, he invited the other farmers to send their children to his house to get the benefit of this instruction.

Religion concerned these farmers but slightly. They had no synagogue, no religious leaders, no schochet and, as far as can be learned, held no religious services. It sounded rather strange to hear about the hogs that were raised in the colony, how they were prepared for food over the winter, and how a young couple married in the colony received a litter of pigs for a wedding gift.

Three years of reverses right at the outset was almost too much to withstand. Yet, the colonists might have continued had their creditors treated them more mercifully. With mortgages in default, the mortgagees began to foreclose. Disintegration was on in full force. Some colonists were fortunate enough to sell out and save a little out of the wreck. Rosenthal was able to exchange part of his farm for a large grain elevator in Mitchell, where he did a thriving business until he was forced out by the big companies which regarded him as too formidable a competitor. Greenberg opened a grocery store on his farm and later moved to Louisville, Kentucky, where he lived for some years before returning to New York. Another colonist, Eleazer S. Marshbeer, found a position as drug clerk in a neighboring town. Later he became a language instructor, and still later returned to New York, where he studied law at the New York University, and served on the District Attorney's staff. Elias Rosenthal, brother of Herman, opened a store in Mitchell. In 1888 he returned to New York, worked for the New York Life Insurance Company, and became a practicing attorney. Some of the colonists engaged in peddling. Others found jobs in Sioux City, Iowa, and other western towns, and some returned directly to New York City.

Grean, a brother of Greenberg, relates that when he

left the colony he had $5.25 in his pocket. At the railroad station he asked the agent for a ticket to any point that could be reached on a $5 fare. Thus he landed in Sioux City with 25 cents in his pocket. There he worked at digging sewers at $1.75 per day, and after working two days lost the job. He obtained employment in a restaurant, where he worked for his board during the winter. Finally, like most of the others, he came back to New York.

Jacobowitz * was the last man to leave. He stuck it out until 1889.

The Jewish Covered Wagon †

It is strange that though seven colonies were planted in Kansas—Moses Montefiore, Hebron, Gilead, Touro, Leeser, Beersheba and Laskar—less authentic data could be uncovered about them than about colonization in the other states. The explanation probably lies in the fact that these colonies were small and short-lived. The writer was fortunate in finding a surviving member of what was likely the most important colony. As this man was the leader, the information vouchsafed by him, making allowance for the vagaries of memory, can be taken as fairly accurate.

No sooner had the ill-fated Arkansas colony come to an end than some of the more courageous and idealistic of the colonists made preparations to try again on a plan which they hoped would rule out the causes of their previous failure. After their return to New York, they held a meeting at which they resolved to establish a colony as

* The known colonists, other than those already mentioned, included the following: Waldman, Levitan, Geshelin, Sokoloff, two Rosenbergs, four Weinshenker brothers, two Weinsteins, Reinstein father and three sons, Godner (ex-soldier who had been in America 20 years) Petrofsky (a poet and newspaper correspondent) Kelman, Bernstein, Stahl, Chazenowitz, Riess and Samuels.

† From the "Jewish Criterion," January 29, 1932.

soon as each had saved at least $200. Michael Heilprin, the patron saint of these "back to the land" idealists, promised to use his efforts to raise as much money as the colonists themselves could manage to get together. This aid unfortunately did not materialize. The members of the group found employment in New York, lived frugally and laid aside in a common fund every dollar not actually needed for bare necessities. They met frequently and went painstakingly at the task of laying plans for their forthcoming colony. Their scheme was to divide their membership into groups of six; four of each group to settle in the colony, two to remain in New York and contribute to the development of the group holdings. The members were to alternate between city and colony, to give everybody the opportunity to work on the land until the time arrived when all could settle permanently.

Correspondence was carried on with the Moses Montefiore Colony which had just been established near Dodge City, Kansas. The leaders assured the prospective colonists that there was ample government land in the immediate neighborhood available for settlement, and proferred their assistance in obtaining it.

- Late in April, 1884, a band of thirty left New York for St. Louis, Missouri. Here they sought out the few erstwhile Arkansas colonists who had settled in that city, and made inquiry of the United States Land Office as to available locations. They bought horses, wagons and implements and sent them by train to Dodge City. The cost of all this, as of their entire trip West, came out of the common treasury.

At Dodge City, the travelers were met by a delegation from Montefiore and proceeded directly to that colony forty miles away. Here they learned to their dismay that all desirable government land had been pre-empted. Bundling themselves into covered wagons, they hired a scout and set out on their wanderings over these western plains in search of a suitable spot for their new colony. For weeks they travelled over trackless prairies at the mercy of marauding Indian bands until worn out by fatigue, suffering from thirst, and reduced to starvation, they finally located a stretch of country in the extreme southwestern corner of Kansas about forty miles from what is now Ford City, then a community of only five families. Here they staked out and filed their claims. Eventually six full sections, an area of 3,840 acres of contiguous land extending over three miles in one direction and two miles in the other, was acquired. Government regulations required the payment of $200 for a quarter section (160 acres) payable in four annual instalments and made it mandatory for the homesteader to build a house, to plow ten acres and to live on the land at least six months before being entitled to a deed.

Upon Michael Heilprin's suggestion, this colony was named Lasker, in honor of Eduard Lasker, the German economist and liberalist, who had died in New York City while on an American lecture tour just preceding the formation of the colony.

The first step of the colonists was to provide shelter. They built a sod house large enough to accommodate all thirty. The lumber for the roof had to be hauled forty miles. The roof, put on with so much labor and hardship, was later swept away in a storm. The next thing was to provide water. The nearest natural source was the Arkansas River. As this was fifteen miles away, no time could be lost in digging a well—a huge task on the prairie where water is obtainable only at great depth. Even with the help of two experienced well diggers, it took two weeks of back breaking toil and the sinking of a shaft two hundred feet deep, to strike water. At its completion, the well cost $500, an enormous sum for those days. Even then, the equipment was so crude that it took twenty minutes to bring up a bucket of water. While the well was being dug the colonists had to carry water from a polluted surface pond over a distance of four miles. Some time later, a second well was dug.

Their immediate needs provided for, the colonists set themselves to erecting separate houses for each individual group. All told, six small houses were built bordering the plowed lane which had been previously furrowed through the entire three-mile tract. These houses were made out of sod strips, plastered on the inside. They contained no flooring and the only lumber used was that for the roof. Attached to each house was a lean-to designed to serve both as a stable for the horses and a barn for the cows and chickens.

The plan of operation was intelligent and unique. Fearful lest divergent religious or economic viewpoints might disrupt the colony, each small group was composed of people of like temperament and was granted autonomy in the conduct of its affairs.

Although this was planned as an agricultural colony, there is little to be said about it from the standpoint of agricultural accomplishment. The colonists planted sorghum which came up well but which could not be sold because of the distance from markets. It had to be used for fuel and fodder. The wheat crop was poor and was used only for home consumption. Eggs sold at six cents a dozen. Vegetable gardens were only of sufficient size to supply home needs. The second season witnessed a terrible drought. The ground was so parched and burnt as to cause almost a complete crop failure. The paltry crop was ravaged by hordes of wild horses that roamed over the prairie. The government had to be appealed to to send cavalry forces to drive these horses to the reservations to which they belonged.

Despite the hardships, perhaps because of them, an active social life developed. Most of the colonists were young. There were only two men over forty, the rest were under twenty-five. There were but two married couples. All were of an intelligent bent. Evenings they met for purposes of discussion and debate. The aggregate of the books which each brought with him made up a respectable library. One group was religiously orthodox in its practice —the others, if not irreligious, were non-religious. Still they all fraternized. On the high holidays, religious worship was conducted in the large sod house which had become a community building. In this, even the non-religious joined to make up the "minyan."

The original plan by which the members were to alternate between city and colony, was followed only in part, but those in the city contributed regularly, sending five dollars and in some instances six dollars out of their meager nine dollars weekly wage, for the support of the colony. Yet, despite this outside assistance, the colony did not endure.

In 1886 a land company began buying up large stretches of land for an irrigation project. Prices boomed, mortgage money was plentiful. The colonists could not put up with crop failure, drought and physical deprivation and hardship. The temptation to take advantage of the inflation was too strong to resist. Gradually they sold out or mortgaged their holdings and the colony rapidly disintegrated. Only two held on with the firm intention to engage in active farming. But the irrigation scheme soon collapsed, the boom died down and these two stalwarts lost out completely.

A Unique Agricultural Colony *

To put this story in its proper setting, we must go back to a few years preceding the time when this history opens. At that period there developed a movement among the Jewish youth in Russia to become more closely identified with Russian life and with Russian affairs. They attended Russian institutions of learning, took up energetically the study of the Russian language, and sought to become thoroughly Russian, part and parcel of their native land. The pogroms that broke out early in 1881 in Odessa, Kiev, Elizabethgrad and other parts of South Russia gave them a rude shock. They realized that there was nothing to hope for in this land of oppression. Stimulated by two Russo-Jewish newspapers and exhorted by individuals, chief among them Manuel Bokhal, there sprang up almost simultaneously in various parts of Russia, principally in Odessa, groups whose objective was to stand together as Jews rather than as Russians. They called themselves Am Olem (the Eternal People). These groups attracted the intellectual Jewish youth and were composed mainly of gymnasium and university students. In the minds of these young people there developed a firm belief that farming is the noblest occupation for man. They were prepared to exemplify these ideals in their own lives through the establishment of model colonies. Some left for Palestine. Many more came here.

The first Am Olem group to emigrate to America left Odessa in September, 1881, and arrived in New York the following January. It was composed of about sixty-five young people. They travelled by way of Austria and Germany and were met at Brody by the representatives of the Alliance Israelite Universelle which had been called

* From "The Reflex," May, 1928.

there to look after the large influx of Russian Jews following the pogroms. Brody, a short distance from the Russian border, had become the rallying point for Jewish refugees. There these Am Olemites remained for a time until arrangements could be made for their further journey.

Some of these youths held rather liberal views in the matter of religion. This brought down upon them the disfavor of the conservative elements in Brody and later at Berlin where they stopped en route. Letters were actually sent to Jewish leaders in America warning them against these young radicals. Thus they incurred the displeasure of some of the very people who might, but for these tendencies, have been ready to help them.

The second group of the Odessa Am Olem arrived in February, 1882, and these two groups were followed within a month by two other groups. The colony in Oregon was made up almost entirely from members of these four groups.

The first task to which these future colonists set themselves was the formulation of a plan to carry out the objectives which brought them over, the establishment of a farm colony somewhere in the United States. They were without funds. They had to live, and, if possible, to save. They had to seek occupations until they could save or raise the money necessary to set up the colony. Besides, investigations had to be made before proper land could be selected. Their radical tendencies had left Jewish leaders cold to their plans. But there was one among them who understood their minds, who sympathized, even though he might not have agreed, with their fanciful if idealistic views, and who was in complete accord with their colonization aims. That man was Michael Heilprin, author and scholar, who threw himself heart and soul into every movement of service to the Jewish immigrant and who is regarded by some as the greatest Jew in America of all times. Heilprin became their staunch friend, and though advanced in years and of modest means, he devoted his time without stint and often at the expense of physical discomfort to win support, financial and otherwise, for their undertaking. Associated with him was Dr. Julius Goldman, then a young lawyer, since risen to eminence in many fields of communal endeavor, who, at the neglect of his own profession, labored earnestly and ceaselessly in behalf of these immigrants.

Impractical though they were, they realized that training acquired through actual work on farms would prove a valuable asset to the future colony. Some of the members therefore looked about for farm jobs. Some went to Long Island, others elsewhere near New York. Two hired themselves out on farms near Hartford. A few went to Indiana and further west. One of these landed at Vincennes, Indiana. Here some Jews offered him positions in the city, which, much to their surprise, he refused. They finally placed him on a farm in the neighborhood where he worked for $8 a month.

These farm workers were instructed to hold themselves in readiness for a call to New York when the time should come for the group to set out on the journey to its own farm. When the call did come to this Indiana farm hand, he found himself penniless though he had worked on the farm for four or five months. That did not dampen his ardor. Walking part of the distance, riding on wagons when he succeeded in getting a lift, he made his way back to New York.

Not all worked as farm hands. There were not enough farm jobs to go round. Moreover, they realized that some would have to seek positions with higher pay if they were to lay by a little for the general fund. But they were not discriminating in their choice of jobs. They wanted work as quickly as possible and no labor was too arduous, too dangerous, or too menial. Some went to Boston to work as longshoremen. Others worked on the railroad that was then being constructed between New York and New Brunswick. They tramped over trestles, slept in railroad yards and on station platforms. Still others worked in the city at whatever presented itself. These, with members of other Am Olem groups, in all about 50 or 60 in number, rented a house on Pell Street which became known as The Commune. Here they put their communistic theory into actual practice. They led a real communistic life. The household tasks were divided and the earnings pooled. Educational meetings were held nightly that extended into the wee hours of the morning. At these gatherings the communistic philosophy was explained and discussed. The plans for the colony were elaborated and perfected. The Alliance Israelite Universelle kept in close touch with them. Michael Heilprin was their constant advisor.

Two scouting parties were sent out to different parts of the country to examine land. One went to the midwestern states and Texas. Its members worked on farms for three months to test out conditions. They found the heat depressing and land arid, and reported unfavorably on colonizing in those parts. The other expedition went to Washington and Oregon. On this committee was William Frey, a non-Jew, a former Russian nobleman, military officer, and Professor of Mathematics in the Military Academy at St. Petersburg, who cast his lot with this group of reformers and immediately became its leader. This committee found land in Douglas County, Oregon, about 250 miles south of Portland. Upon its recommendation, a parcel of 760 acres of land was bought. About 150 acres were fit for immediate cultivation. Most of the rest was a forest. There were two modest farm houses on the property. The price was $4,800. The two thousand dollars required for the first payment was raised through the personal solicitation of Heilprin from a few New York Jews whom he succeeded in interesting in the project.

In July, 1882, a group of about twenty-five prospective colonists started for Oregon. They travelled by steamer to Colon and crossed the Isthmus of Panama, then by steamer to San Francisco and finally again by steamer to Portland. The trip took about a month. Through the intervention of Henry Villard, a close friend of Mr. Heilprin, transportation was obtained at $20 per person, covering the cost of the entire trip. Eight or ten proceeded immediately to the colony. The rest remained in Portland to earn a few dollars and to become better acquainted with the language and the customs of the country. According to the plan mapped out, small groups were to follow one another from New York to Portland and to remain there until summoned to the colony. In the meantime those in Portland were to send part of their earnings to the colonists. The stay in Portland was a trying period for the more restive spirits. One impatient individual disobeyed the injunction and left on his own account for the colony, tramping the 250 miles to get there.

The spring of 1883 saw between forty and fifty people in the colony. Very soon after their arrival a large two-story frame building was put up. The upper story was used for sleeping quarters. On the lower floor there were kitchen, dining room and assembly hall. The colonists planted wheat, oats, peas, beans, and a variety of vegetables mostly for home use. The land was rich and well watered. No great technical knowledge was needed to make it produce. The river and the creeks were full of fish. Sustenance proved no problem.

During the first two years about forty or fifty acres were broken up, which made about two hundred acres fit for cultivation. In addition to raising crops the colonists set themselves to cutting wood from their forest. About four thousand cords were cut in the first two years and sold to the railroad company. Between $7,000 and $8,000 was realized in this way and a further payment of $1,000 made on the contract for the land. Occasionally some of the men worked out at various trades. One, an engineer, earned as much as $6 a day in a machine shop. The wages were placed into the common chest.

This colony was unique in the type of life that prevailed. None of the other colonies founded at this period or, for that matter at any other, was conceived along such distinctive lines. The leading spirit, Frey, had come under the influence of the famous French philosopher, Auguste Comte, exponent of the philosophy of positivism. Frey became a most fervent advocate of that philosophy and many of the colonists became his ardent disciples. The colonists lived under a strict regime. Rigid regulations were in force. Everybody worked. Their fundamental philosophy was the Marxian dictum—"each man works according to his ability, each man receives according to his needs." "One for all, all for one" was their motto. There was no written constitution. There were fixed hours of labor and assigned tasks not only on the farm and in the forest, but also in the kitchen and about the house.

Though the land was fruitful and the food was plentiful, these young idealists led a most frugal existence. Their theory of life forbade them to "gorge" themselves when there were people on this earth suffering from want and hunger. Their diet consisted of beans, peas and coarse bread—food of the simplest kind. The daily food budget was around five cents per person. When it exceeded eight

cents, they reproached themselves as wastefully extravagant.

Imbued with the loftiness of their ideals these youthful
"intelligentsia" did their work, manual and menial, with
joy in their hearts and songs on their lips. Their diversions
were largely intellectual. Nightly they gathered in the assembly hall to discuss, to debate, and to argue. They expounded the theories of positivism. The more learned delivered lectures in their special fields of study. One night a
week was devoted to a "self criticism" meeting at which
the members were encouraged to pass judgment on one another's actions and to suggest means of improving the
affairs of the Colony. The thirst for knowledge was un-
quenchable. The books in the library were read and studied with avidity. Mrs. Frey, who was an accomplished
musician, gave recitals on an organ that had been presented
to the Colony.

Their religion was the "Religion of Humanity." The
moral life of the colonists was unimpeachable. Despite the
very large preponderance of single men—there were only
four or five married couples—they led a most chaste existence. A spirit of brotherhood reigned. This was so striking that a wandering farm expert, a non-Jew who lived in
the Colony a year or so, remarked that in all his wide experience among many classes of farmers in many parts of
the country, he had never come across so remarkable a
group of young people—a group that never quarreled,
that was constantly cheerful, pervaded with idealism, and
every one of whom "labored to save the world." It was beyond his understanding.

The Colony, though composed of newly arrived immigrants, and Jews at that, commanded the respect if not the
admiration of the Christian neighbors. Staid American
farmers travelled long distances to spend a social evening

and brought their wives and daughters to the dances given at the Colony's assembly hall.

Harmony reigned for two years. Then the serenity became disturbed by the intellectual bickerings of the colonists. Two schools of thought had developed. One was composed of the adherents of Frey. These followed him with a zeal and fervor approaching hero worship. Frey's philosophy was clean and noble but Spartan in its severity. In the matter of food he was a rigid vegetarian, to the extent of not only banning meat from his own diet but of refusing to sit at the same table with anyone who ate meat. The other school was also very positive though not positivistic in its views. Its followers were not vegetarians. Though idealistic in their way, they were far more practical in their outlook. This strong diversity of views led inevitably to a clash of opinions. Two groups of young enthusiasts, both idealistic but along different lines, both headstrong, could not live and work together in amity. Realizing that their viewpoints were irreconcilable, Frey and about fifteen of his followers left the Colony. Yet such was the spirit of both factions that no enmity was engendered. They parted as friends with expressions of good will on all sides. The pain of separation was so poignant, the sorrow at the breaking of old friendships so profound that, in the words of a former colonist, "tears fell like rain."

The departure of Frey's party hastened the disintegration of the Colony. A fire which burned down the "community" building and destroyed the library—their most valued possession—accelerated the process. The colonists began to disperse. Some remained in the West, others wended their way back to New York. At the end of about three and a half years, this hoped for Utopia had become a mere matter of history. . . . These dreamers aimed at the stars, and the stars seemed to move further away.

THE PALESTINE COLONY IN MICHIGAN—AN ADVENTURE
IN COLONIZATION *

In the center of the so-called Thumb District of Michigan, about a hundred and twenty-five miles north of Detroit and fifty miles east of Bay City, there is a small village bearing the odd-sounding name of Bad Axe. The story goes that a great many years ago lumbermen camping at this point found an old axe believed to have been left by the Indians. While one of their number was engaged in chopping down a tree the handle of the axe broke. In his anger he cast it aside execrating it as a bad axe. The scene of this incident became known as the place of the Bad Axe, and the village which in time grew up around it inherited that appellation. Up till about 1884 this district contained vast stretches of heavily timbered country, but in the fall of that year destructive forest fires denuded the land of much of its timber. In 1891, when our story opens, this land was covered with a second growth of scrawny brush and poplar, useless for almost any purpose save fuel, and not too good for that. About four miles from the present village of Bad Axe and right in the heart of the region just described, a dramatic venture in Jewish colonization was enacted.

The dramatis personae of this sketch were with one exception Russian Jews living in Bay City, the exception being a German Jew who lived in Detroit. All had been in this country less than four years, excepting one who had been here eleven years. All were peddlers. This was a period of depression, the precursor of the distressing panic that broke upon the country in 1893. Walking from town to town and from village to village, burdened down with heavy packs, these Jewish peddlers were barely able

* "American Jewish Historical Society," No. 29—1925.

to eke out a scanty living for their families. Their contact
with farmers naturally turned their minds to farming as a
means of improving their condition. This thought took
form particularly in the brain of Hyman Lewenberg, the
man who had been in this country the longest. He had
read of the many efforts at Jewish colonization made in
the 'eighties, and conceived the idea of establishing a Jewish colony in Michigan. While peddling around Bad Axe,
Lewenberg had become acquainted with bankers who
owned immense stretches of land in Huron and adjoining
counties. They promised to sell land on easy terms if
Lewenberg could bring together a sufficiently large group
of Jewish purchasers. These negotiations resulted in the
purchase of twelve contiguous parcels of land by Hyman
Lewenberg, Aaron Kahn, Wolf Baerman, Sam Eckstein,
Joseph Beckman, Moses Rosenberg, Abraham Goldman,
Uriah Steinborn, Sam Steinborn, Jacob Lipowsky, Louis
Malinoff and Joe Malinoff in July, 1891.

As far as can be ascertained Louis Malinoff bought 20
acres, Joseph Malinoff and Uriah Steinborn 40 acres each,
and the rest 60 acres each, thus taking up an entire section
of land. The price was $11 an acre for the 60 acre parcels
and $12 for the smaller holdings. The peculiar feature of
the transaction was the nominal cash payment—about $15
per parcel—a total of less than $200, which was probably
all the ready cash of the entire group. Each buyer received
a contract providing for payments in five equal annual instalments with interest at the rate of 7% per annum before maturity and 10% thereafter, title to pass after the
payment of the full purchase price. Louis Kostikoff, Moses
Heidenrich and another bought land that same autumn
upon the same conditions.

The settlers set to work with zest and zeal to establish
themselves in their new home and new calling. Though

imbued with the spirit of the true pioneer, they little realized the stupendous struggle ahead. Attuned to the ideal of establishing a new Zion in free America, they named their new colony Palestine.

Their first tasks were to build small shacks and to clear small patches for fall plowing in preparation for spring planting. A hardware dealer in Bad Axe still remembers selling the saws and axes, implements in the use of which these Jewish peddlers were far from adept. Five or six crude shacks built out of saplings and partially burned logs, each containing one unplastered room with flimsy partitions to separate the sexes, were hastily put together. While the clearing and building were going on, the settlers and their families camped out in the open. When cold weather set in some of the colonists were forced to take their families back to Bay City and to resume peddling during the winter months. Those that remained in the colony were well-nigh destitute and depended for maintenance upon the pittance which their brothers in Bay City could spare from their meagre earnings. Their condition was at times so desperate that it is a mystery how they were able to subsist till spring. It is told that a neighboring German farmer, himself in not too affluent circumstances, doled out to them a small supply of milk and a few loaves of home-baked bread daily for a short time until he himself could no longer afford it. Still they struggled on, undaunted and full of hope, to prepare more land and to put up more buildings for the reception of their fellow colonists the following spring.

An important phase in the history of the colony began at this time. A Jewish peddler who had witnessed the colonists' sufferings brought the story of their heroic struggle to Martin Butzel, a prominent Detroit merchant, with whose firm this peddler had had business dealings. Butzel was known for his broad philanthropies and was at that time the president of Temple Beth El Hebrew Relief Society. A close friend of Butzel and also a member of Congregation Beth El was Emanuel Woodic, an experienced farmer who had had twenty-five years of successful farming back of him. Woodic was then living in the village of Utica, near Detroit, on a small farm where he had retired when his advancing years and his wife's illness compelled him to give up more active farming operations. The story of Woodic's life is of such absorbing interest, full of adventure and pioneering, and his influence on the life of the colonists was so potent that, at the risk of breaking the continuity of this sketch, it is worth while to digress to give a few of the outstanding incidents of his momentous career.

Arriving in 1854 from Bohemia, at the age of 18, Woodic's first job was on a Long Island, N. Y., farm, where he received the princely wage of $6 per month. Later he hired out on a wrecking vessel cruising in Delaware Bay. In 1856 he enlisted in the United States Army. Almost at the very outset of his military career, he participated in the Mountain Meadows Massacre, being one of the few survivors. At the expiration of his term he reenlisted and served throughout the Civil War. His service record is a remarkable history. It includes, among others, the battles of Bull Run, Chancellorsville, Gettysburg, the Wilderness, Spottsylvania, Cold Harbor, Petersburg, and the various battles preceding the evacuation of Richmond. He received a number of wounds, but fortunately none that incapacitated him from service. At the close of the war he was honorably discharged and went to Michigan. There he bought a forty-acre farm in McComb County. For the next twenty-five years, and almost up to the time of the beginning of Bad Axe, he farmed in that section and became known as the foremost farmer in the county, an authority on all farm problems and a leader in the community. Woodic was in 1922 a resident of Detroit, a venerable figure, active and virile, despite the burden of 87 years.

It was natural for Butzel to turn to Woodic as the ideal man to investigate conditions at Bad Axe. When Woodic arrived in Bad Axe in March, 1892, sixteen farms had been taken up, Reuben Neisuler having joined the colony that spring. The population of the colony was then 57, consisting of 16 men, 7 women, 26 boys and 8 girls. They occupied ten shacks. Some of the wives and children were still in Europe. Not more than an acre or two on each farm had been cleared. The sum total of all the livestock was seven horses and two cows. One of the settlers had brought with him a team with which he had made his peddling rounds, another a single horse. Four horses were bought on time and had not yet been paid for. Enough money was scraped together with which to buy the two cows that furnished the entire milk supply for the population.

Upon Woodic's return to Detroit, Butzel called a special meeting of the Beth El Relief Society. Immediately a supply of clothing, groceries and matzoh was sent to Bad Axe, and arrangements made to procure fodder for the livestock. A fund of $1,200 was raised which was entrusted to Woodic to use according to his own best judgment. Because of the intervening Passover holidays and a spell of stormy weather, Woodic could not return to Bad Axe until early in May. His first step was to provide each farmer with a cow. He also bought three plows, three drags, a yoke of oxen, other equipment, and oats, peas and potatoes for planting. He supplied each family with a small quantity of groceries. What is more, he remained in Bad Axe

throughout that spring and summer, teaching these raw
recruits how to sow and cultivate, and later how to harvest
their little crop. Realizing the necessity for more cleared
land, he kept the men constantly at work underbrushing
and clearing. During these operations he installed a temporary sawmill of the crudest type in order to cut the
burned logs—a considerable supply of which had accumulated—into rough boards to be used as siding for the almost open shacks, so as to make them more habitable for
the winter. Not only was Woodic the agricultural advisor
but he acted as the communal leader and arbiter of the
many petty disputes which naturally arose among the colonists. Living accommodations were barely sufficient for
the colonists' own families and Woodic had to lodge in
Bad Axe village. Despite his age he tramped the distance
of four miles each morning and, after a strenuous day's
work under a broiling summer sun, trudged back again
to his modest room in the village. He received no compensation for his self-imposed task. To him it was truly a labor
of love.

At the same time that Butzel appealed to his own relief
society, he also entered into correspondence with the
Baron de Hirsch Fund, which had then been in existence
about a year, and which, Butzel felt, was the proper organization to deal with the problem. As a result, the Fund,
upon motion of the late Jacob H. Schiff, appropriated the
sum of $3,000 to meet the colonists' urgent needs. This
fund was turned over to Butzel as trustee.

By this time the first year had rolled by. Interest and
taxes were due and the colonists had incurred small debts
for groceries and other living requirements. The work
that had been done under Woodic's guidance was merely
preparatory for the following season, but yielded no income. The largest creditor was the land company which,

besides selling the land, had lent its credit for the purchase of merchandise and had also made small cash advances. Early in September, 1892, Butzel took a trip to Bad Axe and personally supervised the distribution of the money made available by the Baron de Hirsch Fund. He paid $2,300 to the company and used the rest to pay other debts and to supply pressing necessities. This money was considered a loan to the farmers and each of the 12 recipients gave a promissory note for the amount received—ranging from $125 to $275—payable in five years with interest at 5%, to be charged only after the first year. As security the borrowers assigned their contracts to Butzel as trustee. Before making any payment to the land company Butzel prevailed upon it to modify the terms of the contracts so as to make the first instalments fall due in 1896—thus obtaining a four year extension—and to change the maturity date of the annual interest payments from July 20 to October 1, the end of the harvesting season. But before the company made these concessions it insisted upon receiving an agreement under which Butzel bound himself to release all interest in the several contracts immediately upon a default in payment, in this way relieving the company from the necessity of foreclosure.

Butzel came back from Bad Axe much impressed with the calibre of the colonists. In his report to the Baron de Hirsch Fund upon the disbursement of its appropriation he wrote:

"These people, both men and women, . . . through industry early and late, in all kinds of weather, seem to have accomplished all that could be expected in such a short time and thus given proof of their sincere intention and earnestness to become farmers in fact. Notwithstanding their present poverty, scanty food and poor habitation, which would discourage others, these families seem to make sacrifices of all personal comforts and stick to farming."

An exhibition of the colonists' products at Temple Beth El during the Succoth holidays of 1892 stands out in a truly pathetic light. This was the means conceived by Butzel and Woodic to interest the Detroit Jews in their neighboring farming brethren. Samples of the few crops raised in the colony were placed on display. Small as it was, this was the first exhibition of farm products raised by Jews to be held in the United States. A small parcel containing two potatoes was sent to the Baron de Hirsch Fund as a memento of the first crop raised in the colony.

Encouraged by the interest which their efforts were arousing and freed from their pressing debts, the colonists worked industriously, clearing land, cutting down saplings, pulling stumps, draining, ditching, preparing more land for plowing, and sowing winter wheat. During this time two more families from Saginaw joined the colony, Michael Jacobson and William Weisberg. Behr Marks, the father-in-law of Moses Heidenrich, and Charles Danto had arrived somewhat earlier. The colony had by this time attracted such wide-spread attention, not only in Detroit but elsewhere, that Bad Axe became a veritable Mecca for Jewish farm enthusiasts. An employee of the realty company vividly recalls a certain morning on which the train from Saginaw brought thirty-three prospective settlers, some of whom came from distant points in neighboring states, and that his company had to provide six teams to convey them through the colony. Every one of these thirty-three became so infused with the "back-to-the-soil" spirit that each paid a small deposit, the total of these deposits amounting to $125. This enthusiasm evidently waned for only one from nearby Saginaw returned to throw in his lot with the colonists.

During the entire winter of 1892–1893 Butzel kept in close touch with Bad Axe, advising and encouraging the farmers, all of whom remained on the land throughout the season. Late in December, 1892, he asked M. Razek, a Jewish resident of Bad Axe, to make a report on the situation of the colony. Razek reported that the colonists were working industriously preparing the land for a large crop that year. They planted over fifty acres of potatoes alone, in the hope that the income would yield them sufficient to clear much of their debt. But they were in desperate need of living necessities to tide them over until the harvest. Butzel sent them a supply of kosher meat and authorized Razek to buy potatoes and flour. That winter was one of the severest ever experienced in the section and Butzel sent a second appeal to the Baron de Hirsch Fund for relief. His plea was a touching one. "It is almost miraculous," he wrote, "with how little they get along." In February, 1893, the Baron de Hirsch Fund made a second loan of $1,000 which Butzel entrusted to Woodic and which the latter in turn lent out to ten of the colonists in amounts ranging from $60 to $250. Like the previous year Woodic was the guiding spirit in the colony. Under his direction the colonists sowed, cultivated, harvested, cleared land and put up buildings. Their livestock and farm equipment were put to constant use. Woodic's active participation was cut short early in the fall through the illness and death of his wife, but the impetus he had given carried the colony along for several years.

During the year 1893 the colony was augmented by three families from Saginaw, J. Levinson and Israel Levinson, brothers, and J. Shepaninski. Sometime later David Graff and Sam Elias also took up farms in the colony. In the meantime there had been some defections because the colony at no time numbered more than sixteen families.

The years 1893 and 1894 marked the height of the colony's agricultural activity. Unfortunately, the potato crops of both years on which the colonists pinned their hopes failed. The autumn of 1893 found them again unable to meet the interest on their land contracts. As before, Butzel came to the rescue. In 1894 the farmers fared better. They made enough for their own maintenance and for the first time were able to make partial payments on their annual interest.

An interesting episode, and one which throws Butzel's broad humanitarian spirit into bold relief, was his efforts to bring over the families of Kahn, Marks and Beckman from Russia. Foreign bureaucratic regulations made this a difficult task but Butzel was relentless. He corresponded with agencies here and abroad for upwards of a year before he finally succeeded in reuniting these families.

During this era of comparative farm activity a laudable communal spirit developed. Almost from the start religious services were conducted every Sabbath morning, and Saturday was a day of cessation from labor. At first worship was held in one of the little shacks, later a small synagogue was built. Part of it now forms the rear of a farm house occupied by a farmer named Drews. A photograph is in the writer's possession. A schochet came from Saginaw, and for a few months during the summer and autumn of 1892 Rev. Charles Goodwin of Bay City, was spiritual leader, cantor and religious teacher, acting in these various capacities without pay. Praiseworthy was the ardent desire to give the children a thorough Jewish bringing up. Hard as it must have been to get together the little money required, a modest Talmud Torah building was erected.

The critical period began in the autumn of 1895. The succeeding years were years of continuous struggle to re-

tain the lands. The colonists defaulted on their contracts
and were in constant danger of eviction. At these crucial
junctures Butzel stood as a bulwark between them and the
real estate company. His nobility of character reveals itself
in his correspondence with the company pleading for
leniency to these struggling colonists.

"You must have patience with these poor farmers
(he begs), be they Jews or Christians. . . . You would
not be so cruel as to set families with small children
out of doors. Do not do what the law allows you but
be kind to your fellow man. (Again he pleads:) I cannot believe that you considered the consequences and
fully comprehended your order for the removal of
those tenants. Just think of the anguish, heartaches,
sufferings and disappointments of women and children to be driven from that which they have toiled
for, for four years, with earnestness praiseworthy to
build up a home for future and good citizenship,—
and just now when favorable indications seem to appear, would you insist to drive them from house and
home just for the reason that each one of the family
heads owes less than $100 for interest past due? I ap-
peal to your own judgment and sense of justice, saying nothing of charity or humanity. Do grant them an
extension that they may try this season once more. I
hope and trust that you will not only grant this request but give them aid, comfort, and advice. This
would give all parties peace of mind, satisfy the teaching of the Savior and the God of Israel alike. The
prayers of the oppressed have never been unan-
swered."

This plea evidently had no effect because the creditor
company persisted in its demands upon the colonists. Besides being behind in their contract payments, the colo-

nists owed the company about $1,300 for merchandise for which they had given joint notes. The company pressed for security covering the crops and movable property and the colonists turned to Butzel for counsel. With his characteristic sympathy, clarity of thought and a comprehensive grasp of the legal intricacies involved, Butzel advised them in the strongest terms not to tie up a single article of personal property. This spurred the company to action and an agent was sent with an officer to serve summonses on all the colonists. Thereupon, a committee composed of Kahn, one of the colonists, and Isaac Shulman, a storekeeper of Minden, a small village near Bad Axe, went to Detroit to report in person to Butzel. Butzel showed that he could fight for the colonists as well as plead for them. In a scathing letter he reminded the company that movable property is exempt by law and that in any event he, as trustee, had a prior claim by reason of the fact that the organizations for which he was acting had spent over $6,000 on the colony, none of which they expected to get back. He pointed out that the real estate improved by the clearing of 165 acres of land, with many new buildings, was much more than ample to secure the company and, he continued:

"I protest against any such unlawful proceedings on your part or the part of your agent to take away any property of whatever nature which is exempt by the law of the state. . . . I shall be compelled to hold you accountable and responsible for all damage thus inflicted."

Butzel's firm stand was effective. The land contracts were again redrawn extending the period of payment to October, 1906, with principal payments of $30 annually to be made in the interim. The new contracts ran to the individual purchasers but, as in 1892, an agreement was entered into under which, in the event of default, the land was to be surrendered without legal process. These negotiations were conducted by Shulman who from this time on took an active interest in the affairs of the colony, particularly during the protracted illness with which Butzel was seized at this stage.

For a short time things ran smoothly. The 1897 crop was again a failure and ruin was once more staring the colonists in the face. A petition was dispatched to the Baron de Hirsch Fund in which the colonists suggested that it might be advisable for the Fund to buy the land outright. An agent from the Fund was thereupon sent to make a special investigation. Some of the passages of his report are worth quoting as proof of the stamina of these settlers.

"Some of them had to sleep on the bare ground, in weather and storm, with the animals of the field as their companions but they braved it all with the ultimate expectation of possessing what they then began to toil for. It should not be difficult to convince you how almost insurmountable were the obstacles they had to contend with and it is surprising that they did not lose heart. That they were industrious beyond measure none can gainsay as their own shoulders served as animals which they had not the means to purchase, and their Christian neighbors testify to their pluck, energy and determination."

The trustees of the Fund considered the matter thoroughly but their conviction was inescapable that further nursing would only prolong the agony. Correspondence, however, ensued with the object to effect an amelioration of the terms of the 1896 contract "that will insure the land to the colonists in the future" but these efforts were without result. All that was left to be done was to stave off the inevitable as long as possible. As a measure of protection to the colonists quit-claim deeds were taken in the name of Henry Rice, a trustee of the Fund, conveying the purchasers' right under their contracts.

From this time on things moved rapidly. Payments on purchase contracts were due, taxes and drain assessments had piled up, and the company began ouster proceedings. Though just out of a sick bed, Butzel once more came to the rescue. His urgent appeal to the Baron de Hirsch Fund resulted in the sum of $1,000 being placed in his hands to avert imminent eviction. On Monday, January 17, 1898, Butzel received a telegram from the company's agent stating that the service of eviction-writs could not be delayed beyond Wednesday. Wednesday afternoon found Butzel in Bad Axe to stay the threatened misfortune. There was then due a total of $1,522.17. Having only $1,000 at his disposal, part of which he desired to reserve for other uses, Butzel was put on his mettle to make an adjustment with the company. With his keen business resourcefulness he succeeded in prevailing upon the company to accept $825 in full settlement. He asked permission of the Baron de Hirsch Fund to use part of the balance for medical attention for the young daughter of David Graff and for the wife of Hyman Lewenberg, both of whom were in a hospital at Detroit, the latter dying of cancer. He also paid the long overdue bill of the local physician, which amounted to $36 for six months. This left $75 which he used the following May for advances in amounts ranging from $5 to $10 towards the purchase of seed.

After Butzel had made this last adjustment he thought that the colonists would be unmolested at least until Oc-

tober, 1899, since the interest and taxes had been paid up
to October 1, 1898, but because some of the colonists
could not pay the small principal instalments, the company early in 1899 again demanded personal security on
pain of ejectment. Butzel once more took up the cudgels
for the colonists and warded off the disaster.

The disintegration of the colony began in the fall of
1899 when three colonists abandoned their farms. In 1900
only eight families remained in the colony and these rapidly disappeared. Except three parcels, all the land finally
reverted to the sellers and was later sold to German immigrants. Lewenberg appealed to the Baron de Hirsch Fund
for a release of the quitclaim deed so that he could save a
little to compensate him for his labor in bringing his farm
"from a wilderness to a home." Butzel seconded his plea
and the quitclaim was released. Lewenberg soon after sold
the farm and realized a few hundred dollars. A year later
Heidenrich made a similar appeal to the Fund and it was
also granted. Heidenrich was thereby enabled to sell his
farm and to carry away from the colony the munificent
sum of $35 for his years of toil. Heidenrich moved to the
village of Bad Axe where he still resided in 1922.

The departure of Lewenberg and Heidenrich marked
the end of the heroic project to establish a new Palestine
amid Michigan's primeval forests. The odds were too
great. The handicap against which this handful of fervent
pioneers had to contend eventually proved insurmountable. A small band of peddlers, utterly devoid of agricultural experience, with an insignificant initial capital, settling on lands that were swampy, cut over, burned out
and infertile, under contracts that were millstones about
their necks, with a serious financial panic breaking out
before they had even had a chance to orient themselves,
most of all, with the specter of the sheriff constantly before

their eyes, the colony was fore-doomed to failure. Success
was impossible.

SOUTH JERSEY COLONIES *

The first of the South Jersey Colonies was founded on
May 10, 1882, by the Hebrew Emigrant Aid Society. It
was named Alliance in honor of the Alliance Israelite Universelle, which contributed the sum of $3,000 toward its
founding. The first group of colonists comprised sixty-
seven families, numbering about three hundred souls.
These settlers hailed from southern Russia, mainly from
Odessa, Kiev, and Elizabetgrad. An option was secured on
a tract of about eleven hundred acres of land, which was
surveyed and divided into plots of ten acres. The land was
completely covered by a dense growth of scrub oak and
pine. The work of clearing the land and cultivating the
soil began at once under the guidance of an experienced
native farmer. They also proceeded with the erection of
houses, and the colonists were meanwhile lodged in three
large buildings, which they humorously named Castle
Garden, erected to provide temporary shelter. The total
cost of this, the Vineland Colony, as it was then called,
was $41,960, of which $12,129, was for land and equipment, $9,897, for houses and the balance for maintenance
and relief.

Meanwhile, in 1883, there was a lull in the arrival of
refugees, and the Hebrew Emigrant Aid Society dissolved.
It was succeeded by the Alliance Land Trust, which was
formed for the purpose of taking over and conserving the
property and the funds of the dissolved corporation, and
to look after the interests of the Alliance Colony. Among

* From "The Agricultural Activities of the Jews in America," by Leonard
G. Robinson. The American Jewish Year Book 5673 (1912).

the trustees were Henry S. Henry, Isaac Eppinger, Leopold Gershell, M. Mendel, Leonard Lewisohn, and the Rev. F. de Sola Mendes. The Alliance Land Trust is still in existence, and retains its interests in the Alliance Colony, although it has done no active work for a number of years.

After the houses were completed, two of the barracks were torn down. The one remaining was converted into a cigar factory in order to provide the new settlers with an opportunity of earning a living until they could see some returns from their land. This infant industry, established in what was practically a wilderness, did not enjoy a long existence. It was replaced by a shirt factory, which lasted less than a year. The hardships suffered by these colonists would be difficult to depict. Some of them had to travel with their wives and children several miles on foot to find work with non-Jewish farmers. After toiling all day they returned home as late as midnight, only to start out again in the small hours of the morning. This was the critical period in the history of the Alliance Colony, and it was mainly through the energetic efforts of public-spirited Jews from New York and Philadelphia, notably Alfred T. Jones and Simon Muhr of the latter city, that the colony was rescued from the fate that befell its contemporaries. The timely aid eventually bore fruit, and many of the colonists were enabled to make considerable progress on their farms. This brought the colony to the favorable attention of the Mansion House Committee of London, which placed the sum of $10,000 in the hands of the Alliance Land Trust, making it possible to secure for the colonists deeds to their farms, which theretofore they had only held under contract.

Following are the statistics of the Alliance Colony for the year 1889:

```
Population (souls) .................  529
Land owned (acres) ............... 1400
Under cultivation (acres) ...........  889
Houses ...........................   92
Barns ............................   63
Horses ...........................   32
Cows .............................   59
```

The history of the Rosenhayn Colony likewise began in 1882, when six families were settled by the Hebrew Emigrant Aid Society. They set to work clearing the land and erecting houses. But in addition to suffering the many hardships attendant upon pioneering, the colonists soon found themselves without funds. Their appeals for aid did not meet with success, and they were compelled to abandon their project and leave the place. In 1887, however, when the success of the Alliance Colony became known, several other families repaired to Rosenhayn and contracted for some land. They continued to live and work in the city until they could earn enough to pay for their land and start farming operations. The following year thirty-seven other families bought land under similar conditions. A large building, called "The Hotel," near the railroad station was rented and converted into a shirt factory, where many of the colonists found employment. As the colonists were obliged to work away from their farms, progress was necessarily slow. But the colonists worked assiduously, and gave as much attention to their farms as they could.

The condition of the colony in 1889, as it appears from the statistics for that year, shows some progress even at that early date:

```
Number of families ................   67
Population (souls) .................  294
Land (acres) ......................1912
```

Under cultivation (acres) 261

Houses 23

Barns 12

Horses 12

Cows 14

In 1882, Michael Heilprin, aided by sympathetic friends in New York, among them Jacob H. Schiff, Jesse Seligman, and Julius Hallgarten, settled seventeen families at Carmel on lands previously occupied by a number of German families who had abandoned their holdings and returned to Philadelphia. Some of the new settlers succumbed to the ordeal of the first two years' privations. But these were replaced by more vigorous settlers from among later comers among the Russian refugees. When these had become fairly established, new arrivals began to swell the number of settlers.

The sudden death of Michael Heilprin deprived the colonists of their best friend. Such organized support as remained was devoted to fostering the growth of Alliance. To avoid the imminent danger of the settlement's failing for want of a temporary helping hand, an appeal was made through the Rev. Sabato Morais of Philadelphia to Baron de Hirsch, who sent $5,000 for distribution among the colonists. The money was allotted to the settlers in various amounts, in accordance with recommendations made by Moses Klein, the agent of the Jewish Emigration Society of Philadelphia, who had been detailed to make a thorough investigation of the needs of each individual colonist. The timely aid thus obtained prevented the disintegration of the Carmel Colony.

The statistics of Carmel for the year 1889, as contained in a report made by Moses Klein, on February 17 of that year, were as follows:

Population (souls) 286
Land (acres) 848
Under cultivation (acres) 247
Houses 30
Barns 25
Horses 11
Cows 11

The same year 1,500 acres of land were added to the original tract of 848, and thirty-six new houses were erected, making the total acreage owned by the colonists 2,348 and the number of houses 66. A sidelight on the economic progress of the colonists in 1889 is their contribution of $47 for the sufferers of the Johnstown flood.

Two other settlements which are virtually a part of these Colonies are Garton Road and Six Points. Garton Road is two and a half miles west of Rosenhayn. It was started by a Russian immigrant in 1888, who purchased twenty acres of bush land near Woodruff on the Central Railroad of New Jersey. He was joined by some of his friends from the Colonies as well as from the neighboring city of Bridgeton. This settlement gradually grew, and now numbers about twenty-four Jewish farmers. It is entirely agricultural. The soil is somewhat better than in the Colonies, and the farmers have been successful almost from the start. Six Points was started in 1907 by the Jewish Agricultural and Industrial Aid Society. It bought several large farms about two miles from Brotmanville, and subdivided them into farms of twenty-five acres. The settlement numbers fifteen families.

One of the first constructive acts of the Baron de Hirsch Fund was the founding of the well-known Jewish settlement of Woodbine in 1891. After investigating sites in various parts of the country, the choice of the Trustees fell upon a tract of land in the northern part of Cape May County, New Jersey, fifty-six miles from Philadelphia and twenty-two miles south of Vineland. A tract of 5300 acres of land was purchased at a cost of $37,500. Of this area about 275 acres were laid out for a town site, and about 2000 acres surveyed into thirty acre farms.

Woodbine, like most of that part of New Jersey, was covered with a dense growth of scrub oak and pine. During the first year the families of the settlers were left in New York until some land could be cleared and buildings erected. The families arrived in 1892 and planting began. The work done by these pioneers was paid for by the Baron de Hirsch Fund and charged to the cost of the farms. In this way the settlers were enabled to earn a living while improving the farms allotted to them. The cost of the farms with the improvements amounted on the average to about $1,000. Not all of the fifty families remained. The hardships were enough to discourage the most optimistic and persevering. Agriculturally Woodbine has not made very great progress. The soil is rather sandy and poor and requires a large quantity of fertilizer to make it productive. There are now about thirty farmers in Woodbine, cultivating about five hundred acres.

Woodbine might be classed as an agricultural-industrial colony. During the early period, when farming to any extent was a physical impossibility, it was found necessary, in order to enable the farmers and their children to make ends meet, to establish some industries where the surplus farming population could find employment. The industrial activities have made better progress than the agricultural, and Woodbine's industrial enterprises comprise a machine-shop employing about one hundred persons, two clothing-factories employing two hundred and fifty persons, a knitting-mill employing one hundred persons, besides a hat-factory and a box-factory. These industries are housed in brick buildings and equipped with the most modern machinery.

In 1903 Woodbine was, by act of the legislature, separated from the township of Dennis and made a separate borough.

NOTE—The later developments in these colonies have been discussed in the early chapters of this book. Woodbine was fully written up in Samuel Joseph's "History of the Baron de Hirsch Fund" published in 1935.

FARM SCHOOLS

The immigration into the United States of the eighteen eighties had a profound influence on the thinking of American Jews who thenceforth were faced with an entirely new set of problems—problems that required an entirely new method of approach. In the effort to integrate the newcomers, several avenues had been explored, farming among them. The colonization experiences of that decade, though dismal, brought to the fore the need for informed leadership.

Two men at that time were inspired by the same vision and moved by the same ideal. Joseph Krauskopf and Hirsch Loeb Sabsovich were both immigrants. Both had imbibed a love for the farm in their native lands. Both had attained station in this country. Both were stirred by the suffering of their fellow Jews. Both saw alleviation and salvation in the Jew's return to the soil. Both were convinced that the keystone of successful Jewish agriculture was agricultural education. Both worked with might and main to build institutions to give concrete expression to their common ideal.

In telling the stories of these two schools, the author has drawn freely upon Samuel Joseph's "History of the Baron de Hirsch Fund" in the case of the Baron de Hirsch Agricultural School, and upon Herbert D. Allman's "A Unique Institution" in the case of the National Farm School.

Barely a year after the first settlers had pulled the stumps and cleared the underbrush at Woodbine, Sabsovich, the superintendent of the colony, was gathering his little flock around him on Saturday afternoons in a makeshift hall for lectures and discussions on problems facing these farm novices. Encouraged by their interest, he secured funds to erect a barn on a farm unit, the upper floor to serve as a lecture room. As the construction progressed, the plan was enlarged to make the entire building available for school purposes. This was the beginning of the Baron de Hirsch Agricultural School in 1891.

The first class was admitted in October, 1894, and consisted of fifteen students, most of them sons of Woodbine residents. The curriculum was restricted. In 1895, twenty-two pupils were enrolled, two from Connecticut. Heartened by these results, Sabsovich urged the Trustees of the Baron de Hirsch Fund to carry out a program of expansion. The Trustees, in turn, obtained from the Jewish Colonization Association an appropriation of $23,850 for the construction of a dormitory and a blacksmith shop and the remodelling of the older structure; also an allowance of $12,000 for current expenses. The school grounds were increased to 200 acres. When the dormitory, the DeHirsch Hall, was completed, fifty students were admitted. They began to come from beyond the immediate environs. Indeed, only seventeen were from Woodbine. An ambitious curriculum was instituted, covering three years and including scientific subjects suited more to an institution of higher learning than to a secondary school.

This was the first of a series of reorganizations that followed each other in rapid succession, indicative of the openmindedness of the Trustees and of their willingness to make the changes dictated by experiences and changed conditions.

In 1899, the Trustees appealed to the ICA for further expansion and the ICA made a contribution toward a $20,000 building fund. A three story brick building was erected containing offices, class rooms, laboratories, gymnasium and an assembly room to seat three hundred persons. The new buildings were ready in 1900, and in the school year 1900–1901, one hundred and twenty pupils were enrolled. Entrance requirements were altered and, to meet the needs of the younger boys and of fresh immigrants, a primary department was instituted.

In 1899 and again in 1900, student strikes broke out attributable to lack of supervision. To remedy the situation, Dr. Boris D. Bogen who had been instructor at the Baron de Hirsch Trade School and the Hebrew Technical Institute, both in New York City, was appointed principal of the school. The teaching staff was enlarged. The farm was expanded to 275 acres. "The school," read a report of this period, "provokes the admiration of all who visit it," and . . . of the dairy, the report added, "perhaps there is none in the state where sanitary conditions are more carefully looked after." Again, "the Woodbine Agricultural School stands now as the leading institution of secondary education in the United States. The Paris Exhibition loudly proclaimed to the world our supremacy. We received a silver medal for our Pomological Exhibit and the Grand Prix for secondary education."

Unfortunately, a fundamental conflict existed during practically the entire life of the school. What was the school's aim? On the one side, Sabsovich, Bogen and some of the Trustees wanted an institution along the line of the agricultural college with its professional and scientific objectives. On the other side, some of the trustees and the ICA held that the aim should be simply to make good farmers. The ICA's agricultural advisor criticized the curriculum as too expansive and the per capita cost as disproportionate. Yet, despite these findings, the ICA continued its support.

Another of the many student strikes which beset the school throughout its history broke out in the spring of 1904 and led to the dismissal of thirty-one boys. Another investigation ensued and harsh criticism was levelled at the school and its conduct. A separate board of trustees for the school was created. Sabsovich resigned to become general agent of the Baron de Hirsch Fund. A new superintendent, Dr. Harold H. Ballard, was appointed in June, 1905, to be replaced in 1906 by Henry W. Geller. Another of the numerous changes in curriculum followed. The dormitory was kept closed for a time, the school term was cut to one year, only to be raised again within six months to two years, classroom studies were limited and more attention was paid to work on a so-called model farm.

These repeated investigations, reorganizations, changes in curriculum, school term, teaching staff and management settled nothing definitely. Within a few years, another investigational study—and a very elaborate one—was decided upon. The debate was on issues involving the very life of the school. Was there a need for a school? Was Woodbine the proper site? Was the cost commensurate with results? Though the argument raged through the rest of the school's history, the decision, most times by divided vote and ofttimes grudgingly taken, was always in the affirmative. But the question of support did not cease to vex the authorities from year to year. The ICA continued to appropriate $20,000 yearly until World War I, coupling each grant, however, with the recommendation "the Council thinks you ought to take active measures in closing the school."

In 1912, there was another student strike and another reorganization. These strikes, annoying as they were, were not as serious as might be supposed. The student body was composed of older youth, mostly fresh immigrants, mature, serious, rearing to get along, impatient, fretful of little things, who felt that they should have a greater voice in determining their course. And these very bickerings

were at least partly responsible for the changes ultimately
decided upon by faculty and trustees. After this strike the
school committee was increased to ten members, the additional members being appointed from Philadelphia to
make closer supervision possible. Thirty-eight visits were
made by Philadelphia committeemen in that year. Geller
resigned and was replaced by Louis J. Cohen. That same
year, Robert D. Maltbie was engaged as Dean in charge of
education while Cohen retained the business management.
Causes of friction between faculty and students were
largely removed. The Alumni Association was reorganized
and Dr. Jacob G. Lipman was elected its president.

The year 1912 was a banner year. There were 664 applications for admission as against a dormitory capacity of
seventy. That same year Maurice Fels of Philadelphia undertook to make a study of all who had attended the
school. The first report came out in 1913, to be revised in
1914. It showed that 900 students had attended the school,
762 for a period of at least six months, and that 285 or
37% were still engaged in some agricultural activity. This
was considered a very good showing.

Yet the basic questions as to the need for the school, its
location, cost, etc., kept bobbing up and additional questions were raised. What effect would the discontinuance
of the school in Woodbine have upon Woodbine Boro?
What effect upon the general situation of Jewish immigrants? Could the Baron de Hirsch Fund provide proper
agricultural education in other secondary schools? A committee of ten thrashed out these questions in detail. After
more than a year's study, the committee came out not only
in favor of continuance of the school at Woodbine but
even recommended its enlargement. Secondary agricultural schools, the committee found, were not adapted to
immigrant Jewish boys. The closing of the school might

be regarded as an admission of the failure of the attempt to train Jewish youth agriculturally. But by the time the report was ready, the World War had broken out. The financial situation of the Baron de Hirsch Fund was affected, and the ICA soon communicated its doubt as to its ability to continue its subsidy. Action on the recommendation of the committee, therefore, had to be held in abeyance.

At about this time, a new rift between superintendent and dean caused the resignation of the former and of five faculty members. Joseph A. Rosen, a graduate of Michigan Agricultural College, was engaged as superintendent in October, 1914. The question of removal continued to be advocated despite the conclusion of the Committee of Ten and Rosen was its firm proponent. In the fall of 1916, Jacob H. Schiff and Julius Rosenwald proffered a joint gift of $300,000 for the purchase of a suitable tract of land for school purposes. After painstaking search, a tract of land was bought at Peekskill, New York, and plans for buildings prepared. Meanwhile Rosen had resigned and Arthur R. Merill, a former director of the Lyndon School of Agriculture in Vermont, was appointed superintendent.

The entrance of the United States into the war caused the number of applicants to drop from a normal of 500 to 50 in 1917. The school at Woodbine was kept going for a while and then the few remaining students were transferred to Peekskill. High costs had caused the postponement of construction at Peekskill. Estimates in 1919 showed that it would cost a million dollars to erect and equip the new school. The suggestion was advanced that the Baron de Hirsch Fund and the Jewish Agricultural Society contribute. Some of the Directors of the Society opposed the diversion of its funds from farm loans and agricultural education. There was also some feeling that the school was no longer needed. The ICA was approached and, when it declined to participate in either a capital contribution or in annual subventions, the trustees decided to give up the project. The land was later sold and the Schiff and Rosenwald contributions were turned back. In the meantime, the school at Woodbine had been closed. The buildings and surrounding land were donated to the State of New Jersey for the establishment of a state institution.

Thus there came to an end an institution that had for a quarter of a century aimed to arouse in Jewish youth the spirit of the farm. After the closing of the school, the Baron de Hirsch Fund for some years made contributions to the National Farm School and set up a scholarship fund to help Jewish boys to enter agricultural schools of both secondary and advanced type.

During the quarter century of the school's life, it performed distinctive services, the results of which are perceptible even today, twenty-five years after its discontinuance. Woodbine was the first school in the United States to impart secondary education in agriculture, and it may not be going too far afield to assert that it blazed the way for the many county and state schools of the same type that have since sprung up. And, when the trustees were faced with the necessity of giving up a Baron de Hirsch Agricultural School, they could do so with small pang. The school transformed raw immigrants of European schooling and background into upstanding Americans. Be their number large or small, Woodbine sent out into the world teachers, scientists, research workers and those who applied the training and skill acquired there on their own farms. Some of those who were content with the humbler role of farmer rose to leadership in their respective communities.

Among the graduates of the school were Jacob G. Lipman; his brother, Charles B.; Jacob S. Joffe; Moses Napthalison Levine; Arthur Goldhaft; Sam Bober, all mentioned elsewhere in this volume. Then there were Jacob Kotinsky, who achieved rank as entomologist in Hawaii; David Eli Fink and Marcus Smulyan, both entomologists in the United States Department of Agriculture; Harry Marmer of the United States Coast and Geodetic Survey; S. A. Goldberg, an outstanding pathologist; Joseph W. Pincus, former head of the JAS Extension Department; David Purmell, teacher at the National Farm School, and others. A number of the key men on the Jewish Agricultural Society's staff received their introduction to agriculture at the Woodbine school, and unknown young men, fledgling teachers while at Woodbine, later attained prominence in wider fields—men like Edward Albert White, Professor of Floriculture at Cornell, Harry Reynolds Lewis, foremost authority on poultry and husbandry and until recently Commissioner of Agriculture of Rhode Island; Elmer Seth Savage and Harry Lucien Garrigus, both authorities on animal husbandry and professors of that subject at Cornell and Connecticut, respectively. Also Albert Edward Wilkinson, horticulturist at Connecticut; O. Williams of the United States Department of Agriculture; Clinton V. Ballard, leader in county agent work; John Horowitz, long administrator of the ICA's Argentine colonies; and other less known but nevertheless distinguished men.

"Professor Sabsovich has established an institution which rendered an important service at a time when other institutions of a like nature were not available. He fulfilled a great public need. He laid the foundation of character; he taught many young men the power of ideals and devoted service." Thus wrote Jacob G. Lipman, Sabsovich's early disciple and the school's most distinguished alumnus, in a tribute to the memory of the man who gave him not only education but the vision and inspiration which put him on the path that brought him renown.

In 1894 Dr. Joseph Krauskopf, Rabbi of Congregation Keneseth Israel of Philadelphia, on a trip to Russia, primarily made to study the conditions of the Jews, met Count Leo Tolstoy. Together they visited the Jewish agricultural school in Odessa, where they were impressed by the ardor and zeal displayed by the students. Tolstoy had already become known as the prophet of the simple life and it is quite probable that his words set the spark to the thought that had lain dormant in Krauskopf's mind for some time. "Lead the tens of thousands of people of your cities to your idle fertile lands and you will bless not only them, but also your country and spread a good name for your people throughout the land; for all the world honors and protects the bread producer and is eager to welcome him. Begin with the young and the old will follow." Inspired by Tolstoy's exhortation, Krauskopf lost no time in translating thought into deed, into building something which, next to his calling, was to become the consuming passion of his life.

On April 10, 1896, the National Farm School received its charter "for the training of youth to become scientific and practical agriculturalists." Soon thereafter, with $6,500 raised by lecturing and $3,500 laid aside from clerical perquisites, Krauskopf bought a 122 acre farm a mile from Doylestown, Pennsylvania, 26 miles from Philadelphia. The proceeds of a second lecture tour plus donations yielded another $10,000 for the erection of a dormitory later to be known as Pioneer Hall. The building was dedicated and the school formally opened on June 20, 1897.

But there were no pupils and no faculty. By September, fifteen boys had been gathered together. Living accommodations lacked comfort and some of the boys became restive and homesick and did not remain long.

The beginning was haphazard. Because of lack of student material, there was no adequate selection. Boys went there because everything, even clothing, was free. There was no systematized curriculum. Discipline was poor. The boys were unpopular among the townfolk at Doylestown. Indeed the school almost went on the rocks the very first year. But Krauskopf was not disheartened. When the venture was dubbed "Krauskopf's dream" and many said that "it is best that it die young," he kept making converts, raising funds and preaching his gospel in season and out of season until his scoffers became his supporters.

The first faculty consisted of Dr. Krauskopf, a head master, a matron, and three instructors. To judge by the account written by an early graduate many years later, the instructors were little more than farm managers or supervisors. Overworked and underpaid, they were compelled to oversee all farm operations. The farm had to be worked. It had to bring returns. At the outset no outside farm labor was hired; farm duties came first. Classes for study were held only as convenient.

To give the school direction and guidance, John Hosea Washburn who had been Professor of Chemistry at Connecticut and who had received his Ph. D. degree at Goettingen, was appointed Director in 1900. With Krauskopf, he shared the travail of the school's formative years. Allman characterizes him as "a brilliant scholar and teacher, rugged, dynamic, sincere."

The next decade or more was an uneventful epoch. The plant remained fairly static, there was little new construction and, in the words of a graduate, life "was all Pioneer

Hall." Washburn accomplished more than could be expected with his meager facilities. Krauskopf had to be constantly on the hunt for money to carry on.

The school differed from Woodbine. It was conceived and conducted along different lines. The Baron de Hirsch School was started primarily to strengthen the Woodbine colony. Its first aim was to reach the Jewish farm boy, while the National Farm School went immediately to the city for its student body. Except in its early years, Woodbine drew upon youth of some maturity, the National Farm School catered to younger boys. Woodbine was designed for Jewish boys. The National Farm School has always proclaimed its non-sectarian character although its support, with the exception of a modest state appropriation, has come almost in toto from Jewish sources. There were also differences in curriculum and in outlook. The National Farm School, probably due to money stringency, stressed the commercial side of its farm operations. At Woodbine, that phase was subordinated to instruction. Like Woodbine, the National Farm School had its occasional flare-ups between student body and faculty.

In 1917 Dr. Bernhard Ostrolenk succeeded Dr. Washburn as Director. During his administration, the school made rapid growth. Land, buildings and equipment were added. There was modernization in all directions. School organization was improved, contacts between teachers and students were encouraged and a new school spirit based on better order, higher social, civic and esthetic values was engendered.

In the first year of Ostrolenk's incumbency, the family of Morris Lasker presented in his memory a three story brick building which cost $92,000 to erect. That inaugurated a building program which lasted over twelve years and resulted in developing a campus which has evoked the

admiration of visitors for the beauty of its structural
scheme and the harmonious planning of its graceful buildings. The original plan conceived an administration building, recitation hall, laboratory, chapel, student dormitories,
mechanics building, dean's residence, athletic field and
grandstand. These were to constitute the academic group.
Then there were to be dairy buildings, poultry houses, hay
and cowbarns, piggeries, greenhouses and storage houses.
A sum of approximately $525,000 was raised to carry out
this program.

In 1917 a stone poultry house costing $7,000 was built.
The following year, the Edward Hirsh Botanical Laboratory was donated by Mr. and Mrs. Harry B. Hirsh in
memory of their son. This was followed in 1921 by the
erection of a residence for the dean costing $15,000. The
next year witnessed the building of the Rebecca F. Louch-
heim Auditorium-Gymnasium presented by Mrs. Louch-
heim's children. To replace Pioneer Hall which was destroyed by fire in 1923, an imposing three story building
was erected costing $150,000 and named Ulman Hall in
honor of Rosetta M. Ulman, whose estate furnished $80,-
000 for the building. In that year also, Segal Hall, the gift
of Adolph Segal, was remodelled and enlarged. In 1924
Abraham Erlanger presented a 205 acre farm; and soon
thereafter, another farm of 138 acres; in the following
year, the Erlanger Model Dairy Barns were erected by the
school at a cost of $67,000. Also in 1924, a complete mod-
ern sewage disposal plant was installed.

Dr. Krauskopf died on June 12, 1923. By the terms of
his will, his valuable library was bequeathed to the school.
The bequest expressed the hope that his books would be
housed in a room which was to be a replica of the library
in his home in Germantown. After his death, the Board
of Trustees decided upon a tribute which went far beyond

their leader's hopes. They built the Krauskopf Memorial Library and Forum Building at a cost of $81,500 of which $15,000 was subscribed by friends and admirers. This building is the spiritual and cultural center of the school.

The generosity of Mr. and Mrs. Nathan Straus provided the Straus Model Dairies in 1925, including a complete pasteurization plant and a dairy laboratory. Two years later Eisner Hall, one of the earliest buildings, was completely remodelled, and in 1928, Penn Hall, another early building, was remodelled for dormitory purposes. A modern heating plant, artesian well and chlorination system were installed. With the exception of a roadside market, a battery of individual garages, a Colonial Gateway Building and minor improvements, the construction program came to an end with the erection of the Herbert D. Allman building in 1929, put up at a cost of $77,000. This building houses the administrative office and the farm mechanics department and is said to be one of the finest structures of its type.

The twenty-fifth anniversary of the founding of the school occurred in June, 1922, and the festivities were made a gala occasion. Conferences attended in the aggregate by thousands of persons were held on school grounds. A former Governor of Pennsylvania, the publisher of the New York Times, a former Ambassador to Japan were among the speakers. A campaign to raise a Silver Jubilee fund of $1,000,000 for building and endowment was inaugurated as a tribute to Dr. Krauskopf. The Trustees subscribed $50,000. Felix M. Warburg and Mortimer M. Schiff each contributed $25,000. Before the celebration was concluded a total of $166,000 had been pledged. During the progress of the campaign $250,000 was raised from citizens of Philadelphia. These funds provided the sinews for the expansion already discussed.

Shortly after the Silver Jubilee, Dr. Krauskopf fell ill and died within a year. Many people had always been apprehensive that Dr. Krauskopf's passing would mean the passing of the school. It was Krauskopf's energy, personality, passion, his enthusiasm and self-denial that had sustained the school. With Krauskopf removed, could the school go on? Fortunately he had surrounded himself with a group of men imbued with something of his own spirit and tied to him with such bonds of devotion that they carried on with a feeling of dedication the work of their revered leader—men like Herbert D. Allman, Harry B. Hirsh, Adolph Eichholz, Hart Blumenthal, Alfred M. Klein, Isaac H. Silverman, Joseph N. Snellenberg, Dr. Louis Schlesinger and Leon Merz. Upon Krauskopf's death, Hirsh acted as president. He was succeeded by Allman who presided over the destinies of the school until his retirement in 1937, since which time Joseph H. Hagedorn has filled the post.

The Silver Jubilee had its reverberation in an event that followed closely on its heels and drew nation-wide attention. "Uncle Abe" Erlanger had given generously of both time and money and had established a New York City office which he financed and directed for the purpose of soliciting funds for the school. To his former contributions he added $10,000 in 1926 and his brother, Charles, matched this with a like amount. Erlanger's plans were ambitious. They envisaged a school of large dimensions drawing its pupils from every state in the union and sending back its graduates to all parts of the nation to enter into farming in all its business and professional aspects.

Beginning soon after the war, there had been a noticeable drift from farm to city. Many of the nation's best thinkers on farm problems had become alarmed at seeing so much fine human material drained from the country's farms. The governing board of the school backed Erlanger in his expansion plans. But it was desirous of checking its own judgment with that of leaders in agriculture, business and government who, because of their more detached view, could weigh the problem dispassionately, free from preconceived opinions. Erlanger, therefore, staged a conference to which he invited the governors of the states and the mayors of the large cities to attend or to send representatives. The conference was held in New York City during the first week of June, 1926, followed by sessions at the Farm School. It was attended by over two hundred and fifty delegates, among whom were the representatives of thirty-five governors and fifty mayors. The sessions were interspersed with banquets and entertainments. There was a galaxy of speakers drawn from many parts and from many callings. Among them were Assistant Secretary of Agriculture, R. W. Dunlap; Ex-Governor Lowden of Illinois; Martha Van Rensselaer, Director of the College of Home Economics of Cornell; Sophie Irene Loeb, President of the Child Welfare League of America; Dr. H. B. Knapp, Director of New York State Institute of Applied Agriculture; Benjamin F. Yoakum, railroad magnate and agricultural expert; Dr. C. W. Warburton, Director of the Extension Service of the U. S. Department of Agriculture; Dr. Thomas D. Wood, Professor of Physical Education, Teachers College, Columbia University and many other men and women of prominence. President Coolidge sent greetings and Secretary of Agriculture Jardine sent an address to be read to the assembled delegates.

The conference culminated in a set of resolutions, one of which declared: "We recommend that in our opinion $100,000,000 would not be too much to collect in the next ten years to expand this type of agricultural education. Therefore we declare to the National Farm School that no matter what may be their budget for the extension of this work, we pledge our hearty and continued support and backing to their efforts." Following these resolutions, a resolution was adopted calling for the raising of $15,000,-000 "to carry out a comprehensive program of national expansion." The directors later reduced the sum to $5,-000,000 to be collected over a three-year period because they felt that the larger sum could not be immediately utilized to best advantage.

Erlanger established a suite of offices in New York City for the conduct of the campaign and threw himself wholeheartedly into the task. But the hopes he cherished were not destined to be realized. The strain of hard labor in his advancing years was too much to bear. Without his guiding genius the campaign bogged down. Later the economic depression set in. Only a minute fraction of the projected fund was raised. Erlanger defrayed the total cost of conference and campaign—and it came to a sizable amount. In addition, he issued a volume reviewing the proceedings of the conference which he titled "An American Contribution," which is likewise a contribution to the noble man who made the conference possible.

In 1927 Ostrolenk was succeeded as dean by C. W. Goodling of the Pennsylvania State College, who in turn was succeeded in 1939 by Harold B. Allen who had been engaged in agricultural education in the Near East since 1926 and who had been Director of Education of the Near East Foundation since 1930. In that capacity Allen had helped to organize rural education in Greece, Albania, Bulgaria, Syria, Turkey and Palestine. Dr. Allen became president while Mr. Hagedorn became chairman of the Board of Trustees.

The school's present curriculum covers a period of three years with credit for one year given to students who have taken a high school course in vocational agriculture. The first year and a half is given over to mandatory courses. After that, the student can take special courses in general agriculture, horticulture, floriculture, landscape gardening, animal husbandry and poultry husbandry.

A recent study shows that since its inception, approximately 1,100 students have been graduated from the school. A study made by the Alumni Association in 1938 indicated that of 648 graduates heard from, forty-eight per cent had remained in agriculture or related occupations. In the late summer of 1940, the school made a careful check of graduates of the years 1935–1939. There were 181 graduates in the five years and occupations of 143 were ascertained. The study showed that 130 (72 per cent of total graduates) were in agricultural occupations, 13, (7 per cent of total graduates) were in non-agricultural employment; the occupation of the remaining 38 (21 per cent of the total) was not established.

Of the graduates, Jacob Joseph Taubenhaus and Bernhard Ostrolenk have already been sketched. Then there are such men as Samuel Brody, Professor of Dairy Husbandry in the University of Missouri; Bruce Mayne, entomological expert of the United States Public Health Service; Abraham Miller, the president of American Bulb Company; Samuel Rudley, a prominent Philadelphia landscape architect; Dr. Sol Shapera, a well known veterinarian in Mamaroneck, N. Y.; Ira J. Mills, a nationally known breeder of milk goats and president of the Delaware Valley Milk Goat Association; Julius Ulman, the owner of the well known Ulman Dairies in Georgia; Samuel Kogon, landscape engineer in the New York City Department of Parks, where, it might be added, about twenty graduates of the school are employed. Three of the graduates are engaged in colonization work in Palestine. Other graduates hold supervisory and managerial jobs and, of course, there are some graduates who conduct farms of their own.

BOARD OF DIRECTORS
OF
THE JEWISH AGRICULTURAL SOCIETY, 1942

Reuben Arkush	Alfred Rheinstein
Alexander S. Bing	Arthur M. Reis, Jr.
Harry H. Cohen	Francis F. Rosenbaum
Gabriel Davidson	Wolfgang S. Schwabacher
Richard S. Goldman	Lewis L. Strauss
George W. Naumburg	Harold J. Szold

Honorary President...........Lewis L. Strauss

OFFICERS, 1942

President.....................Francis F. Rosenbaum
Vice-President...............Wolfgang S. Schwabacher
Secretary...........................Reuben Arkush
Treasurer.......................Richard S. Goldman

DIRECTORS OF THE JEWISH AGRICULTURAL
SOCIETY, 1900–1942

Reuben Arkush..................1922
*Mark Ash......................1903–1907
*Eugene S. Benjamin.............1900–1941

* Deceased.

*Abraham Bijur.................1922
Alexander S. Bing..............1942
*Henry Budge...................1900–1902
Harry H. Cohen................1942
Gabriel Davidson 1941
*Julius Goldman................1900–1903
Richard S. Goldman............1932
*William B. Hackenburg..........1900–1902
*Alfred Jaretzki.................1902–1925
Alfred Jaretzki, Jr...............1925–1936
*Jacob G. Lipman...............1914–1939
*Morris Loeb...................1900–1912
*Eugene Meyer.................1902–1909
Eugene Meyer, Jr...............1909–1913
Henry Morgenthau, Jr...........1925–1934
George W. Naumburg...........1932
*Sigmund Neustadt..............1900–1902
*Marx Ottinger.................1900–1901
*Francis D. Pollak...............1913–1916
Arthur M. Reis, Jr..............1942
Alfred Rheinstein...............1934
Joseph A. Rosen........1919–1922; 1923–1925
Francis F. Rosenbaum...........1923
*Solomon G. Rosenbaum..........1907–1919
Wolfgang S. Schwabacher........1937
Fred M. Stein..................1900–1904
Percy S. Straus.................1902–1932
Lewis L. Strauss................1920
*Cyrus L. Sulzberger.............1902–1932
Harold J. Szold................1940
Morris D. Waldman.............1919–1920

STAFF OF THE JEWISH AGRICULTURAL SOCIETY, 1942

Gabriel Davidson.................Managing Director.

Philip R. Strisik..................Assistant Manager.

George Goward..........................Consultant.

David B. Alcott.........................Consultant.

Joseph Blaustein........In Charge Farm Employment Department.

Jacob M. Maze†...........In Charge Farm Settlement Department.

Milton N. Simons†.........Assistant, Farm Settlement Department.

Benjamin Sacks..Assistant, Farm Settlement Department.

Edward A. Goodwin.......In Charge Rural Sanitation Department.

Benjamin C. Stone..In Charge Agricultural Education and Extension Department. Editor "The Jewish Farmer."

Abraham Dobin......Itinerant Agricultural Instructor.

Benjamin Miller......Itinerant Agricultural Instructor.

Israel Bernstein.......Itinerant Agricultural Instructor.

Herman J. Levine......In Charge Ulster-Sullivan Office.

Samson Liph...............In Charge Western Office.

Ethel Honig...............................Cashier.

Meyer Ashendorff†...........................Clerk.

Samuel Axelroth..Cooperating Representative. (National Refugee Service, Inc.)

† On leave to U. S. Army.

Index